BOEING
The Complete Story

First published in 2008 in the French language by ETAI

This English-language edition published in March 2010

A catalogue record for this book is available from the British Library

ISBN 978 1 84425 703 4

Library of Congress catalog card no. 2009936972

Published by Haynes Publishing, Sparkford, Yeovil, Somerset BA22 7JJ, UK

Tel: 01963 442030 Fax: 01963 440001

Int. tel: +44 1963 442030 Int. fax: +44 1963 440001

E-mail: sales@haynes.co.uk

Website: www.haynes.co.uk

Graphic design by Sophie Jauneau

Typeset by Dominic Stickland

Printed and bound in the UK

Jacket illustrations

Front Main picture: Virgin Atlantic's Boeing 747-4Q8, G-VFAB, *Lady Penelope* (Ian Black). Insets (from left): P-26 pursuit fighter; B-52 strategic bomber; 787 Dreamliner.

Back (from top): Replica of the first Boeing, the B & W seaplane, at the company's jubilee celebrations in 1966; front sections of B-17 fuselage awaiting assembly; the KC-135 entered service with the Strategic Air Command from 1957; a model of the supersonic transport in NASA's Langley Research Center wind tunnel, July 1973.

BOEING
The Complete Story

Alain Pelletier
Translated by Ken Smith

Haynes Publishing

One of the rare survivors among American civil airliners from the 1930s, this Boeing model 80A is the jewel of the Seattle Museum of Flight. (A. Pelletier)

Contents

>> Introduction 006

>> Foreword 008

CHAPTER 1

>> The first steps of a giant (1910-1932) 010

The very first Boeing 013
Difficult times 015
The Boeing Airplane Company emerges from the red 018
The first fighter planes 019
Making money from the mail 021
A new family of fighter planes 024
Towards new standards of air travel 030
Bill Boeing thinks big 031
Monomail: the plane that delivered it all 033

CHAPTER 2

>> The turning point (1933-1939) 040

The first modern airliner 041
The end of a dream 046
The era of the giants 048
The birth of a legend 050
The Stratoliner 054
The reign of the Clippers 057
Stearman: biplanes and tradition 061
The eve of battle 063

CHAPTER 3

>> The war years (1940-1945) 064

The Stratoliners and Clippers go to war 067
From the Sea Ranger to the 'Lone Ranger' 069
Down in Wichita 070
The Flying Fortress: queen of the skies 071
'Grand Pappy' 083
B-29: the plane of all the superlatives 083
Sixteen planes a day! 093
From bombers to cargo planes 094
The last fighter 095

CHAPTER 4

>> The dawn of a new era (1946-1956) 098

A super Superfortress 104
Stratojet: the first modern bomber 110
Diversifying and enlarging the range 116
The birth pangs of the B-52 118
The 707: icon of air travel 123
The flying petrol station 131

CHAPTER 5

>> Changing times (1957-1969) 134

The search for the B-52's successor 135
The Space Shuttle's forerunner 137
The 707 family 138
Big changes 144
Missiles to the fore 145
TFX: the myth of the common-user aircraft 146
The gamble with the 727 148
The race for a supersonic transport 150
CX-HLS: an HGV in the skies 152
Birth of a winner 154
The Jumbo and air travel for all 155
Boeing at the heart of the space programme 161
Boeing broadens its range 165
And diversifies 168

CHAPTER 6

>> From the edge of the abyss
to the pinnacle (1970-1996) 170

Pulling out all the stops 173
A limited military market 173
A new generation of airliners 176
Climbing back to the top 184
Cooperation to reduce risk 191
Towards heavy commercial transport 192
Remote-controlled planes get off the ground 193
Vertol and the hardy Chinook 193
New types of missile 198
A major player in the conquest of space 202

CHAPTER 7

>> Endless horizons (1997-2008) 206

An era of mergers 207
The purchase of McDonnell Douglas 209
A new generation of 737s 210
A return to the defence market 212
The growth of the 700 family 214
Boeing keeps on growing 217
Boeing leaves its historic cradle 218
The amazing Sonic Cruiser 220
The repercussions of 9/11 223
A brand-new kind of plane 227
The birth of the 787 227
The rejuvenated 747 231
Endless horizons 237

>> Appendices 239
Bibliography, acknowledgements and photograph credits

At the 'Defenders of Liberty' show, which took place at Barksdale base, Louisiana, two Fortresses made this conspicuous fly past: a B-52H Stratofortress from the 2nd Bomb Wing and the B-17G Flying Fortress from the Lone Star Flight Museum at Galveston, Texas. (USAF/MSGT A. Kaplan)

Introduction

>> The aeronautical industry is a world without pity. It destroys the weak and leaves by the wayside those who make the wrong choices. Very few aeronautical enterprises can take pride in having got through the last century and survived to the present. Boeing is one of them who can. Nonetheless, the road that has brought it to its present-day success has been full of pitfalls, and significant ones, too, as the Seattle firm's very existence has more than once been at risk. On four occasions, Boeing's future has rested on the success or failure of a single aircraft. On each occasion, the men in charge at Boeing have bet on the future and in doing so risked all. On looking back, it is surprising to find that the firm's history has been a succession of highs and lows – indeed very high and very low at times – punctuated by spectacular comebacks.

This is the story we have tried to tell in this book, through all the vicissitudes in the life of the company and its products, many of which have long since been forgotten, while others have achieved the status of icons. In the collective subconscious, the Flying Fortress, the 707, the 747 Jumbo Jet and the B-52 are names irrevocably associated with the name of Boeing.

Today, Boeing has become what is generally known as a 'Global Player' as its technological and industrial strength has spread into so many fields: civil and military aircraft, weapons systems, missiles, electronic systems and spacecraft – little seems to have escaped its attentions. In all these fields, Boeing plays a dominant role and the coming years are opening up new and unlimited horizons.

Foreword

>> No author could fill enough pages to do justice to such a vast subject as the history of the Boeing Company. Indeed, in 256 pages, we are conscious of having skimmed over the surface without going into great detail about the history of the various models of aeroplane and spacecraft. For this reason we have included a certain amount of information in appendices at the end of the book. For a detailed history of each model, we refer the reader to the numerous monographs available in the literature of aviation. The present volume aims to be as non-technical as possible. For clarity, some remarks concerning the presentation of economic and technical information are provided.

Commercial and financial results relate to the calendar year and contracts to the fiscal year (FY), which runs from July of the year in question to July of the following year. Costs and budget figures are quoted in US dollars. Commercial (orders, deliveries) and economic (turnover, profits etc) figures are taken from the annual reports. For orders of airliners, we have used 'net orders' (ie, taking into account cancellations and take-up of options during the year).

For the most part, technical details and performance figures come from official documents (the manufacturer's archives and US Air Force and Navy technical documents). Weights given are for typical configurations, but can vary considerably and have a substantial effect on performance, so that figures for the latter should be taken as indicative only. They depend upon the speed of the engine, the weight of the aircraft, the height at which it is flying, the nature of the mission and the flight plan. For these reasons, the reader may come across differing figures.

Finally, power output is expressed in both horsepower (hp) and kilowatts (kW). Likewise, engine thrust is given in kilograms and kilonewtons (kN).

The replica of the first Boeing made its
first flight at Seattle on 25 May 1966.
(P.M. Bowers collection)

CHAPTER 1

The first steps of a giant

>> On Wednesday 25 May 1966, just east of Seattle, a flimsy-looking biplane took off from the calm waters of Lake Washington, lifted into the air by the power of its 170hp Lycoming engine. The occasion was the culmination of a decision taken a year before to build a replica of the very first Boeing, the B & W. The seaplane formed the centrepiece of the celebrations marking the jubilee of America's biggest aeroplane manufacturer on 15 July of the same year. A few months before, Boeing had announced the launch of the world's biggest airliner, the 747. Fifty years separated the tiny 1,270kg B & W and the 300-tonne giant!

Nothing in William Edward Boeing's origins had predisposed him to make a career in aviation. The son of an Austrian mother and a German father who had made his fortune in the timber and iron ore business in Minnesota, he was born on 1 October 1881 in Detroit, Michigan. He was just eight years old when his father died. His mother then decided to send him to a private school in Switzerland to receive the strict and serious education that his late father would have wished for him. On his return to the United States, where he had no particular connections, the young 'Bill' Boeing continued his studies in several private schools before going to Yale's Sheffield Scientific School, followed by a trip to the west coast where he, too, started a career in the timber trade, which, in 1903, was in full swing.

Boeing decided to settle in Hoquiam, a small port situated on the mouth of the Chehalis at the far end of Grays Harbor bay. He was then just 22 years old. Within a few years, he had made enough money to consider working on something bigger. So, in 1908 he moved north and settled in the southern part of Seattle, on the shores of Lake Washington. Attracted by anything new, he decided, in January 1910, to go to Los Angeles for the first big American air show[1]. Held on the lands of the Dominguez Ranch a few miles south of the city, the show attracted the very best flyers and no fewer than 20,000 spectators a day. Captivated, Boeing constantly badgered the Frenchman Louis Paulhan to take him for a ride in his Farman biplane. While the Frenchman did agree, the flight never

1. The Los Angeles Show took place over the period 10–20 January.

materialised. Deeply disappointed, Boeing returned to Seattle, with a greater determination than ever to learn more about the science of aeronautics. However, he was to wait some time before anything came of it.

On 10 March 1910, Boeing acquired a shipyard owned by a Mr Ed Heath and started building a yacht. At the same time, he began to frequent the Seattle University Club and got to know a young naval lieutenant named Conrad Westervelt. The two men got on well, especially as Westervelt had attended the Belmont Park (New York) Air Show at the end of October 1910. The naval engineer had completed a course in aeronautics at the Massachusetts Institute of Technology (MIT) and had been sent to Belmont Park at the express request of the US Navy. For some months, the two men's aerial ambitions were restricted to flights of fancy until the much-hoped-for day dawned. In the summer of 1914, a pilot by the name of Terah Maroney brought a Curtiss seaplane to Lake Washington to take part in festivities celebrating Independence Day.

Remembering his disappointment in 1910, Boeing asked Maroney if he would take him for a flight. Maroney agreed and on 4 July 1914, sitting on the lower wing of the flimsy biplane, Boeing got his maiden flight, followed shortly afterwards by Westervelt. Despite his excitement at his brief aerial foray, Boeing nonetheless kept a cool head, remarking afterwards to his friend: 'Maroney's plane isn't that

William E. Boeing. (Collection M. Olmsted)

William Edward 'Bill' Boeing

Detroit, Michigan, 1 October 1881–The Taconite, *28 September 1956*

After studying in Switzerland and Yale University, from where he graduated in 1904, this son of a German immigrant took over his father's timber business and established the Greenwood Timber Company. In 1915, in association with a naval lieutenant, G. Conrad Westervelt, he built his first plane, the B & W. Encouraged by this, he founded, in the following year, the Pacific Aero Products Company, which, on 26 April 1917, became the Boeing Airplane Company. As an aware businessman, Boeing expanded his firm by building Thomas-Morse fighters and rebuilding DH-4 biplanes.

After going through a difficult period where he was reduced to making furniture and motor boats, 'Bill' Boeing showed great foresight in creating an international postal route between the United States and Canada. In 1921, he married Bertha Potter Paschall, who bore him one child, William Boeing Jr. Alongside his industrial activities he was, for many

years, one of the leading figures in the development of air transport in his country. In 1927, he founded the Boeing Air Transport Corporation, which later became one of America's biggest airline companies: United Airlines.

In 1929, Boeing was instrumental in the formation of a huge aeronautical group, the United Aircraft & Transport Corporation (UATC), the result of a merger of several aeronautical manufacturers and airline companies. However, UATC was destined not to last very long, as it was broken up in 1934 under the anti-trust laws. Piqued, Boeing withdrew from business. A few months later, however, he received one of the highest of American distinctions when he was awarded the Daniel Guggenheim Medal.

After retiring to 'Aldarra', the property he had built for himself in the Seattle suburbs, Bill Boeing lived long enough to be present at the Boeing 707's first flight. He died on 28 September 1956 on board his yacht *Taconite*.

great. I think we could make a much better one.' 'Sure we could,' replied Westervelt. The great Boeing adventure had just begun…

>> The very first Boeing

Without further ado, fired with enthusiasm, the two men determined to go into aeronautical construction. They asked Herb Munter, a local pilot, to join them in their plans to build and fly a seaplane, or rather two of them, designated by their initials, B & W. While Westervelt worked on the design of the two machines, Boeing made contact with one of the great names of American aviation, Glenn Luther Martin, so as to learn the basics of flying from him. Thus, in the autumn of 1915, he went to Griffith Park, Los Angeles, where he not only made his flying debut, but also bought a Martin model TA seaplane for the tidy sum of $10,000. On his return to Seattle, Boeing started a flying club, while the construction of his own seaplanes got under way. Unfortunately, Westervelt was transferred to the east coast before the first one could be completed. It needed more than this to discourage Boeing, who decided to carry on alone.

The construction of the B & Ws – christened *Bluebill* and *Mallard* – was finished by the middle of 1916. Their design was relatively simple, consisting of a parallelepipedal fuselage on which were mounted the two large, rectangular wings of unequal span. The engine was a 125hp, four-cylinder Hall-Scott. Only the flight controls

William E. Boeing (left) and his wife. The other two people have not been identified. (DR)

were original: there was no rudder-bar and changes of direction were accomplished by means of a wheel mounted on the joystick.

On 15 June 1916, when the time came to fly *Bluebill*, Herb Munter was late arriving. Fed up with waiting, Boeing decided to take the controls himself. As a result, when Munter did arrive, it was to find that Boeing had already taken the seaplane to the far end of the lake

Powered by a modern Lycoming GO-435 engine of 170hp, the B & W replica flying over Seattle. (Boeing)

where he had turned and was revving for take off. The seaplane got airborne for a distance of about 400 metres, before touching down again on the water. Back at the lake shore, Boeing handed over to Munter, but told him not to attempt a take off. However, a few days later that was exactly what he did, much to Boeing's annoyance. As for *Mallard*, Munter flew it for the first time in November 1916[2]. In the meantime, on 15 July 1916, William Boeing had founded his Pacific Aero Products Company with a capital of $100,000. He owned 998 of the 1,000 shares, and had his cousin Edgar N. Gott as vice-president and James C. Foley as company secretary.

The main building of the boatyard served as the factory premises. This large wooden structure, painted all over in red apart from the white door- and window-frames would enter into legend under the name of the 'Red Barn'. It is in existence to this day and, fully restored, it forms part of the Seattle Museum of Flight (see page 238).

Boeing wasted no time in hiring new collaborators, chief among whom was Tsu Wong, a young Chinese who was fascinated by Gustave Eiffel's work and was one of the few people in the area who was qualified in aeronautics. At the same time, he financed the construction of a wind tunnel at the University of Washington. Wong was given the task of designing a new plane called the C-4. This designation indicated that it was both the third plane built by Boeing and the fourth he had owned[3]. The plane differed considerably from the B & W and was partly inspired by the Martin TA. Its dihedral wings were staggered to give greater stability. The engine was a four-cylinder, in-line Hall-Scott A-7A developing around 100hp. It made its first flight on 15 November 1916 over Union Lake. Herb Munter established that the rudder was much too small and the plane was taken back into the shops to have it modified. Thus the model C flew again on 9 April 1917, with a new fin and rudder.

With the departure of Westervelt, Boeing was left on his own to lead the firm. On 9 May 1917, he changed its

(Boeing)

Edgar N. Gott

1887–1947

A cousin of William Boeing, Gott graduated in chemistry from the University of Michigan in 1909 and soon moved to the Pacific Northwest to devote himself to the timber trade. After eight years in the business, he was brought in to be vice-president and general manager of Boeing's company. Gott, who was subsequently president from 1922 to 1925, helped the company to emerge from the post-war slump. Under his leadership, Boeing designed its first fighter aircraft and built a reputation for being an excellent military aircraft constructor. Edgar Gott left Boeing in 1925 to take the vice-presidency at Fokker Aircraft Company, followed by the presidency of Keystone Aircraft Corporation the next year. He was later appointed president of Consolidated Aircraft Corporation. His final post, during World War II, was as chairman of the San Diego War Transportation and War Housing Commissions.

name to the Boeing Airplane Company and at the same time took on new staff. On 4 June 1917, he recruited two graduate engineers from the University of Washington at a salary of $90 a month: Clairmont L. 'Claire' Egtvedt and Philip G. Johnson, who were soon to become pillars of the company and ultimately chairmen too.

---

2. In 1918, after having been offered to the US Navy, the two planes were sold to the New Zealand Flying School in Auckland for $3,750 each.

3. In 1925, when Boeing adopted model numbers to identify his planes, the C-4 was retrospectively renamed model 2.

The Boeing C-4 (model 2) was notable for its very offset wings, which increased its stability. (Boeing)

» Difficult times...

By 1917, 28 people were working for the company, a total that naturally included engineers, but also pilots, carpenters, shipwrights and...seamstresses. The lowest wage was 14 cents an hour, whilst the pilots could earn as much as $200 or even $300 a month. However, business was hardly flourishing. Despite everyone's efforts, the B & W didn't sell. At one point, Boeing was forced to dip into his personal fortune to pay the wages, a matter of $700 a week. By the end of 1917, planes flown by Americans were seeing action for the first time in the European war zone. Westervelt told Boeing that the Navy had a great need for training machines. For the model C, this was an opportunity not to be missed. However, the seaplane could not have made the journey all the way from Seattle to Pensacola, Florida, where the senior officers of the Navy were meeting to make their procurement plans. Two model Cs (C-5 and C-6, improved versions of C-4) were therefore dismantled, packed into cases and sent by train. On 17 July 1917, factory director, Claude Berlin, and test pilot Herb Munter reassembled the planes and flew them in front of an audience of officers.

The two machines put on such a good show that the Navy ordered 50 of them. It was Boeing's first production order. Delivery of the model Cs began in April 1918 and the last was handed over to the US Navy the following November. Nonetheless, it was vital to win further contracts. On 14 May 1918, Boeing, who had maintained his contacts with the Navy, called Edgar N. Gott from San Diego to tell him to get ready to build some HS-2Ls. These were large, single-engined patrol seaplanes designed by Curtiss. On 29 June, Boeing signed a contract worth $116,000 with the US Navy for the production of 50 HS-2Ls. But on 11 November, when

On 2 March 1919, Bill Boeing (right) and Eddie Hubbard prepare to climb aboard the C-700 before making the first international mail flight. (Boeing)

the guns fell silent in Europe, the order was suddenly halved[4]. By this time, the company had 337 employees on its books.

The situation deteriorated rapidly. The military was no longer buying planes and, on the civil market, Boeing was confronted with a mass of new, surplus military planes flooding the market at knockdown prices. Fighting for survival, the firm was forced to diversify into furniture and motorboat construction[5]. Losses reached

---

4. The Curtiss HS-2L was also produced by Standard, Lockheed, Gallaudet and LWF.

5. These boats, christened 'Sea-Sleds', were built under licence from the Sea-Sled Company in Boston. Ten of them were sold via advertisements placed in Seattle newspapers, although rumours circulated that the buyers were alcohol smugglers.

(Boeing)

Clairmont L. 'Claire' Egtvedt

Stoughton, Wisconsin, 18 October 1892–October 1975

Of Norwegian origin and a native of Wisconsin, this Washington State University engineering graduate was barely 25 when, on 4 June 1917, he was taken on by William Boeing as a designer. His engineering talents were soon recognised and allowed him to rise rapidly to the post of chief engineer, followed, in 1926, by general manager. He was appointed president on 2 August 1933, a post that he held until 1939. After Boeing's departure in 1934, 'Claire' Egtvedt also held the post of chairman of the board before being officially appointed to the position on 9 September 1939, when Phil Johnson

took over as president. It was at this time that he got the company involved in building big four-engined planes like the 307 Stratoliner, the 314 Clipper flying boat and the B-17 Flying Fortress bomber.

After Johnson's sudden death, Egtvedt took the presidency again for a while until William Allen was nominated to the post in the autumn of 1945. Recognised as the father of the B-17, Egtvedt was a driving force in the development and career of this legendary aircraft, which prompted some to claim that he had played a not inconsiderable role in the Allied victory. Clairmont Egtvedt took his retirement on 24 April 1966.

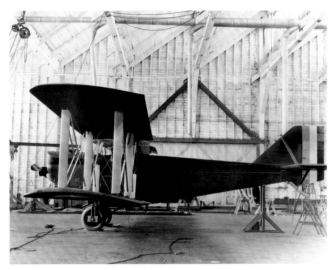

Powered by a new, 18-cylinder W-engine, the GA-2 never got beyond the prototype stage. (Boeing)

around $90,000 and staffing was cut to just 56 people. 'We can't go on like this forever, confided Boeing to Gott. 'If we don't find work that will bring in a regular income, we are going to have to shut down[6].' Fortunately, Joe Hartson, Boeing's representative in Washington, got wind of the Army's requirement to rebuild and modernise a large number of British de Havilland DH-4s. It was a piece of good fortune, provided that they could secure a favourable contract. Hartson negotiated skilfully while Phil Johnson organised production so that the job was done as efficiently as

possible. A deal was struck and modernisation of the first batch of 50 planes began in November 1919. The contract had come at just the right time, allowing Boeing to get out of the red. And it was to be followed by several others, as Boeing rebuilt 354 DH-4s between 1919 and 1924.

Meanwhile, William Boeing had had various aircraft designs built, but none made it into production. Boeing's first non-seaplane aircraft were two EA models[7]. Derived from the Boeing C, they were delivered to the US Army in January 1917. After the series of 50 model Cs (numbered C-650 to C-699), Boeing had a 51st one built for his own requirements, designated logically enough C-700. It was with this plane that Boeing was to make a mark in aviation history. On 3 March 1919, he and Eddie Hubbard took aboard a bag containing 60 letters and flew it from Vancouver, British Columbia, to Seattle, thereby making the first ever international mail flight.

Having accumulated considerable know-how in floatplane construction thanks to the HS-2Ls, William Boeing started to sell small floatplanes to leisure pilots allowing them access to the hundreds of small lakes that dotted the north-western United States. He began with the B-1, a smaller machine than the HS-2L, powered by a V6 Hall-Scott L-6 propulsion engine of 200hp, which made its first flight on 27 December 1919.

Unfortunately, the B-1 didn't sell and it was acquired by Edward Hubbard in 1920. After fitting it with a 400hp V12, he used it for eight years in mail

Like several other manufacturers, Boeing rebuilt British de Havilland DH-4 biplanes, designating them DH-4M. (Doug Olson collection)

The GA-1 ground-attack aircraft was designed by the US Army's engineering division and built in a small run. The third figure from the left is probably Bill Boeing. (P.M. Bowers collection)

service between Seattle and Victoria[8]. Two smaller derivatives of the B-1 were built in 1920: the BB-1 three seater with a 130hp Hall-Scott L-4, which was sold to a Canadian company, and the BB-L6 conventional, non-floatplane using the BB-1's wings on a new fuselage and powered by a 200hp Hall-Scott L-6. First flying in May 1920, this aircraft is reputed to have been the first plane to fly over Mount Rainier, which at 4,391 metres is the highest peak in Washington State.

The company certainly could not have hoped to survive on these few planes alone. It remained in business thanks to orders from the US Army. On 15 June 1920, after an invitation to tender, the Army asked Boeing to build 20 armoured GA-X (Ground Attack eXperimental) ground-attack planes. Designed by McCook Field Engineering Division's military engineers, the GA-X was a large three-seater tri-plane powered by two V12 Liberty 435hp propulsion engines. For the time, its armament was formidable, consisting of a 37mm cannon and eight 7.62mm machine guns.

Designated GA-1, the first production model flew in May 1921, but weighted down by its armour, handicapped by inadequate engine cooling and poor visibility for the crew, the plane performed particularly poorly. The initial order was therefore halved. Sticking to their guns, the McCook Field engineers persevered with their notion of an armoured ground-attack plane. They asked Boeing to build two prototypes of a new plane (designated GA-2) to be fitted with a new 750hp engine with 18 cylinders arranged in a W configuration. Taking off from McCook Field in December 1921, it too failed to distinguish itself by its performance and soon disappeared into obscurity. As for the ten GA-1s, they went into service with the 90th AS (1921–1922) then the 104th AS (1922–1923).

6. Quoted by H. Mansfield in Vision, the Story of Boeing.

7. The EA designation indicated Boeing E for the Army. In 1925, it was retrospectively named model 4.

8. Restored, the B-1 has been on show since 1954 at Seattle's Museum of History and Industry.

This MB-3A of the 6th Pursuit Squadron suffered damage on landing, May 1924. (R.L. Cavanagh collection)

>> The Boeing Airplane Company emerges from the red

In autumn 1920, the famous Pulitzer Trophy Race was scheduled to take place at Mitchel Field, Long Island near New York City. On Thursday 23 November, among the eight planes on the start line were two prototypes of the Thomas-Morse MB-3 fighter. They were piloted respectively by Captain Harold Evans Hartney and Second Lieutenant Leigh Wade. The first of these two planes came in second, just behind the Verville VCP-R, at an average speed of 148mph. It is likely that this performance exerted a not inconsiderable influence over the decision of the Air Service to order extra MB-3s, particularly with the manufacturer not missing out on the chance to gain publicity for the achievement. Following the rules in force at the time, the Army issued a request for tenders for the construction of a batch of 50–200 planes. Six manufacturers responded, offering to build 200 MB-3s at the following prices:

Dayton-Wright	$2,201,000
LWF	$2,133,000
Curtiss	$1,982,000
Thomas-Morse	$1,926,000
Aeromarine	$1,832,000
Boeing	$1,448,000

Despite the original intention to order four batches of 50 planes from four different builders, Boeing's bid was so attractive (25% less than Thomas-Morse's and 34% less than Dayton-Wright's) that Major Reuben H. Fleet, then in charge of Engineering Division contracts, gave the whole order to the young Seattle firm. A contract was signed on 21 April 1921 to supply two hundred planes and the necessary spare parts for a total sum of $1,837,626. There is little doubt that Boeing's ownership of spruce plantations, whose timber was then extensively used in aircraft construction, allowed him to slash his prices and win the contract hands down. This manna from heaven allowed Boeing to contemplate the future with greater peace of mind. The planes were designated MB-3A and incorporated some significant improvements, among which were new radiators and a reinforced skin[9].

Thus after three lean years, 1922 began much more auspiciously for Boeing. On 3 January 1922, perched

An end-of-series MB-3A, distinguishable by its enlarged rudder. The nose and spinner appear to be painted white.
(J.W. Underwood collection)

on the back of a lorry, the Boeing Airplane Company's managing director addressed his employees to tell them that they would be receiving a New Year's present of a £500 insurance policy. A few months later, on 3 May 1922, William Boeing carried out a reshuffle of company posts. He became chairman of the Boeing Airplane Company while Edgar N. Gott was appointed president, Philip G. Johnson vice-president and Clairmont L. Egtvedt was made company secretary.

The first production MB-3A was completed in the spring of 1922 and flew for the first time on 7 June of that year. Production proceeded quite rapidly as the 200th and final plane was wheeled out of the workshops six months later, on 27 December 1922. Meanwhile, the MB-3A achieved another distinction when, on 14 October 1922, Lieutenant Donald F. Stace won the John L. Mitchell Trophy Race at Selfridge Field, Michigan, at an average speed of 148mph. The first 100% American production fighters, the MB-3As would remain in service until 1926, not only in the United States, but also in Hawaii and the Panama Canal Zone.

In February 1923, the Army asked Boeing to rebuild the fuselages of three DH-4s with arc-welded steel tubes using a process developed in-house. These planes, designated DH-4M (M for modernised), would thus see their potential extended substantially. The order was followed by two further contracts for the rebuilding of 50 followed later by 133 DH-4Ms[10]. Other smaller orders came in over the months throughout 1923 and 1924.

» The first fighter planes

In the same year, 1923, the USAAS launched a programme of experimental prototypes aimed at finding a replacement for the MB-3As. The programme turned out to be a disaster with none of the six experimental fighters proving capable of exceeding 150mph![11] It was time for the manufacturers to take the initiative. Flushed with its success in competition[12], the Curtiss Aeroplane and Motor Company proposed a new fighter adopting certain features of its racing planes. The military, which had swallowed up considerable sums of money in their prototype programme, were somewhat unwilling to commit themselves to further expenditure. However,

A Boeing PW-9 was delivered to NACA in January 1927. It is seen here being set up in the Langley Research Center's wind tunnel. (NASA/LISAR)

MB-3As were used in the filming of Wings, the first American feature-length aeronautical movie. (DR)

9. This reinforcement proved necessary after a number of incidents where planes had lost part of their skin in mid-flight.
10. Contract no. AC1173-23 of June 1923 for 50 planes at a total cost of $157,000 followed in July 1923 by a revised order for 33 planes at a total cost of $263,300.
11. These six fighters were the Dayton-Wright PS-1, the Engineering Division TP-1, the Fokker PW-5, PW-6 and PW-7, and the Loening PW-2A.
12. Particularly with the Curtiss Army R-6 and the Navy's Curtiss CR in 1922.

This Boeing PW-9 (registered 25-301) from the 19th Pursuit Squadron is known for having been flown by Claire Chennault, who would later form the famous 'Flying Tigers'. (R.L. Cavanagh)

Boeing delivered 41 NB-1 trainers to the US Navy from late 1924. Here we see one of them at the Langley Research Center, in October 1926. (NASA/LISAR)

they were prepared to provide an engine, fittings and armaments as long as Curtiss would bear the costs of construction. Thus was born the Curtiss model 33 fitted with the excellent Curtiss D-12 V12 engine of 440hp, which during tests had had no difficulty reaching 170mph. Won over, the Air Service quickly acquired three prototypes designated XPW-8 (PW for Pursuit Water-cooled).

Following Curtiss's example, Boeing had undertaken the design of a fighter at its own expense. The model 15 had some similarities to the Curtiss D-12. Much influenced by the Fokker F.VII, it had a fuselage constructed from arc-welded steel tubes with fatter, more-tapered profiles to the staggered wings, which were also of different spans. Construction began in January 1922 and the first prototype flew on 2 June 1923 piloted by Captain Frank Tyndall. This prototype was also bought

by the Army who, after preliminary tests, ordered two more prototypes. All were designated XPW-9.

The tests demonstrated that the XPW-9 met not only the Army's needs, but also those of the Navy. Consequently on 19 September 1924, an initial order was sanctioned for 12 PW-9s, followed by a second in December for a further 18 planes, costing $14,000 each. The first Boeing PW-9 was delivered on 30 October 1925 and the final one on 18 December, indicating how rapidly the Seattle factory worked. For its part the Navy acquired 16 model 15s (which they designated FB-1) the first of which was delivered to the US Marine Corps on 1 December 1925. Subsequently, the USAAS submitted orders for several batches of improved PW-9s (25 PW-9As, 40 PW-9Cs and 16 PW-9Ds), while the Navy took a few planes of equivalent type (two FB-2s, three FB-3s and one FB-4).

One of the ten Boeing FB-1s used by the Marines. This plane probably belonged to the VF-1M squadrons based at Quantico. On the engine housing can be made out the name of the pilot, Blackwell. (US Navy)

A newly built model 40A. It has not yet received its registration number, but is carrying the insignia of Boeing Air Transport Corporation. (Boeing)

The Boeing NB-2 (model 21) was almost identical to the NB-1. This one (registered A6778) was used by NACA at Langley Field in the early 1930s.

At the same time, Boeing was working on other types intended for the Navy, beginning with the model 50, a large, two-engined seaplane designed by Isaac Laddon (who was responsible for the GA-1 and GA-2) and the model 21, a trainer biplane developed from the model 15 and supplied with a 200hp Lawrance J-1 engine. The latter flew on 20 October 1923 and spawned two production versions: 41 examples of the NB-1 and thirty NB-2s. Boeing sold five further planes in Peru. So, including all versions, Boeing sold 157 model 15 derivatives, which for the time was a more than respectable commercial performance.

» Making money from the mail

During the year 1925, the American Postal Service realised that the venerable DH-4s that made up their postal fleet had had their day. It therefore invited tenders from different manufacturers with the proviso that the 420hp Liberty engine be used as there were still considerable stocks of these. Boeing put in its bid with the model 40 on which design work began on 7 April 1925. Built essentially from wood apart from the front part of the fuselage, the model 40 was a very conventional design capable of carrying 450kg of mail. It first flew on 7 July 1925, but failed to win any orders, which went instead to Douglas with its model M-1, 50 of which were acquired by the Postal Service.

The period was marked by some changes at the head of the company: Philip G. Johnson (aged 26) was named president in place of Edgar N. Gott, who left Boeing to become vice-president of Fokker Aircraft Company; on 13 February 1926, Bill Boeing was re-elected chairman of the board.

The Boeing model 40 would have sunk into oblivion had it not been for the passing of the Air Mail Act. This law, better known as the Kelly Act from the name of Congressman Clyde Kelly, who was chairman of the postal committee, permitted air mail to be carried by private operators[13]. At the beginning of 1926, numerous routes went over to private operation, with only the transcontinental New York–San Francisco route being operated by government pilots and

---

13. The transfer of all the routes took place between April 1926 and August 1927.

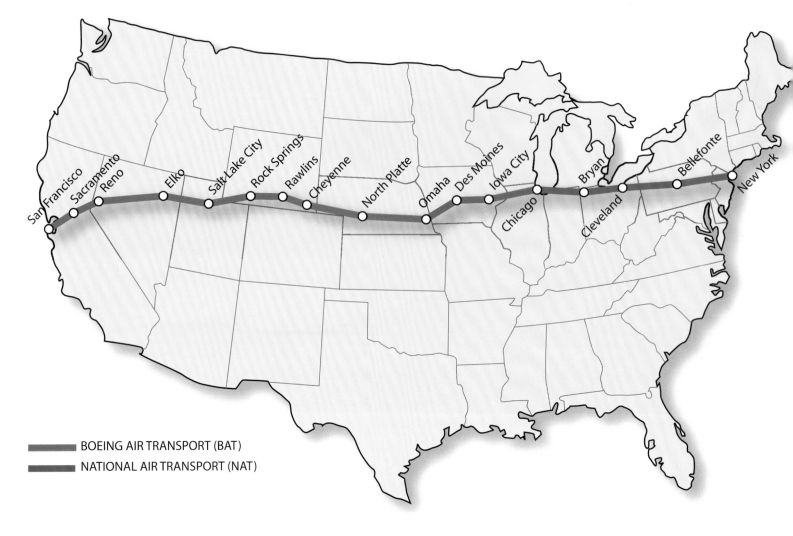

The Boeing Air Transport postal routes complemented those of National Air Transport. (A. Pelletier)

BOEING AIR TRANSPORT (BAT)
NATIONAL AIR TRANSPORT (NAT)

planes. Consequently, on 25 November 1926, the Postal Service put out a tender for the carriage of mails on the San Francisco–Chicago and Chicago–New York routes. Several operators entered bids on the basis of using existing planes. When he got wind of the tender, Edward Hubbard, who was already responsible for the mail contract between Seattle and Victoria, persuaded Boeing to put in a bid with a much-improved version of the model 40.

In a short time, the design department had completed work on a new model, the 40A. The plane benefited from the new nine-cylinder 420hp Pratt & Whitney Wasp radial engine, which allowed radiators to be dispensed with, payload to be increased and performance to be substantially improved. This engine was the first in a long series of radial engines that would revolutionise American aviation. As Boeing later said, his planes were designed 'to carry passengers and mail, not water and radiators'. In another departure, the model 40A had a small cabin for two passengers. Exploiting all these features, Boeing was able to put in his bid at a lower cost than that of any of his competitors. He undertook to carry mail at $1.50 per pound weight for the first 1,000 miles and

15 cents per pound for each additional 100 miles, while his nearest rival, Western Air Express, was asking $2.24 and 24 cents respectively. For a while, Harry S. New, the Director-General of the Postal Service had doubts about Boeing's bid, but Senator Wesley Jones assured him that Boeing was a serious and reliable person. New was forced to bow before the evidence and the Boeing Airplane Company won the order. On 28 January 1927, Boeing signed a contract with the US Postal Department to carry the mail between Chicago and San Francisco (a distance of 1,918 miles) using 25 model 40As, starting on the following 1 July. A few months later, on 20 May, the model 40A made its first flight and, by 15 June, all the planes were ready to go into action. On 30 June 1927, Boeing created a new company for the purpose, the Boeing Air Transport Corporation (BAT), which, as well as handling the mail and passengers, trained the pilots and built airfields and maintenance centres.

Bill Boeing's wife, Bertha, inaugurated BAT's postal service on 1 July 1927 by christening the first model 40 City of San Francisco. Because of Prohibition, the traditional champagne was not available, so orange soda was used instead. Jane Eads, a journalist on the daily *Chicago Herald & Examiner*, was the first passenger (see panel). From now on, it took no more than 48 hours to get the mail from New York to San Francisco. Nonetheless, the New York–Chicago section was still undertaken by train, as it was considered too risky for planes. From Chicago, the model 40As took over all the way to San Francisco with stops at Iowa City, Des Moines, North Platte, Cheyenne, Rawlins, Rock Springs, Elko, Reno and Sacramento, as well as refuelling at Omaha and Salt Lake City. From the very first month of the service, BAT made money. By the end of the first year, the company had transported 379 tonnes of mail, 67 tonnes of cargo and 1,863 passengers. On 1 January 1928, for the sum of $94,000, BAT acquired a 73% share in Pacific Air Transport managed by Vern Gorst, and a route linking Seattle and San Francisco was opened. Marine searchlights were installed on the hills along the coast to guide the pilots. Together, these two routes became known as the 'Boeing System'.

Passengers climb into a Boeing model 40B's cramped cabin. At this time, passenger comfort was more or less non-existent. (UAL)

Jane Eads: the first transcontinental passenger

On Friday 1 July 1927, a few weeks after Charles Lindbergh's historic Atlantic crossing, a young woman became the first passenger on a regular flight to cross the United States. A journalist, Jane Eads had been assigned the job by the editor-in-chief of the daily *Chicago Herald & Examiner* intending to cut the ground from under the feet of the *Chicago Tribune*, which had had a similar plan. For the 21-year-old woman, dressed for the occasion in a knee-length skirt, cloche hat and a feather boa, it was no ordinary first, as she had not even flown before!

She was quite simply terrified, but the desire to make a scoop was paramount. The plane was a Boeing Air Transport model 40A that had just completed its first transcontinental mail trip between San Francisco and Maywood Airfield in Chicago. On this Friday morning, Miss Eads climbed on to the plane's wing and slipped into the cabin, which, as well as being particularly cramped, had no ventilation system whatsoever. It is hard to imagine today what discomfort she had to bear inside the noisy cabin that had been turned into an oven by the summer heat of 1927. As on the outward journey, the flight had to be undertaken in several stages. It had been arranged that at certain stopping points the journalist would hand over a few hastily written notes to the Western Union operator who would then transmit them to the editor in Chicago. On each occasion, the mail and the passenger had to change planes and be taken on by a new pilot. Ira Biffle was the first pilot as far as Iowa City, then on to Nielson Field, near Omaha, Nebraska.

There, Jack Knight took over for the section to North Platte, Nebraska and on to Cheyenne, Wyoming. For the penultimate stage, Hugh Barker flew via Rock Springs, Wyoming, and Salt Lake City, Utah, to Reno, Nevada. After a final stop at Sacramento, California, it was an exhausted Jane Eads whom C. Eugene Robinson deposited at Crissy Field on 2 July at 19.20 after a journey lasting a mere 23 hours 50 minutes!

(Boeing)

By 1928, and by then with 800 employees, Boeing had become one of the largest aeronautical manufacturers in the United States. On 31 October 1928 came the creation of the Boeing Airplane & Transport Company, incorporating both the aeroplane manufacturing and commercial transport sides of the business. The model 40 was a great success and production eventually reached 91 planes, the last of which were delivered in 1932. After the model 40A came the 40B with a more powerful 525hp Pratt & Whitney Hornet engine. It flew for the first time on 5 October 1929 and was the first model 40 to be equipped with a two-way radio designed by Thorpe Hiscock, William Boeing's brother-in-law. Finally, the model 40C had a cabin for four passengers.

A Boeing F4B-1 from the VB-1B 'Red Rippers' squadron taking off from the aircraft carrier USS Lexington. *(US Navy)*

>> A new family of fighter planes

None of these commercial activities prevented Boeing from remaining fully active in the military field. On 7 October 1926, the first production FB-5 undertook its maiden flight, opening the way for a series of 27 FB-5s for the unique American aircraft carrier, the USS *Langley*. These planes differed considerably from their predecessors, notably in the layout of their wings and the undercarriage. Though they gave satisfactory service, they were destined to last only two years with the Navy, thanks to its decision to have only radial-engined planes, these being lighter and more reliable than the old Liberty.

Thus was born the model 54 (FB-6), an FB-5 powered by a Pratt & Whitney 425hp Wasp, followed by the model 69 (XF2B-1) using the same engine. The tests led to a production run of 32 F2B-1s costing $12,650 apiece with its first deliveries made on 20 January 1928. The F2B-1 underwent a steady development, being succeeded by the F3B-1 (model 74). Boeing produced a prototype, financed from its own resources, and this made its first flight on 2 March 1927; 73 were acquired by the Navy. At the same time, Boeing was fulfilling an order for the construction of three torpedo biplanes designed by the Naval Aircraft Factory and designated TB-1. It was a development of the Martin T3M that made use of a steel-tube structure and could be fitted with either wheels or floats. The first one flew on 4 May 1927 and the cost of the three planes came to $199,000.

Fighter planes intended for the Army followed a parallel course of development to that of the Navy fighters. Three successive experimental planes appeared: the XP-4 (model 58) with a supercharged 510hp Packard engine, the XP-8 (model 66) powered by the new 600hp Packard V6, and the XP-7 (model 93), which was the last Boeing fighter to have a liquid-cooled engine, specifically a 600hp Curtiss Conqueror.

This Boeing F4B-2 was used by NACA to test a T-shaped tailplane. (NASA/LISAR)

The prototype XF2B-1 was derived directly from the Army's XP-8 prototype. Its Pratt & Whitney Wasp radial engine was partially enclosed, a solution not retained on the production series. This plane, which has not yet been delivered to the US Navy, still awaits its markings and roundels. (NASA/LISAR)

The model 77 (F3B-1) was a carrier-based fighter that was supplied to the VF-1B, VF-2B and VF-3B squadrons until 1932. (NASA/LISAR)

A Boeing F4B-2 from the VF-5 squadron comes in to land on the carrier USS Lexington on 29 January 1932. (M. Olmsted collection)

This Boeing P-12E (registered 31-559) preserved at the US Air Force Museum in Dayton, Ohio, is wearing the colours of the 6th Pursuit Squadron. (R.L. Cavanagh collection)

This Boeing YP-12K, fitted with skis, was used by the 27th Pursuit Squadron. The white bear painted on the engine cowl indicated its participation in winter exercises. (M. Olmsted collection)

During the winter of 1927–1928, although not having been requested to do so by the military, the Seattle design office started work on plans for new fighters as short-term replacements for the PW-9s, F2Bs and F3Bs. Developed and built at Boeing's expense, models 83 and 89 led to a whole family of planes that would be very popular with the Army and the Navy and be produced in no fewer than 586 examples. There was basically nothing new in the structure of the planes; on the contrary, they used only tried and tested methods and the two models were very similar apart from the undercarriage.

The model 83 made its first flight on 25 June 1928 and was handed over to the Navy three days later. The model 89 was taken by train to Anacostia, where it flew on 7 August. Both planes had a Pratt & Whitney 450hp R-1340B Wasp engine. The tests led to an order of 27 production planes (F4B-1) the first of which flew on 6 May 1929, with completion of the order on 22 August. The corresponding planes for the Army (model 102) were designated P-12. The first one flew on 11 April 1929 and the last example of an initial batch of ten was delivered a fortnight later. These planes gave birth to a succession of progressively improved versions. The Navy took 21 F4B-3s and 92 F4B-4s, the last of which were delivered in 1933, while the Army acquired 90 P-12Bs, 96 P-12Cs, 35 P-12Ds, 110 P-12Es and 25 P-12Fs as well as testing various experimental versions such as the turbocharged XP-12K and XP-12L and the injection-engined XP-12K. Boeing also developed different versions specifically for export grouped under the generic 'model 100' designation, a few of which were sold to Thailand. The P-12s and F4Bs forged an excellent reputation among pilots, both for their legendary robustness and their performance. 'They were built like houses and a pilot could rely on their near-indestructibility to carry out manoeuvres unknown to pilots of earlier generations', according to the aerobatic flyer Frank Tallman[14].

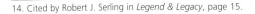

14. Cited by Robert J. Serling in *Legend & Legacy*, page 15.

The final PW-9D was experimentally fitted with a Curtiss V-1570 Conqueror engine and designated XP-7. Despite an undeniable improvement in performance, the XP-7 remained a prototype. (P.M. Bowers collection)

The last production PW-9 was fitted with two identical wings of the same profile as the Boeing model 103A, as well as a turbocompressor. Thus modified it was designated XP-4 and delivered to the Wright Field test centre on 27 July 1926. (P.M. Bowers collection)

Colonel Henry H. Arnold posing with Bebe Daniels, the musical comedy star, in front of a Boeing P-12E, in the early 1930s. (USAF)

The XTB-1 prototype (registered A-7024) in April 1927 before it had made its first flight. The fuselage structure was from steel tubes, with Duralumin for the wings. (AAHS)

The many coats of the P-12

The Boeing P-12 was the backbone of American fighter units in the 1930s. A total of 366 aircraft, in different versions, was delivered between February 1929 and May 1932. They were supplied to many units, with a glimpse of some of them here.

1. P-12C no. 21 from the Skylarks aerobatics team based at Maxwell Field, Alabama, around 1933. (M. Olmsted collection)

2. P-12B no. 9 as flown by the squadron leader of the 95th Pursuit Squadron, part of the 1st Pursuit Group based at Selfridge Field, Michigan. It carries the 'Kicking Mule' insignia, with two red bands around the fuselage. (B. Swisher via M. Olmsted)

3. P-12E no. 43 as flown by the leader of the 35th Pursuit Squadron's A Patrol, part of the 8th Pursuit Group based at Langley Field, Virginia, about 1934. It carries the 'Leaping Panther' insignia, with a yellow band around the fuselage. (Doug Olson collection)

4. P-12Es from the 27th Pursuit Squadron, part of the 1st Pursuit Group based at Selfridge Field, Michigan. They are carrying a falcon insignia and have a broad red band on the fuselage. (USAF)

5. P-12E no. 1 as flown by the squadron leader of the 24th Pursuit Squadron, part of the 6th Composite Group based at France Field, Panama, in 1934. Its insignia represents a leaping tiger. The two bands around the fuselage and the engine cowling are painted red. (R. L. Cavanagh collection)

6. P-12C no. 62 as flown by the leader of the 36th Pursuit Squadron's A Patrol, part of the 8th Pursuit Group based at Langley Field, Virginia, in February 1939. It carries the 'Flying Fiend' insignia and has a red band around the fuselage. (Doug Olson collection)

7. P-12E no. 42 from the 77th Pursuit Squadron, part of the 20th Pursuit Group based at Barksdale Field, Louisiana. Its insignia represents a hand of cards. (M. Olmsted collection)

8. P-12B no. 8 from the Bolling Field (Washington DC) detachment. Its insignia is an image of the Capitol in Washington DC. (M. Olmsted collection)

9. P-12C no. 12 of the 3rd Staff Squadron based at Fort Leavenworth, Kansas. The engine cowling and the wheel hubs are painted in blue and yellow chequerboard. (R.L. Cavanagh collection)

10. P-12E no. 1 as flown by the squadron leader of the 34th Pursuit Squadron, part of the 17th Pursuit Group based at March Field, California, about 1934. It carries the 'Thunderbird' insignia and has black and white bands around the fuselage and the engine cowling. (USAF)

This Boeing model 80A (serial number 1082) was the second aircraft in the series. It was registered as C224M, later NC224M. It was fitted with illuminated signs to carry out night-time publicity flights in the Los Angeles area. This aircraft survives today and is exhibited at Seattle's Museum of Flight. (P.M. Bowers collection)

>> Towards new standards of air travel

In spring 1928, nine years after the B-1 seaplane, the model 204 (B-1E) appeared, a four-seater commercial seaplane derived directly from it. Ten 410hp Wasp-engined planes were built between May 1928 and April 1929. In fact these were the last Boeing aircraft built specifically for private, civilian customers. In 1929, after Boeing had formed Boeing Aircraft of Canada with the Hoffar-Breeching shipyard of Vancouver, four further model 204s were constructed under the name of 'C-204 Thunderbird'.

The Boeing B-1 saw use in Canada from 1920 to 1923. Its registration number started with an N, indicating that its owner was American, but the letters CA show that it was registered in Canada. (P.M. Bowers collection)

The success of carrying passengers on the mail planes encouraged manufacturers to develop aircraft specially designed to transport passengers. Thus Ford introduced a family of three-engined monoplanes of all-metal construction that relegated wooden planes such as the Fokkers to the level of antiques. To compete with Ford, Boeing offered the rather conventional – for its time – model 80. While it was triple-engined, using three 410hp Pratt & Whitney Wasps, it was still a part-metal, part-wood biplane. The 12-seat passenger cabin was very comfortable. The walls were lined with mahogany ply and the Duralumin floor was rubber-carpeted. There were 12 leather-covered seats in the cabin (in four rows of three), luggage racks and individual reading lamps. In addition – a supreme luxury – it was equipped with ventilation and there was even hot water in the toilets.

The model 80 first flew in August 1928 and four were put into service on the San Francisco–Salt Lake City route. They were soon followed by ten model 80As, a more powerful version for 18 passengers powered by 525hp Pratt & Whitney Hornet B engines. Although it was not obvious, this model possessed an interesting innovation: a large part of its structure consisted of square-section aluminium tubes bolted together, achieving a substantial reduction in weight. Only the front part of the fuselage retained molybdenum-chrome steel-tube construction. The cabin was divided into two sections, the first for 15 passengers and the second (situated immediately behind the cockpit) for three passengers.

The port-side Pratt & Whitney Hornet engine on a model 80A. This nine-cylinder radial engine developed 525hp. (A. Pelletier)

On 1 May 1930, BAT began a daily service between San Francisco and Chicago using its Boeing 80As. The 20-hour flight cost $200[15]. In all, 11 model 80As were delivered for use by BAT. Later, model 80As made the first night flights between Salt Lake City and Oakland, a distance of 634 miles. The 80As could also be used to carry mail. In about a quarter of an hour, the seats could be removed and the cabin transformed into an airborne sorting office.

On Thursday 15 October 1929, the port of Seattle was witness to an incident that remains unresolved to this day. It was on this day that the big Soviet Tupolev ANT-4 seaplane landed near the Sand Point naval base, this being one of the stopping points on an attempt to fly between Moscow and New York[16]. The all-metal plane had been designed by the German firm of Junkers, a pioneer in this method of construction.

According to the Russians, Boeing engineers had taken part in the plane's repair and replacement of the floats with wheels. They had used the opportunity to look over the plane, taking note of various structural features, and they used these in the design of future Boeings, in particular the model 247. For its part, Boeing declared that it had no record of having taken any part in these repairs. The truth probably lies somewhere between the two versions. It would be hard to imagine that Boeing's engineers would not have tried to get a look at the ANT-4, if only to confirm the worth of their own designs.

» Bill Boeing thinks big

During their first two years of service, the model 40s covered around 5,500,000 miles, carried 1,300 tonnes of mail and transported 6,000 passengers. This success was chiefly due to the reliability and performance of the Pratt & Whitney Wasp engine. Pleased with these results, William Boeing proposed a merger to Pratt & Whitney's managing director, Frederick B. Rentschler[17], who managed to convince his friend Chance Milton Vought to join them in the new group, which was formed on 1 February 1929 under the name of the United Aircraft & Transportation Corporation (UATC). Its headquarters was established at Hartford, Connecticut where the engine maker already had his

15. The outward flight left Chicago at 8.00am and arrived in San Francisco at 4.30am the next morning. On the return, it left San Francisco at 8.00pm and arrived in Chicago at 6.00pm the following day.

16. The expedition lasted from 23 August to 1 November 1929. The crew consisted of Shestakov and Bolotov (pilots), Sterlingov (navigator) and Fufayev (mechanic).

17. Frederick Brant Rentschler (1887–1956).

The unique Boeing model 226 was a luxury version for the directors of Standard Oil. The cabin had been refitted to accommodate just eight passengers. (Boeing)

factory. Financial support was provided by the National City Bank of New York, whose president, Gordon S. Rentschler, was Frederick B. Rentschler's brother. UATC held the capital of Boeing Airplane Company and its subsidiary Hamilton Metalplane Division (which it had just acquired), of BAT Incorporated and its subsidiary PAT, of Pratt & Whitney Aircraft Company, of Chance Vought Corporation and of Hamilton Aero Manufacturing Company. Half of the shares were held by Pratt & Whitney and the other half by Boeing, Hamilton and Vought. Each firm continued to trade under its own name. This alliance resulted in standardisation of the use of Pratt & Whitney engines and Hamilton propellers on all Boeing planes unless customers requested otherwise.

UATC grew rapidly with other firms joining: on 30 July 1929 it was Sikorsky Aviation Corporation, based in New England; on 15 August 1929 Stearman Aircraft Company based in Wichita, Kansas and, in September 1929, the Standard Steel Propeller Company of Pittsburgh. The latter was merged with Hamilton to form the Hamilton Standard Division. Finally, John K. Northrop spent a brief spell with UATC, after financial problems brought about a merger in October 1929. On 1 January 1930, a new division of Boeing was created, the Northrop Aircraft Corporation, with Bill Boeing as chairman of the board, W. Kenneth

This photograph, undoubtedly taken on the ground, shows one of the very first air hostesses on board a Boeing model 80A. (Boeing)

Jay as president and John K. Northrop as vice-president. Despite all this, Northrop's situation barely improved, leading UATC, on 1 September 1931, to reorganise Northrop and Stearman[18] as one group based in Wichita. Refusing to go to Kansas, John K. Northrop resigned from UATC in January 1932.

On 7 May 1930, the first transcontinental air network was officially set up. On 31 March the

A Boeing model 80A has survived to this day and is on show at Seattle's Museum of Flight. (A. Pelletier)

Both by its structure and its aerodynamic qualities, the Monomail model 200 marked an important stage in the history of Boeing aircraft. This plane's fuselage was painted green and the aerofoil surfaces were in grey and orange. (Boeing)

previous year, UATC had bought up a third of the shares in NAT (National Air Transport), the company running the Dallas–New York route, via Chicago. Just eight weeks later, UATC had taken over full ownership of the firm. On 30 June UATC bought VAL (Varney Air Lines), and on 31 August all the shares in Stout Air Services were transferred to NAT. With the liquidation of Stout AS, UATC had control of four companies: BAT, PAT, NAT and VAL.

Eight days later there followed another great innovation for the time: the model 80 would from now on have an air hostess on board to take care of anxious or sick passengers. On 15 May 1930 Ellen Church, a qualified nurse, joined the crew of a model 80A on its flight from Chicago to San Francisco, and thus became the world's first air hostess. During the ensuing weeks, seven more stewardesses – as they were called – were taken on[19].

On 1 July 1931, United Airlines Incorporated was formed to oversee the management of the various airline companies owned by UATC, which, in the manner of the aircraft manufacturers, continued to operate under their own names.

---

18. Lloyd Stearman had left UATC in 1931 in a disagreement about certain aspects of company policy.

19. The recruitment criteria for these first stewardesses were as follows: to be a qualified nurse, to be no older than 25, be under 1.62m in height and to weigh no more than 52kg. The salary was $125 a month for 100 hours of flying.

>> Monomail: the plane that delivered it all

In the spring of 1930, following the very conventional model 80, Boeing's research department designed its first truly modern aircraft, the model 200 Monomail. The head of the design department, Charles 'Monty' Monteith, was convinced that, faced with the big three-engined Fokkers and Fords, there was a place for a much smaller, more powerful aircraft using cutting-edge technology. Jack Northrop had also come to the same conclusion with his Alpha model. Thus was born the Boeing model 200 Monomail, designed from the outset to carry mail and cargo only (hence its name). It combined an all-metal, semi-monocoque fuselage, a low-slung, unsupported, cantilevered, deep-profile wing, an enclosed Pratt & Whitney radial engine, a metal propeller with adjustable pitch, and a retractable undercarriage (one of the first of its kind). Though modern in so many ways, the Monomail retained a few traditional features, such as an open-air cockpit.

The plane made its first flight on 6 May 1930 in the expert hands of Eddie Allen. It flew appreciably faster than any of the military aircraft in service at the time. Powered by the 575hp Hornet B engine, it put up very fine performances for a plane of its size. It could achieve 158mph and carried more than a ton of cargo. Slim Lewis, BAT's chief pilot, demonstrated its strength

The second Monomail had a cabin for six passengers. Its fuselage was later lengthened to accommodate two more passengers. (Boeing)

A camouflaged Boeing Y1B-9A from the 2nd Bombardment Group during manoeuvres in 1933. (USAF)

a few weeks later by executing a triple loop-the-loop. Nonetheless, the plane was handicapped by its propeller, which, thanks to the ground-adjusted pitch feature, did not allow the pilot to make the most of the advantages offered by a modern airframe. The following August, an improved version appeared, the model 221, also going under the name of Monomail and able to carry six passengers and 340kg of

baggage. The model 200 itself was lengthened so as to be able to take passengers and became the model 221A. The two planes were used on the Boeing System, but were not put into production because of their cost. The Monomails were modified several times to test various technical features, but above all they were the inspiration behind the design for the first modern American bomber, the B-9, and formed the basis of the model 247, an aircraft that would revolutionise air transport.

Until the early 1930s, bomber aircraft in the United States, as in Europe, had been more-or-less successful derivatives of concepts dating from the First World War. The only development had been in the use of metal. For its part, the US Army Air Corps had a fleet of several dozen large and slow Keystone biplanes. In Seattle, the Boeing team set about designing two twin-engined bombers, the 214 and 215, of identical construction to the Monomail. The two planes differed from each other only in their engines. The model 214 used 600hp, V12 Curtiss GIV-1570C Conquerors, while the model 215 made use of Pratt & Whitney SR-1860B Hornets. The model 215 was ready by the spring of 1931 and, bearing a civil registration, made its first flight on 13 April. The tests proved most satisfactory and, on 14 August, the USAAC acquired both this plane and the model 214, which had not even flown at this stage. This purchase was followed by an order for a small batch of five aircraft for evaluation, designated Y1B-9A (model 246) at a unit price of $92,359. At Boeing, the enthusiasm with which the Air Corps had ordered the Y1B-9As led to the expectation of significant orders. They had reckoned without the competition. A short time later, the Glenn Martin Company presented its own bomber. Arriving after the Boeings, the Martin model 123 put up superior performance and won the much-coveted orders. The B-9 was a victim of its open cockpit and an inadequately sized bomb bay, obliging it to carry its bombs externally. Delivered from June 1934, the Martin B-10, and later B-12, would remain service until the arrival of the Boeing B-17 at the end of the 1930s.

In May 1928, having finally abandoned traditional biplanes, Boeing's design department responded to a

A Boeing P-26A in the wind tunnel at Langley Research Center, May 1934. (NASA/LISAR)

A Boeing Y1B-9A bomber under construction in February 1932. It is interesting to note that the metal structure is a direct copy of the wooden structures previously used. (Boeing)

The XP-9 was the first single-wing fighter built by Boeing. It had an entirely metal structure and was powered by a 600hp Curtiss SV-1570 engine. Its performance was disappointing and the aircraft managed only 15 hours' flying time. (USAF)

request to tender from the Army with a small single-winged, all-metal fighter, the model 96 (XP-9). With its Duralumin-skinned semi-monocoque fuselage and 600hp Curtiss V12 engine, it seemed every bit the racing plane. It first flew on 18 November 1930, but sadly the expected performance was not achieved. Far from being discouraged, in September 1931 the Seattle engineers set to work on a completely new fighter design. Once again, Boeing built it at his own expense, the Army providing just the engines and

fittings for the three prototypes. It was therefore under the experimental designation of XP-936 that the new aircraft first flew on 20 March 1932. With the results obtained from the initial tests, the Army bought two of the three prototypes, changing their designation to XP-26. Although of metal construction, the small monoplane's wings were stiffened with struts and the fixed undercarriage was covered in substantial fairings. Despite its toy-like appearance, thanks to its big Pratt & Whitney radial engine and stocky fuselage the XP-26 could fly 30mph faster than the fighters then in service[20]. With such performance, the Army was not slow to order 111 P-26As at a cost of $9,000 each, an order that was soon increased to 136 planes. Production of the monoplanes began on 11 January 1933 and, a fortnight later, the last biplane designed by Boeing and built at Seattle, the model 236 (XF6B-1), made its first but ultimately fruitless flight. A page was about to be turned.

In these early years of the 1930s, the Boeing Airplane Company remained resolutely focused on the future despite the buffeting it had gone through. Its management had energetically negotiated the corner that would put it on the road towards a successful future. The best was yet to come...

---

20. Actually, the Boeing P-12F. It also had a faster rate of climb (690m per minute as against 540m per minute).

The Boeing YP-29A was based on the experimental XP-940 fighter, with a substantially modified cockpit and engine housing. (NASA/LISAR)

An impressive formation of around 20 Boeing P-26s in the dawn light. (AFFTC)

The many coats of the P-26

Boeing delivered 36 P-26s to the US Army Air Corps between 1933 and 1936. The planes equipped 17 pursuit squadrons forming six pursuit groups and bore some of the most colourful decoration in the history of American aviation. Here are a few examples.

1. The P-26 as flown by the leader of the 1st Pursuit Group based at Selfridge Field, Michigan. The 1st PG's insignia on the cowling was accompanied by the motto: 'Win or die'. Its pilot, Colonel Ralph Joyce, commanded the unit from 1934 to 1937. (F.C. Dickey Jr collection)

2. P-26 no. 94 of the 17th Pursuit Squadron, part of the 1st Pursuit Group based at Selfridge Field, Michigan, in late 1940. It bears the 'Snow Owl' insignia and the fuselage band is white. (M. Olmsted collection)

3. P-26 no. 23 from the 94th Pursuit Squadron, part of the 1st Pursuit Group based at Selfridge Field. The diagonal fuselage band was painted red. (R.L. Cavanagh collection)

4. A line-up of P-26s from the 26th Pursuit Group based at March Field, in 1934. The aircraft in the foreground, no. 102, is the group commander's. The markings are in red and yellow and the insignia is accompanied by the motto 'Ever into Danger'. (USAF)

5. A camouflaged P-26 of the 34th Pursuit Squadron, part of the 17th Pursuit Group, at March Field. (M. Olmsted collection)

6. P-26 no. 15 from the 6th Pursuit Squadron, part of the 18th Pursuit Group, at Wheeler Field, Hawaii. The cowling markings were in red. (R.L. Cavanagh collection)

7. P-26 no. 43 from the 73rd Pursuit Squadron, part of the 17th Pursuit Group based at March Field. Markings were red and yellow. (R.L. Cavanagh collection)

8. P-26 no. 7 was one of three in the Bolling Field detachment. The engine cowling was red and yellow. (M. Olmsted collection)

9. P-26 no. 90 from the 95th Pursuit Squadron, part of the 17th Pursuit Group based at March Field. The markings were blue and yellow. (R.L. Cavanagh collection)

10. P-26 no. 40 from the 19th Pursuit Squadron, part of the 18th Pursuit Group based at Wheeler Field, Hawaii. The two fuselage bands and the engine cowling were yellow (M. Olmsted collection)

This model 247 is one of three that have survived. It is the 47th aircraft from the production series and has been restored to flying condition. (Boeing)

CHAPTER 2

The turning point

>> By the end of 1933, the future of the aviation giant that was the United Aircraft & Transport Corporation seemed assured, despite the economic crisis. Technologically, Boeing's design department had managed change successfully, which was not always the case with other manufacturers, some of whom would go out of business because of a failure to adapt.

>> The first modern airliner

In 1932, capitalising on its success, Boeing's design department started work on the development of a new airliner for United Air Lines. UATC expected to buy around 60 examples so as to compete with TWA's Ford Trimotors and American Air Lines' Curtiss Condors. At a total cost of $4,000,000, it was the biggest civil airliner order up to that time.

Several lines of development were pursued by 'Claire' Egtvedt's team, among them a comfortable 50-seat plane as well as a smaller aircraft where comfort would be partially sacrificed in favour of superior performance. Boeing's chief engineer, Charles N. 'Monty' Monteith, was an ardent supporter of the second option and strongly opposed the construction of an aircraft bigger than those already in service. In his view, building three planes for six passengers was

less costly than building one plane for 18 passengers. The Seattle engineers worked on several preliminary plans for aircraft with between ten and 15 seats, two engines or three, and biplanes or monoplanes. After much discussion, a design for a small, fast, twin-engined monoplane for ten passengers was chosen, although the idea of a larger plane was not yet dismissed.

Phil Johnson sent F. B. Rentschler the preliminary design specification for a fast transport aircraft, bearing the model 247 designation, to replace the models 40 and 95. Compared with planes then in service, the model 247 was at the very least revolutionary. Aside from its monocoque metal frame with anodised skin, it had 550hp Pratt & Whitney S1D1 Wasp radial engines turning fixed-pitch, three-bladed propellers. Its deep-profile, cantilever wings possessed a large spar that dispensed with the need for struts (unfortunately, the spar cut through the cabin and passengers had to climb over it to reach their seats) and it had the benefit of an electrically powered retracting undercarriage. While not considered in the early stages, space was made in the course of the design for a co-pilot and a stewardess. The cabin was sound-proofed, carpeted and air-conditioned. At the front, on the partition, there was for the first time a light to indicate to passengers when they should buckle their seat belts and extinguish cigarettes. Less powerful than the Fords and Fokkers then in service, the Boeing 247 was more compact, faster and would show that it could not merely fly, but also climb, on only one engine[1].

Drawing on their experience with the Y1B-9 bomber, the engineers were sufficiently confident to bypass the prototype stage and start straight away on the first production aircraft. The first Boeing 247 flew on Wednesday 8 February 1933 with Les Tower (a former Montana cowboy) at the controls and Louis Goldsmith as co-pilot. The plane put up an excellent performance from the start, even better than the design team had expected. In consequence, UAL had no hesitation in confirming its order. To meet the deadlines imposed by UAL, who wanted to get the

aircraft into service as soon as possible, Boeing was obliged to organise its plant into three different shifts. There were now 2,200 workers on the books. Once again, Phil Johnson's know-how worked miracles: UAL received its first plane on 30 March 1933 and 14 more arrived in April, followed by ten in May, ten in June, 11 in July and, finally, ten in August[2].

The Boeing 247 entered service on 1 June 1933 on the transcontinental New York–San Francisco route with three daily trips, replacing the Boeing 80As. The journey, which lasted about 20 hours[3], cost $160 single and $260 return. In the same month, UAL also put 247s into service on the New York–Chicago route, with six flights a day[4]. By August, there were ten flights a day between these two cities and, on the 15th of that month, the 247s entered service between Chicago and Dallas–Fort Worth. However, it was discovered that if the Boeing 247 was forced to fly on only one engine it could barely get above 600 metres, posing problems at airfields situated at altitude, such

---

1. By comparison, the Boeing 247 had a cruising speed of 155mph against the Ford 5-AT-B's 120mph.

2. The allocations to the different UATC companies were as follows: 21 planes to NAT, 19 to BAT, 8 to PAT, 7 to UAL and 4 to VAL.

3. The flying time from New York to San Francisco was 21 hours 30 minutes westbound and 20 hours eastbound.

4. The flying time from New York to Chicago was 5 hours 30 minutes westbound and 4 hours 45 minutes eastbound.

Model 247s for United Air Lines under construction in the Seattle shops. In the foreground is the 11th aircraft of the production run, registered NC13311. It entered service with UAL/Varney Airlines on 25 April 1933. (Boeing)

Two model 247s were bought by Lufthansa in 1934. This one, registered D-AGAR, was wrecked on the ground after a collision with a French airliner at Nuremberg on 24 May 1935. (DR)

as Cheyenne in Wyoming. The problem was solved by fitting new Hamilton Standard two-blade propellers with variable pitch, which increased the altitude at which single-engined flying was possible to 1,200 metres as well as significantly improving the distance needed for take-off, the rate of climb and the cruising speed, the latter going from 165mph to 170mph.

With its huge order, UAL left the other companies little hope of getting hold of any Boeing 247s before this order was fulfilled (a clause in the contract actually specified this). This apparent success would soon rebound on Boeing and UAL. Indeed, unable to obtain

any 247s for his company in a satisfactory time-frame, Jack Frye, the president of TWA, turned to Douglas, asking the Santa Monica firm to design a 'made-to-measure' aircraft at least equalling the performance of the Boeing. Thus was born the DC-1, the direct ancestor of the legendary DC-3. As history would show, this aircraft would totally eclipse the otherwise promising career of the Boeing 247. The prototype DC-1 flew on 1 July 1933, one month to the day after the 247's entry into service. On 19 February 1934, Eddie Rickenbacker and Jack Frye took it on a record-breaking flight linking Los Angeles and Newark in

The model 247D's cockpit had everything needed in a modern airliner. The engine throttles and fuel-supply controls were located on the right in front of the co-pilot's seat. (Boeing)

The model 247D's cabin was relatively spacious, but the wing struts crossed the aisle at the centre, obliging passengers to step over it to get to their seats. (Boeing)

The second production-series model 247D was registered NC13361. It is seen here on 21 September 1934 awaiting delivery to United Air Lines. It was in use by this company until August 1942 before being requisitioned by the USAAF. After the war it was sold to Mexico. (Boeing)

13 hours 4 minutes – six hours less than achieved by the Boeing 247. Boeing's head start had gone.

Starting in autumn 1933, in an attempt at publicity, UAL's Boeing 247s distinguished themselves with a series of speed records. On 25 September, C. T. Robertson flew from Kansas City to Chicago at an average speed of 204mph. The next month, A. W. Stainback linked Salt Lake City and Cheyenne in 1 hour 59 minutes. At the end of the year, John Wolf flew from New York to Cleveland in 1 hour 55 minutes, while George Boyd took only 38 minutes to link Salt Lake City to Rock Springs.

Even better, the following year was marked by the third place gained by Roscoe Turner in the legendary London to Melbourne race, when he came in behind the British de Havilland DH88 Comet racing plane and a KLM Douglas DC-2. These performances were like a thunderbolt to the European manufacturers, leaving them stunned. They had just discovered that American airliners could put up almost the same performance as the best racing planes. Worst of all, they suddenly realised that they had no planes of the calibre of the DC-2 or the 247 under development[5]! (see panel on page 45). It can be said without fear of contradiction that the London to Melbourne race marked a turning point in aviation history.

Despite all this, the 247's entry into service was not without its setbacks. There were several fatal accidents in 1933: on 12 May, while being delivered, a NAT

Boeing 247 hit a hillside near Provo in Utah; on 10 October another 247 crashed at Chesterton, Indiana, after an explosion in an item of cargo, killing seven people[6]. That, at least, was the conclusion reached by the commission of enquiry undertaken by the Department of Commerce, making this the first act of sabotage against an airliner. On 9 November, a PAT 247 crashed in fog at Portland, Oregon, killing four people. Finally, on 24 November, a NAT 247 crashed at Ottawa, Illinois, causing the death of three people[7].

While the 247s were criss-crossing the United States, Boeing's engineers were working on ways to improve the plane, coming up with the 247D, with new engine housings designed by NACA and all-metal control surfaces. These improvements brought an increase in the cruising speed of 7mph and of the range to 840 miles[8]. At the same time, Boeing was looking for new outlets for its 247 and designed a military version, the model 247Y, armed with three machine guns. This plane went to China and was used by the military governor of Hubei province.

5. The DC-2, which carried three passengers and 408kg of mail, had arrived second, making 18 stops while the DH88 Comet had made just five.

6. The plane was not at fault. The enquiry showed that the explosion had come from a 'dangerous package' that had been loaded in the cargo bay without proper checks.

7. It is worth putting the number of accidents in context: in 1933, there were about 100 accidents and other incidents of all kinds among the 504 airliners in service. During that year, these planes carried 568,940 passengers, 3,545 tonnes of mail and covered 54,642,545 miles.

8. This figure was obtained by running the engines at 62% of full power; at 75%, it was no more than 750 miles.

Roscoe Turner and the Boeing 247

In early 1933, Sir MacPherson Robertson, a very wealthy 75-year-old Scotsman, owner of MacRobertson Chocolate Company and MacRobertson-Miller Aviation, announced his intention to sponsor an air race between London and Melbourne to celebrate the Australian city's centenary.

For journalists, the Melbourne Centenary Air Race soon became the race of the century. The start date was set for 20 October 1934. Competitors were to pass through five compulsory check points (Baghdad, Allahabad, Singapore, Darwin and Charleville) and the winner would pocket the tidy sum of £10,000.

By 1 June 1934, the closing date for entries, there were no fewer than 64 competitors. Among them was Roscoe Turner, media darling who had just won the Thompson Trophy and was known to the public as 'America's Aerial Speed King'. Aware of the increased publicity that a win would bring him, Turner started looking for sponsors and soon managed to convince Pratt & Whitney, Boeing and United Airlines to back him. For

'Claire' Egtvedt, it was the perfect opportunity to demonstrate the reliability of the Boeing 247. He therefore agreed to have one of the 247Ds that had been sold to UAL modified by replacing the seats with additional fuel tanks, taking the capacity up to 5,380 litres. Unsparing in his efforts, Turner looked for other sponsors, none of them to be sneezed at: H.J. Heinz Company, MacMillan Petroleum Corporation, William Randolph Hearst and Warner Bros. He also recruited two crew members – Clyde E. Pangborn as co-pilot and Reeder Nichols as navigator. The Boeing was transported to Britain by sea and, after a few ups and downs, reached Mildenhall ready for the start. Unfortunately, it was deemed too heavy according to the race rules and it had to have some of its fuel removed, obliging Turner to make a stop at each check point.

Eventually, on 20 October 1934, there were just 20 aircraft on the start line. A draw was made for the order of take-off and the Boeing 247 was second to go, 45 seconds after 06.30 GMT. After stops at Athens, Baghdad

Roscoe Turner with the actress, Mary Pickford. (DR)

and Karachi, the American crew lost three hours trying to find the runway at Allahabad. They then cleared the subsequent stages (Alor Star, Singapore, Koepang, Darwin, Charleville and Bourke) without a hitch, before crossing the finishing line at Melbourne at 03.43 GMT and landing at Laverton 15 minutes later. The Boeing came in third behind Scott and Campbell Black's de Havilland Comet and Parmentier's Douglas DC-2 with an overall time of 92 hours 55 minutes 38 seconds and a flying time of 85 hours 22 minutes 50 seconds. It was an outstanding performance for an airliner.

As soon as he heard about the aircraft's arrival, 'Claire' Egtvedt telegraphed Roscoe Turner: '...the boys are all proud of your outstanding accomplishment and fully appreciate what you and Panghorn have done by successfully completing such a lengthy flight over strange terrain. We also appreciate that you were flying a commercial transport plane where dependability was first consideration in design.'

The model 247 no. 5 flown by Roscoe Turner in the London–Melbourne Race. (DR)

Unfortunately for Boeing, the 247 would have a limited career: two years later, UAL ordered its first DC-3s and sold its 247s to smaller companies. What had been the first modern airliner slipped slowly into oblivion. Nonetheless, four Boeing 247s have survived to the present day, one of which has been restored to airworthiness[9].

>> The end of a dream

Despite the model 247's relative success, UATC's situation at the start of 1934 was not outstanding. The group had to face up to its problems. After the loss of the contract for the B-9 medium bomber to the Martin B-10 and the end of the P-26 series, whose production had not been particularly profitable, interest from the military was at its lowest. In addition, the development of the Sikorsky S-42 seaplane had been extremely expensive and, finally, engine production had suffered from serious strikes at Pratt & Whitney. 'Claire' Egtvedt, who had been appointed president of Boeing Airplane Company on 2 August 1933, took matters in hand, deciding that the company's future lay in the manufacture of large airliners developed alongside bombers. Current problems, however, were nothing compared with what was to come.

The journalist Fulton Lewis Jr. had discovered that some of the postal contracts had been given to companies that had not been best placed in the

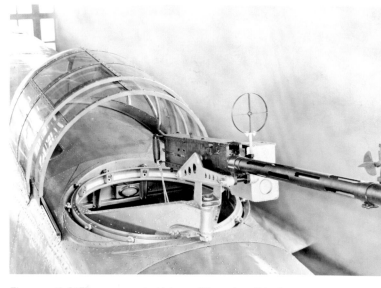

The seventh 247D was converted into a military aircraft in January 1937 and delivered to Marshal Chang Hsueh Liang. Pictured is one of the three 12.7mm machine guns with which it was armed. (Boeing)

bidding. With this information, he approached the Alabama Democrat senator Hugo Black, who set up a special commission to look into these practices. Starting in January 1934, the commission began hearings with the senior managers of the postal administration and chairmen of the airlines. Jumping the gun somewhat, Black hastily concluded that the companies in question were run by a money-grabbing, corrupt 'bunch of crooks' and that the postal contracts

The 18th model 247 was delivered to National Air Transport on 3 May 1933 and, after numerous changes of ownership, it ended its career in Canada with Chevron Standard Ltd of Calgary who donated it to the National Aviation Museum, Ottawa, on 11 February 1967. (J. Gerritsma)

Philip Gustav Johnson

(Boeing)

Seattle, Washington, 5 November 1894–Wichita, Kansas, 14 September 1944

The son of Swedish immigrants, Philip Gustav Johnson gained his engineering degree at Washington State University before joining Boeing in 1917 as an industrial designer. With his gift for organisation, he found himself three years later as head of the Seattle factory. In 1921, Phil Johnson became vice-president and was appointed general manager the next year. Continuing his rise through the company hierarchy, he was just 31 when he became president of the Boeing Airplane Company, in 1926. Following the reorganisation undertaken by Boeing and Rentschler, he took over at United Air Lines, then at UATC, in 1933. He was obliged to leave this post the following year when the group was broken up. However, Johnson soon bounced back and was for a time director of the Kenworth Motor Truck Corporation before leaving for Canada in 1937 to take over at Trans Canada Airways (TCA). Two years later, he rejoined Boeing as president with the task of putting the company's production on to a war footing. One result of this was the mass production of the B-29 heavy bomber at Wichita, Kansas. It was while on a visit to this plant, on 14 September 1944, that he died of a heart attack.

had been signed to benefit friends of Herbert Hoover's Republican administration. He went as far as asserting that the procedures for agreeing the contracts were riddled with irregularities. William Boeing soon became a target.

Hugo Black's allegations, which were later shown to be unfounded, put UATC in the spotlight. The odour of scandal spread rapidly in the media. On 9 February 1934, Philip G. Johnson resigned the chairmanship of UATC and left for Canada to found Trans Canada Airlines. To put an end to the scandal, on 19 February, the Democrat president, F. D. Roosevelt, decreed the cancellation of the postal contracts and asked General Benjamin D. Foulois, chief of the Army Air Corps, to organise the carrying of mail on a restricted number of routes using military planes and crews. It proved to be a disastrous decision. There were 66 accidents causing the death of 12 pilots. On 8 May 1934, Roosevelt and the new director general of the postal service, James Farley, decided to call a halt to the situation and once again entrust carriage of the mail to private firms, under certain conditions. In particular, companies that had previously carried the mail were barred. However, the drawing up of the new regulations left a lot to be desired. To get around the ban, all a company had to do was change its name[10]. The most restrictive originated with Black himself: on 12 June 1934, he pushed through a new Air Mail Act (also known as the 'Black-McKellar Bill') that forbade aeronautical companies from simultaneously owning both manufacturing firms and airlines. It was clear from this decision that UATC was the leading group in the firing line. The industrial empire built up by William Boeing and Frederick Rentschler was evidently doomed to dismemberment.

UATC was split into three parts. Pratt & Whitney, Vought, Sikorsky and Hamilton formed the United Aircraft Manufacturing Company while the airline companies – BAT, PAT, NAT, VAL – and the Boeing School of Aeronautics (a subsidiary of BAT based in Oakland, California) became the United Air Lines Transport Corporation. Finally, the Boeing Airplane Company was reorganised in Delaware on 19 July to become an independent entity. It would henceforth consist of the Boeing Aircraft Company in Seattle, which controlled the Boeing Aircraft Company of Canada Ltd, and the Stearman Aircraft Company of Wichita. 'Claire' L. Egtvedt became president of the new Boeing Airplane Company.

UATC officially ceased to exist on 26 September 1934. Profoundly affected by the dismantling of the empire he had built and by the way in which Congress had treated it, William Boeing had resigned from his post of chairman of the board a few days earlier, on 18 September. He sold off most of his shares and left the world of aviation for good in favour of breeding horses. His one consolation was to receive the Daniel Guggenheim Medal in recognition of the role he had played in the development of American aviation. From that day on, he was to play no further significant part in the enterprise he had created 18 years earlier.

Following the split up, Boeing had no more than $582,000 in liquidities, out of which they had to pay salaries and other costs. Staff numbers dropped below 700, and this figure could have fallen even further had

9. The four Boeing 247s are located respectively at the National Air & Space Museum in Washington, the Museum of Flight in Seattle, the National Aviation Museum in Ottawa and the Science Museum at Wroughton, UK.

10. According to some sources, Jim Farley himself made the companies aware of this flaw in the regulations. Thus American Airways became American Airlines and Eastern Air Transport became Eastern Air Lines.

The XB-15 outside Boeing's Seattle plant. This view gives a good impression of the bomber's large wing-surface area, unique of its type. (P.M. Bowers collection)

The XB-15's flight deck was very spacious. Behind the pilot's (left) and co-pilot's (right) seats were the radio operator's (left) and navigator's (right) posts. The twin doors at the end gave access to the bomb compartment. (Boeing)

the employees not accepted part-time working and half salaries. On the broader front, the year 1934 had not been as bad as all that for the American aviation industry. A total of 1,615 aircraft had been built, about 300 more than in the previous year. Of this number, 437 were military planes and 490 had been exported. The year 1935 would see production rise slightly[11].

» The era of the giants

In the spring of 1934, a boost came from the USAAC. On 14 May, 'Claire' Egtvedt and C. A. Van Dusen, director of the Glenn L. Martin Aircraft Company, were invited to Wright Field by General Conger Pratt to receive a most unexpected request. The head of the Air Corps, Benjamin Foulois, was convinced of the worth of very-long-range bombers. In his view, a bomber with a range of 5,000 miles would be able to assure the defence of Hawaii and Alaska. The Materiel Division had therefore drawn up a specification for an experimental bomber capable of carrying a 900kg bomb load over 5,000 miles at a speed of 200mph. The two manufacturers were invited to come up with their plans by the following 15 June 1935. Martin proposed its model 145 and Boeing proposed its model 294, a four-engined plane designed by a team headed by Egtvedt and R. A. Minshall. Like its competitor, the model 294 was to be powered by Allison V-1710 V12 engines. Boeing's proposal was accepted. A contract[12] for the construction of a prototype designated XBLR-1 (Experimental Bomber Long Range) was signed on 29 June 1935.

---

11. In 1935, the United States produced 1,710 planes, of which 459 were for military use. Source: AIA Facts & Figures.

12. Contract no W535-AC-7618 at a cost of $704,367.55.

An impressive view of the XB-15 in flight. (Boeing)

The XBLR-1 did not keep this designation for long, being renamed the XB-15 to conform to the system currently in force. The XB-15 was an amazing aircraft for its time, especially because of its size, with a 45.41m wing span and 458m² wing surface. As there were no Allison engines available, it was temporarily supplied with four of the less powerful 850hp Pratt & Whitney R-1830-11 engines. The deep wing profile was directly inspired by that of the B-9, and the fuselage, of semi-monocoque design, was fitted out with long-range flight in mind. It thus had a place for a navigator, couchettes and a kitchenette for the crew. The engines were accessible in flight via passages inside the leading edge of the wings. For defence, the XB-15 had six machine guns mounted in six different turrets. The three bomb bays were large enough to carry bombs from 45kg up to 900kg.

The building of the prototype took quite a long time, requiring around 670,000 hours of work. It first flew on Friday 15 October 1937 with Edmund 'Eddie' Allen and Major John D. Corkille of the Air Corps as crew. After several familiarisation flights, the plane finally arrived at Wright Field in December ready for intensive tests. It began its long military career on 6 August 1938 when it was taken over by the 49th Bombardment Squadron at Langley Field, Virginia.

On 24 January 1939, a terrible earthquake hit 11

The XB-15's nose. The articulated mounting of the glazed nose cone, ball turret and 12.7mm machine gun allowed the gun to fire in all directions. (Boeing)

towns in Chile, killing 30,000 people, injuring 50,000 and leaving hundreds of thousands without shelter. The American Red Cross asked President Roosevelt for help with the relief work and the big four-engined plane carried 1,470kg of medical supplies to the area.

A few months later, on Saturday 10 June 1939, the XB-15 took off again towards the south on another unusual mission. At the request of the president, the plane flew back the body of the Mexican pilot Francisco Sarabia to his home country. A few days earlier, he had been killed when his plane was wrecked in the waters of the Potomac River after he had completed a record flight between Mexico and New York[13]. Following these highly publicised events, the XB-15 broke some new records. On Sunday 30 July 1939, in the hands of Major Haynes, it took off from Patterson Field, Ohio, beating two records for load-carrying at altitude, when it carried 14,117kg at 2,000m followed by 9,986kg at 2,500m. Three days later, on 1 August, it easily established a further record: in a flight lasting 18 hours 40 minutes 47 seconds, the Boeing XB-15 carried a load of two tonnes over 3,107 miles, at an average speed of 166mph. At the end of the flight there was still sufficient fuel in the tanks for a further 600 miles!

» The birth of a legend

On 8 August 1934, before the XB-15 had even flown, the USAAC sent Boeing, Douglas and Martin a circular containing the specification for a new multi-engined bomber. It stipulated, among other things, a maximum speed of 200–250mph at 3,000 metres, a cruising speed of 170–220mph, between six and ten hours' flying time, a service ceiling of 6,100–7,600 metres and a two-tonne bomb load. The only thing not specified was the number of engines. While Boeing's teams were heavily involved in the construction of the XB-15, Egtvedt nevertheless took the risk of taking on the project of developing a smaller four-engined aircraft than the XB-15, accompanied by a civilian derivative. The two planes received model numbers 299 and 300 and priority was given to the bomber.

The model 299's starboard waist gun was inherited from the design for the XB-15. (USAF)

Monteith appointed E. G. Emery as head of project 299, with Edward Curtiss Wells, aged just 24, as assistant. On 26 September, Boeing's director allocated a budget of $275,000 to the project. The development costs would run to an additional $150,000.

The engineers employed the same structural methods developed for the XB-15, in particular the principle of a semi-monocoque structure with a load-bearing skin. Created by a team of eight men, the model 299 was a resolutely modern plane. It had a retracting undercarriage, a side-by-side cockpit, disc brakes, electrically operated bomb doors and variable-pitch, constant-speed propellers. The engines were 750hp Pratt & Whitney R-1690 Hornets with a 6,435-litre fuel tank. By contrast, Martin and Douglas worked on twin-engined designs: Martin on an improved version of the B-10, the model 146; Douglas on a derivative of the DC-2, the DB-1 (Douglas Bomber One).

The model 299 was shown to the press at Boeing Field on 17 July 1935. The stunned journalists came

13. On 24 May 1939, Francisco Sarabia had flown from Mexico City to New York, a distance of 2,350 miles, in 10 hours and 47 minutes.

The prototype B-17 on its unveiling to the press. This aircraft, then carrying civilian registration marks, is often referred to as the XB-17, even though it was never officially designated as such. (USAF)

The model 299 crashed at Wright Field on 30 October 1935. (USAF)

With its 31.63-metre wing span, the Y1B-17 had sufficient space for big flaps of 7.45-metre width that could be lowered to a 60° angle. The aircraft was fitted with pneumatic de-icers on the leading edge. (P.M. Bowers collection)

This B-17B, modified to a B-17C, belonged to the Wright Field test center's Materiel Division, as indicated by the letters MD painted on the fin and left wing. (P.M. Bowers collection)

Powered by its Wright R-1820 Cyclone engines, this Y1B-17 steadily gains height. (USAF)

Four Boeing Y1B-17s from the 2nd Bomber Group flying in formation over Manhattan. (M. Olmsted collection)

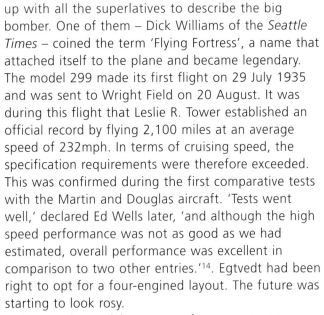

During anti-aircraft manoeuvres in May 1938, this Y1B-17 from the 20th Bomber Squadron was given a temporary coat of brown and green camouflage. (USAF)

up with all the superlatives to describe the big bomber. One of them – Dick Williams of the *Seattle Times* – coined the term 'Flying Fortress', a name that attached itself to the plane and became legendary. The model 299 made its first flight on 29 July 1935 and was sent to Wright Field on 20 August. It was during this flight that Leslie R. Tower established an official record by flying 2,100 miles at an average speed of 232mph. In terms of cruising speed, the specification requirements were therefore exceeded. This was confirmed during the first comparative tests with the Martin and Douglas aircraft. 'Tests went well,' declared Ed Wells later, 'and although the high speed performance was not as good as we had estimated, overall performance was excellent in comparison to two other entries.'[14]. Egtvedt had been right to opt for a four-engined layout. The future was starting to look rosy.

Among the model 299's new features was a system that enabled the control surfaces to be locked to prevent high winds from moving them while parked – a clever idea but one that would turn out to have fatal consequences. On 30 October 1935, with just one test flight remaining, the crew forgot to unlock the system.

The model 299, piloted by Major Ployer P. Hill (head of the Wright Field test-flight section), crashed on take-off at Wright Field. Leslie Tower, who was on board as an observer, died from his burns, and the $432,034 prototype was destroyed[15].

While the design of the plane was not at fault, the US Army Staff asked for the model 299 to be removed from the competition and an order for 133 DB-1s (B-18) to be placed. According to sources at the Department of War, the model 299 may have been rejected by the AAC for this contract, but aircraft from this manufacturer were not excluded from future Army orders[16]. Fortunately for Boeing, the heavy-bomber concept had such ardent partisans (among whom were General Hap Arnold and General 'Tooey' Spaatz) in the Air Corps that a recommendation was made for 65 Boeings to be ordered with a corresponding reduction in the number Douglas planes. The Army opted for a compromise, confirming the Douglas order as well as

14. Quoted by Mary Wells Geer in *Boeing's Ed Wells*, page 59.

15. The team consisted of four men from the Materiel Division: Major Ployer P. Hill (pilot), Lt. Donald L. Putt (co-pilot), John B. Cutting (engineer) and Mark H. Koogler (mechanic)..

16. Op. Cit. page 64.

acquiring 13 pilot-production Boeings on 17 January 1936. These aircraft were initially designated YB-17, later changed to Y1B-17. They differed from the prototype in their more powerful Wright Cyclone R-1820-39 engines, which delivered 1,000hp at take-off and 850hp at 1,500 metres, as well as a modified undercarriage, a reduced crew of six and a new oxygen-supply system. The first one flew on 2 December 1936 in the hands of Major John D. Corkille.

Boeing's factory proved to be too cramped for the simultaneous construction of XB-15s and YB-17s, so on 8 March 1936 Boeing acquired a 27.7-acre site on Marginal Way, Seattle, between Boeing Field and the Duwamish Canal, to build a second factory (named Plant 2, with the original building becoming Plant 1) at a cost of $235,410.

But Boeing was far from being out of its troubles. The B-17's development encountered substantial technical problems at great expense to the manufacturer. The Wright Cyclone engines were prone to overheating, which caused numerous breakdowns. On 7 December 1936, on its third flight, the first YB-17 encountered two problems simultaneously: the pilot had made extensive use of the brakes while taxiing and retracted the undercarriage immediately after take-off allowing no time for the brakes to cool. Two of the engines then overheated, forcing the pilot to make an emergency landing. However, the hot disc brakes had locked on, preventing the wheels from turning freely. As soon as the plane touched down it overturned. Fortunately, no-one was injured and Congress did not revoke the contract, but it did order an extra 52 B-18s. The B-17 was facing one piece of bad luck after another and nobody seemed to want it, apart from the Air Corps Staff.

Y1B-17 no. 63 from the 96th Bomber Squadron. The insignia were painted on the nose; the spinners were black and the front part of the engine cowlings was red. (J.R. Pritchard collection)

The B-17B differed from the Y1B-17 in its larger rudder and flaps, as well as its modified nose. The spherical turret was removed, giving the bomber better visibility. (P.M. Bowers collection)

This was one of 20 B-17Cs delivered to the RAF. It is registered as AN521 and was delivered to 90 Squadron on 25 May 1941. It then served in Egypt with 220 Squadron and was wrecked in an accident near Shallufa on 10 January 1942. (Boeing)

This B-17C, photographed on 28 August 1940, clearly shows the ventral 'bathtub'. This version was supplied with Wright R-1820-65 Cyclone engines and its defensive armament had been completely revised. (P.M. Bowers collection)

The YB-17s were allocated to the 2nd Bombardment Group base at Langley Field, Virginia. On 5 August 1937, this unit had a total of 12 aircraft, with the 13th remaining at Wright Field to continue the testing programme. The Air Corps organised a big publicity campaign to polish the plane's image. On 16 May, four aircraft commanded by Colonel Olds undertook an 11-hour flight during which they flew over 20 US cities. On 15 February 1938, in a bid to show the new bomber's range, six planes took off from Langley Field heading to Buenos Aires for the investiture of the new Argentinean president, Roberto M. Ortiz. The aircraft flew over a crowd of two million people who had gathered in Buenos Aires. The following August, three planes flew to Bogota. Finally, in May, the YB-17s took part in manoeuvres organised by Major-General Frank Andrews and distinguished themselves by locating the 'enemy' fleet represented by the Italian liner Rex. With this achievement, the Air Corps demonstrated that it

could intercept an enemy ship well out to sea[17]. At this time, a 14th YB-17 airframe, originally intended for static tests, was put into flying order for the purpose of turbo-compressor tests. The tests, carried out in early 1939 at the builder's expense, gave astonishing results. At 7,600 metres, the maximum speed rose to 271mph and the ceiling was increased to 11,600 metres.

Thanks to all this, but also as a consequence of the rapid deterioration of the situation in Europe, Congress began to take a new look at the B-17. Contracts were signed for 39 B-17Bs and 38 B-17Cs[18]. These aircraft benefited from a number of improvements, notably to the turbo-compressors, flaps and enlarged rudder. The first B-17B was accepted on 29 July 1939 and the last on 30 March 1940; the first B-17C flew on 21 July 1940. The career of the Flying Fortress had finally begun.

» The Stratoliner

In the civil aviation field, the situation continued to develop. Thanks to his contacts in the Army, Tommy Tomlinson[19], TWA's chief engineer, managed to get a flight at the controls of a B-17 and, impressed, organised a meeting with Jack Frye, four engineers and Boeing's commercial manager, Fred Collins, with the idea of working on a commercial version (the model 300). The aircraft designed by Boeing's engineers used the same aerofoils, tailplane and engines as the model 299. It could carry 33 passengers by day and 25 at night (16 on couchettes and nine in seats). The concept gradually evolved into the model 307 Stratoliner.

By the time it appeared in March 1936, the Boeing 307 differed substantially from the 299. The circular-section fuselage was pressurised using a system that, at 4,500 metres altitude, reproduced the pressure encountered at 2,500 metres. It was a first for a plane of this size and for an airliner. The 307 was thus able to fly above much turbulence, thereby considerably

The Boeing 307 Stratoliner was the first pressurised airliner. Pictured is the third aircraft in the production run in Pan American Airways' colours. (Boeing)

SA-307B no. 1996 while in service with Royal Cambodian Air. It was sold to Aigle Azur Indochine on 16 September 1955. (DR)

The second SA-307B for TWA was registered as NX1940 for publicity purposes; its original registration had been NX19906. (Boeing)

improving passenger comfort. On 1 January 1937, a contract worth $1,590,000 was signed with TWA for the delivery of six planes (plus seven on option). They were to be delivered during the second half of 1938, but, in June 1938, with three of the aircraft in the final stages of assembly, the contract was broken by a default in payment.

Nevertheless, Eddie Allen made the first flight on 31 December 1938 and found that the plane behaved extremely well. In the ensuing weeks, Allen and Julius Barr continued the test programme without any untoward incident. A few months later, news came out that Howard Hughes had become the principal shareholder in TWA, thus restoring confidence in the

firm. On 18 March 1939, Harlan Hull went to Boeing to take part in a demonstration flight for two representatives from the Dutch airline, KLM. During the flight it was intended to observe the behaviour of the aircraft at low speed with two engines on one side out of action. At 3,000 metres, the plane stalled and went into a tailspin. It crashed in a wood not far from

17. When the YB-17s took off from Mitchell Field on 12 May 1938 at 8.30am the *Rex* was still over 700 miles offshore; the liner was intercepted at 12.25pm.

18. B-17B by contract no AC10155 of 17 August 1937, RB-17C by contract no 13257 of 20 September 1939.

19. Daniel W. 'Tommy' Tomlinson (1891–1996) distinguished himself with his experimental high-altitude flights with the Northrop 'Experimental Overweather Laboratory'. In 1930, he wrote *The Sky's the Limit*.

The three Stratoliners used by Pan American Airways were named (from front to back) Clipper Comet, Clipper Flying Cloud and Clipper Rainbow. (Boeing)

The only survivor, the third of the SA-307s, as exhibited at the Pima County Air Museum in Tucson, Arizona, in 1976. It has since been fully restored and returned to flying condition. (A. Pelletier)

Alder, Washington, killing all ten people on board[20]. According to witnesses, the plane had been coming out of the tailspin when the wings and tailplane broke off.

The enquiry conducted by Boeing and the Civil Aeronautics Authority (CAA) went on for several months before the probable cause of the accident was determined. It was attributed to the wing breaking off during an intentional tailspin. The section of wing broke away and tore off a piece of the tailplane.

Naturally, this tragic accident delayed the programme, but did not put it in doubt. Modifications made included enlarging the flaps with a view to reducing buffeting[21], the introduction of slots so as to improve lateral stability at low speeds, and an increase in the area of the fin. Test flights started again on 18 July 1939 with a second plane, and pressurisation tests began on 8 July when the aircraft reached a height of 6,700 metres. Negotiations between Boeing, TWA and Howard Hughes had resumed in June and it was agreed that TWA would buy five aircraft and Hughes one. Deliveries would not take place before the beginning of 1940 because of the modifications and the need for certification by the CAA.

Despite their great similarity, the aircraft ordered by TWA and PAA were certified separately. The PAA version was certified on 3 March 1940 and the TWA version the following day. Deliveries to the two companies began immediately. PanAm's planes were given names of meteorological phenomena (Rainbow, Comet and Flying Cloud), while those from TWA received names of Indian tribes (Navaho, Cherokee, Apache, Zuni and Comanche).

---

20. Julius Barr (pilot), Jack Kylstra (project leader), Peter Guilonard (KLM), Albert Gillis von Baumhauer (KLM), Ralph Ferguson, Harlan Hull (TWA), George Schairer (Boeing) and three other Boeing technicians.

21. Buffeting is a random vibration that generally occurs at around stall speed.

Boeing 314 no. 4, registered as NC18604, was launched on the morning of 6 March 1939. It is seen here at speed in San Francisco Bay. (Boeing)

>> The reign of the Clippers

In 1934, Wellwood E. Beall, the head of Far East sales, was in China having just negotiated the sale of P-26 fighters, when he was recalled to Seattle to take up a job in the design department. He arrived in the summer of 1934 to the task of designing a large commercial flying boat. The idea had come to him after he had learnt that PanAm (PAA) was considering the use of flying boats to link the United States with China via Hawaii, Midway, Wake, Guam, Manila and Hong Kong. Thus, when PAA asked Boeing to come up with a flying boat design, their thoughts on the project were already well advanced. On 21 July 1936, PAA signed a contract for the building of six model 314 flying boats (a contract containing an option for a further six planes) at a unit cost of $512,000. The whole contract, with spares included, amounted to $4.8 million.

Constructed to the same principles as the Martin M-130, the model 314 could carry a payload marginally superior to its empty weight, which was quite exceptional for the time, but would characterise the new generation of American aircraft[22]. It was able to carry up to 74 passengers (38 if fitted out with couchettes) and a ten-person crew. In fact, when in commercial service, it carried fewer passengers. The wing was mounted in the high position and sponsons were fitted on either side of the hull in preference to

Boeing 314 no. 2, California Clipper, registered as NC18602, seen at its moorings at Port of the Trade Winds between Treasure Island and the Bay Bridge. This was the first Clipper to be delivered to Pan Am, on 26 January 1939. (Boeing)

wing floats. The crew's quarters were on a separate deck from those of the passengers, and the passenger accommodation was divided into nine compartments. The engines were Wright Double Cyclones delivering 1,500hp at take-off. Despite this, the model 314 was to be the last large flying boat to be put into service by an American airline.

---

22. The model 314's empty weight was 18,190kg and the payload was 19,230kg, giving a total loaded weight of 37,420kg and a payload/empty weight ratio of 51/49.

Left: The left side of the Clipper's dining room with its door leading to the 'flipper'. Right: The ladies' bathroom in the Clipper was located at the forward left of the passenger deck. (H. Hazewinkel collection)

Left: This close-up shows the access door to the forward compartment, as well as the American flag that been painted on a few weeks before the attack on Pearl Harbor. Right: This photo, taken during maintenance work on the engines, shows the access hatches to the cockpit and cargo compartment. (Boeing)

Boeing undertook to deliver the first example within 14 months (ie, by September 1937), so that PAA could open its transatlantic route in the summer of 1938 at the latest. To hold to such a short schedule, Boeing re-used a number of sub-assemblies from the XB-15 bomber (in particular the wings, tailplane and engines). Nevertheless, the programme encountered delays and the first model 314 took off nine months late, on 7 June 1938, and was delivered to PAA 15 months late. On 26 January 1939, the CAA gave its consent for PAA to fly the model 314 in commercial service. Although designed for the Atlantic crossing,

the first two 314s were put into service in the Pacific. The other four flying boats were allocated to transatlantic flights.

On 3 March 1939, the wife of the US president, Eleanor Roosevelt, christened the *Yankee Clipper* in Washington DC, the ceremony being broadcast by radio to the Boeing workers in Seattle. From 26 March to 16 April, the *Yankee Clipper* made route-learning flights and, on 20 May 1939, the first regular transatlantic mail flights began. Leaving Port Washington, New York, at 13.07 with 14 crew members and 753kg of mail, the plane arrived at

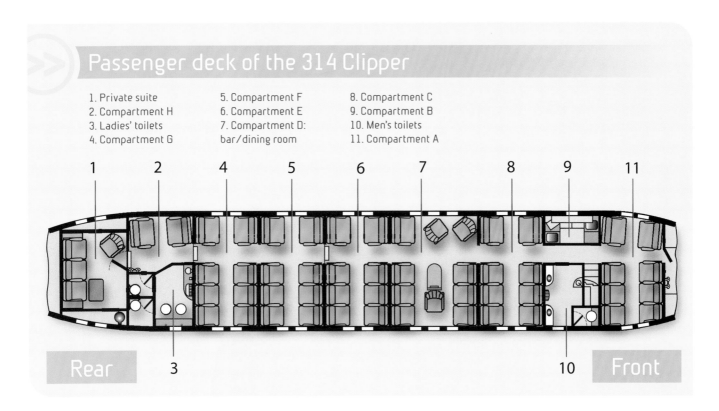

Passenger deck of the 314 Clipper

1. Private suite
2. Compartment H
3. Ladies' toilets
4. Compartment G
5. Compartment F
6. Compartment E
7. Compartment D: bar/dining room
8. Compartment C
9. Compartment B
10. Men's toilets
11. Compartment A

Rear

Front

Horta in the Azores at 04.29 the following day after a 2,375-mile flight lasting 13 hours 22 minutes[23]. Then the *Yankee Clipper* took off from Horta at 10.48 heading for Lisbon, where it touched down at 18.42. The following morning, at 06.25, it left Lisbon for Marseille, landing there at 14.45. Marseille was to be the route's final destination, but for this inaugural flight the *Yankee Clipper* flew on to Southampton. The next day, it began its return flight, reaching Port Washington on 27 May at 14.49.

Two hours later, the *Atlantic Clipper* took off from Port Washington for Europe. Crossing the Atlantic had now become a matter of routine. The first crossing

23. In fact, the aircraft arrived in the Azores just before sunrise and it had to wait until daylight before it could touch down.

Named Bristol, registered as G-AVBZ, and duly camouflaged, the first model 314A flew on 20 March 1941 and was used by BOAC on transatlantic flights. (P.M. Bowers collection)

The model 314's spacious flight deck. The navigator's large table was located behind the pilot's seat. (Boeing)

To save precious time during the 314's design, the design team used the same aerofoils as on the XB-15 bomber. (Boeing)

with passengers on board[24] was made on 17 June, but the first scheduled flights with fare-paying passengers did not start until 8 July 1939 when the *Yankee Clipper* carried 17 passengers and 186kg of mail. The sixth and final 314, *American Clipper*, entered service on 5 August 1939. But, on 1 September, Europe slipped into war and the crossings were henceforth diverted to Foynes in Ireland and Lisbon with a stop in the Azores. On 20 December 1939, the *American Clipper*, which had left New York seven days earlier, touched down again in the city after the 100th transatlantic flight. During these 100 crossings, the Clippers had amassed a total of 393,214 miles.

24. These were no-fare-paying passengers: 16 journalists and two PAA employees.

Boeing's Super Clipper

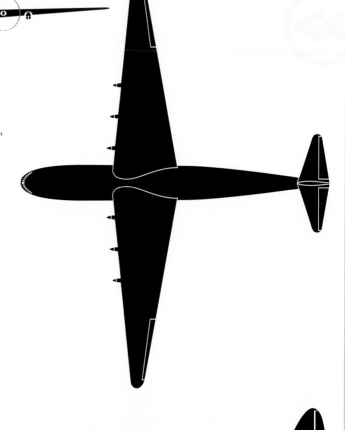

By late 1937, Pan American's monopoly over transoceanic flights was beginning to be questioned, especially by competitors such as TWA. The detractors saw two main risks: on the one hand, the monopoly acted as a disincentive to fare reduction; on the other, it acted as a brake on technological progress, with Pan Am content to carry on using its existing aircraft. To force a change, the company decide to organise a media stunt. On 9 December 1937, it launched an invitation to tender for the design of a Super Clipper. Seeking maximum impact, the authors went as far as adding the signature of the legendary Charles Lindbergh to their document, even though he had not worked for Pan Am for at least two years. Not even consulted, Lindbergh protested, but in vain...

Five manufacturers took the bait: Boeing, Consolidated, Douglas and Sikorsky decided to respond, while Seversky, who had not originally been consulted, managed to slip into the field. Considering the project unworkable, Glenn Martin turned it down. And it has to be said that the specifications were ridiculous, for the period, at any rate. The plane had to be capable of carrying 11.3 tonnes (including 100 passengers) over a distance of 5,000 miles at a cruising speed of 200mph! Achieving such a performance would have required a whole battery of 2,000hp to 2,500hp engines, which at the time did not exist, other than in engineers' imaginations.

Seattle's design department came up with the model 326, a large flying boat with six 2,500hp turbo engines. With a 76-metre span (compared with the Boeing 747's 64 metres) the model 326 had particularly well-thought-out aerodynamics. The fuselage was divided into 50 cabins spread over two decks, 28 of which were classed as 'special', having their own toilet facilities. The upper deck had two luxury cabins fitted out with a table, two stools and a bench seat that could be converted into a couchette. With a take-off weight of 118 tonnes, the Boeing 326 would certainly have met the specification criteria, but in the end Pan Am ruled that none of the proposals was acceptable. There the matter remained – and the company maintained its transoceanic monopoly for a few years more.

>> Stearman: biplanes and tradition

In September 1931, UATC had decided to merge two of its subsidiaries, Northrop Aircraft Corporation and Stearman Corporation, into a single company, the Stearman Aircraft Corporation, based in Wichita, Kansas. In May 1933, J.E. Schaefer was appointed chairman of Stearman, which now became the Boeing Division of Wichita. When UATC was dismantled, Boeing dragged Stearman in its wake. It was therefore under less than happy circumstances that two engineers from the Wichita Boeing Division set to work, at the company's expense, on the design of a new training biplane for the Army. Harold Zipp and Jack Clark took no more than 60 days to design and build the prototype of the Stearman model 70 (this was the seventh aircraft designed by Stearman, the model 7 following models 1 to 6). The plane, appearing in December 1933, was a conventional biplane with a 215hp Lycoming R 680 3 engine, featuring welded steel-tube construction capable of bearing heavy loads.

Although it had not been designed in response to any particular request nor to any precise specification, the model 70 was evaluated in March 1934 by the Navy, then by the USAAC, who gave it a provisional designation of XPT 943. At the time, the two branches of the armed forces were on the look-out for a new trainer. The Navy immediately authorised an order for 61

Thousands of American pilots were trained on the Stearman PT-17. Surrounded by planes, female trainees are deep in discussion; Avenger Field, 12 January 1944. (USAF)

examples of an improved version, the model 73, designated NS 1, which was distinguished by its Wright R-780-8 Whirlwind engine (requested and supplied by the Navy). For its part, the Air Corps, restrained in its ambitions by budgetary concerns, did not authorise an immediate order. However, its comments were taken into account by Stearman, who quickly developed a new version, the model 75. Eventually, in 1936, after lengthy tests, the Army signed a contract for a first batch of 26 aircraft, designated PT-13 (PT for Primary Trainer).

The Stearman A75s for the Peruvian Air Force were supplied with Continental R-670 engines. (Stearman)

A Stearman 76C3 for Brazil. An engine cowl has been fitted and it is armed with two machine guns. (Stearman)

At this time, Stearman was looking to sell aircraft wherever it could and searched for outlets in the export market. The idea was that less wealthy countries could create a fighter force at relatively lower cost by acquiring an armed version of the model 76 biplane. These planes were recognisable externally by their cowled engine and single, small-calibre machine gun mounted on the lower wing. From 1936 onwards, 78 model 76s were sent to equip the embryo air forces of Argentina, Brazil, the Philippines and Venezuela. Luckily, 1937 saw a second order from the Air Corps for an additional 92 model 75s. These aircraft, delivered under the PT-13A Kaydet designation, had a 220hp Lycoming R -680-7 engine and improved instrumentation. They opened the way for big future orders.

>> The eve of battle

The world was now going through the last moments of peace. On 9 September, Philip G. Johnson returned from Canada to take the chairmanship of Boeing, while 'Claire' Egtvedt became chairman of the board. However, the Seattle firm's future was still far from being assured. The contract for the 13 YB-17s turned out to be loss-making, as did the production run. For the year 1939, Boeing registered a loss of more than $3 million. The American aviation industry's total production for 1939 amounted to 5,856 aircraft, of which 2,195 were military planes and 1,220 were exported. These figures represented a considerable increase over those for the preceding year[25].

---

25. The 1938 figures were: 3,623 aircraft built, of which 1,800 were military planes; 875 aircraft went for export. Source: AIA Facts & Figures.

Many PT-17s were sold to Central American and Latin-American countries, like these four aircraft destined for Cuba. (Stearman)

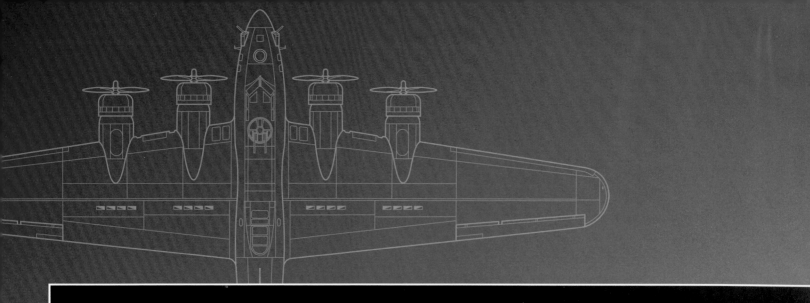

On 19 May 1942, a B-17F-40-VE (numbered 42-6021) built by Lockheed Vega warms up its four 1,380hp Wright GR-1820-97 engines before delivery to a combat unit. (Lockheed)

CHAPTER 3

The war years

>> In Europe, the shock provoked by the knowledge of German rearmament unleashed a hunger for modern armaments amongst the French and British military staff. The two countries dispatched missions across the Atlantic to place a flood of orders quite unlike anything the manufacturers had previously experienced. All the big American aviation companies were soon involved in the Europeans' desperate binge-buying. In 1938, France and Britain placed orders worth $400 million and, in the first six months of 1940, between 1 January and 16 June, the two countries ordered 10,848 aircraft. Furthermore, so as to get hold of the equipment as quickly as possible, they went to the extent of paying out of their own pockets to make good any gaps in the means of production of their suppliers.

U p to the time when the Europeans started to place their orders – the effect of which was not immediately felt – the American aviation industry had experienced modest growth. In 1939, with a turnover of $280 million (of which $67 million were exports) and 64,000 employees, it had climbed to only 41st place amongst the country's industries.

After the stimulus provided by the two procurement delegations came a second stimulus, no less substantial – the 'blitzkrieg' launched by Hitler's Germany. This electrified the American government to such an extent that, on 16 May 1940, President Roosevelt asked for annual aircraft production to be increased immediately to 50,000 (36,500 for the Army and 13,500 for the

Navy). Remember that 1939 had seen a total of 'only' 2,195 military aircraft produced. The president was thus asking for this figure to be increased 20 times! To draw an even more striking comparison, he was asking the industry to produce in one year almost one and a half times as many warplanes as had been turned out since the historic flight of the Wright brothers[1].

Such figures indicate the magnitude of the problem the aviation industry now confronted. Conventional methods of managing industrial production clearly would not suffice. To meet the challenge, the National Defense Advisory Commission (NDAC) was set up in May 1940 under the direction of the former head of General Motors, William S. Knudsen.

1. Between 1912 and 1939, the American aviation industry had produced 31,869 military aircraft and 1,006 civil aircraft. Source: AIA Facts & Figures.

This unprecedented restructuring covered:
- the improvement and optimal use of existing plant
- the building of new factories
- the conversion of non-aeronautical industries, such as automobile, to aviation
- dispersal of production centres across the country to reduce their vulnerability and to take account of available labour (at that time 80% of the industry was concentrated near the coasts and 45% of airframes were built in southern California)
- new management methods[2]

To deal with the building of new plant, the NDAC put out contracts called Emergency Plant Facilities (EPF), under whose terms the builder would finance his own expansion, whilst the government would undertake to meet the costs incurred after a period of five years. Several plant expansions were undertaken, but in practice this measure proved unsatisfactory and led to the creation on 22 August 1940 of the Defense

At the beginning of the war in Europe, Boeing built some Douglas DB-7s for the French Air Force, but, following the French defeat, the majority were delivered to the Royal Air Force as Boston IIIs. (P.M. Bowers collection)

B-17 production was shared among different manufacturers to cope with the growth in orders from the US Army Air Force. This view shows the preparation of fuselage parts. (Lockheed)

In 1942, TWA's model 307s were requisitioned by the Army Air Transport Command and were re-designated C-75. This is the fifth C-75 (number 42-88627) in 1944 after being reconditioned prior to its return to civilian life. (P.M. Bowers collection)

Plant Corporation (DPC), a government organisation that financed and built factories and then leased them to manufacturers.

As a specialist in large planes, Boeing did not immediately benefit from the European orders, which were mostly for fighters and medium bombers. Among the numerous orders from the French government were some twin-engined Douglas DB-7Bs. As part of the plan to spread production among manufacturers, 'Claire' Egtvedt negotiated the construction of 380 DB-7Bs of which 240 were destined for France and the remainder for the Air Corps. The first contract was signed on 18 May 1940, but events meant that none of the planes was delivered to their original customer. Following France's defeat, French orders were taken up by Britain, who used the planes under the 'Boston III' designation. The first one flew on 24 July 1941 and deliveries ran from October 1941 to March 1942. The American orders[3] received the designation of A-20C Havoc. In the course of the war, Boeing was to construct further aircraft designed by other manufacturers, including 362 Consolidated PBY-5 Catalina seaplanes in its Canadian plant and 750 Waco CG-4A transport gliders at Wichita.

» The Stratoliners and Clippers go to war...

On Wednesday 12 March 1940, Pan American Airways took delivery of its first Boeing 307, the *Clipper Rainbow*, followed in May by the *Clipper Flying Cloud* and in June by the *Clipper Comet*. Starting on 4 July, the company put them into service in South America (via Paramaribo, Cayenne and Belem). TWA put their planes into service four days later on the New York, La Guardia–Burbank route via Chicago, Kansas City and Albuquerque, while claiming in its advertising that it was the first to use four-engined aircraft, to have a pressurised cabin and to fly above the weather[4]. This commercial transcontinental flight was achieved in 12 hours 13 minutes[5].

However, the Boeings' use in commercial service was short-lived. On 24 December 1941, two weeks after the Japanese attack on Pearl Harbor, the two companies'

---

2. Despite the huge machinery set in motion, the aim was not achieved: in 1940, only 6,028 military aircraft were built. The target was not met until three years later, in 1943, with output of 85,433 aircraft.

3. Nineteen of the DB-7s built by Boeing were delivered to the USSR and one to Brazil.

4. The 1940 advertising claimed: 'TWA. First to bring you four engines, super-charged cabin, Overweather flying.'

5. The return trip between La Guardia and Burbank was made in 14 hours 9 minutes.

One of the model 314s used by the US Navy during the war. It has been given two-tone blue camouflage typical of that era. (Boeing)

planes were requisitioned by the US Army Air Force. Those belonging to TWA were purchased by the government and designated C-75 in line with the military nomenclature then in use. PAA's aircraft remained in the company's ownership, but were used under contract by the Army. These well-appointed four-engined planes were stripped of their civilian fittings and used as cargo planes from February 1942. One of their first missions consisted of carrying anti-tank shells and medical supplies to British troops fighting in Libya. In their military guise, the C-75s accumulated some 45,000 hours' flying, covering 7.5 million miles and making no fewer than 300 transatlantic crossings.

Towards the end of 1944, with new transport aircraft (Douglas C-54s) taking over, the Stratoliners were returned to civilian life. TWA's went back to Boeing where their wings were replaced by those from the B-17G and their electrical systems by those from the B-29. The pressurisation system, which had been little used, was removed and the capacity increased to 38 passengers. Thus modified, the planes were designated SA-307B-1.

The fate of the Boeing 314s was similar to that of its land-based counterparts. At the end of March 1940, PAA moved its flying-boat base from Baltimore to La Guardia and, on 16 April 1940, the *Atlantic Clipper* broke the record for the crossing by linking Lisbon to La Guardia in 26 hours 2 minutes[6].

From 18 June 1940, the frequency of crossings rose from two to three per week. In the Pacific, after PAA had obtained authorisation to start a regular service from the United States to New Zealand, the first flight between San Francisco and Auckland was made on Friday 12 July 1940 by the *American Clipper* in 52 hours 12 minutes. However, the first proper commercial link with New Zealand did not begin until two months later, on 11 September[7].

In November, PAA requested authorisation to carry

---

6. The previous record had been held by the *Yankee Clipper* with 27 hours 43 minutes.

7. For this flight, the *American Clipper* carried mostly mail in the form of 125,000 'first-day covers', some express cargo and 16 non-fare-paying passengers.

passengers to Manila and Singapore, this being granted on 30 April the following year. The *California Clipper* made the first San Francisco–Singapore flight between 3 May and 10 May 1941. In the meantime, on 30 August 1940, Britain had acquired three of the six A-314s ordered by PAA. BOAC used them over the Atlantic on special missions[8]. On the American side, six days after the attack on Pearl Harbor, PAA's Clippers were acquired by the government, although the company continued to operate them on behalf of the US Navy. They were to serve until 16 November 1945, when PAA resumed its commercial flights between San Francisco and Honolulu. But the era of the big flying boats was coming to its end. They were in use for just a few more months and the last PAA Clipper flight took place on 10 April 1946.

>> From the Sea Ranger to the 'Lone Ranger'

Even before America had entered the war, she had felt the need to wield the air power necessary to protect her possessions in the Pacific. Distances were considerable in this part of the world and, at the time, they could be covered only by the big flying boats. This was why the US Navy asked Boeing, Consolidated, Martin and Sikorsky to design large, long-range patrol and bomber flying boats. Boeing came up with the model 344, a twin-engined plane of enormous dimensions[9] capable – on paper at any rate – of remaining airborne for three days and covering 4,245 miles! It owed this performance to its very long wings, to the use of a new wing profile developed for the B-29, and to 36,240 litres of fuel contained in the wings. Ordered on 29 June 1940 and designated XPBB-1 Sea Ranger by the Navy, the first and only prototype flew on 19 July 1942.

Since 2 September 1941, the US Navy had settled upon the little town of Renton, on the shores of Lake Washington, to build a factory that would produce its first batch of 57 of these flying boats. Unfortunately, the XPBB-1's promising career was to be halted there, the missions that it was designed for being carried out by existing aircraft. The US Navy cancelled the order and handed the Renton plant over to the Army, receiving in return the Kansas City plant where it would produce the twin-engined PBJ-1 conventional planes[10]. The Renton factory would henceforth be dedicated to the production of the future B-29. As for the unique XPBB-1, it served as a training and test-bed aircraft until the end the war.

---

8. These special missions consisted chiefly of carrying allied VIPs.

9. With its 42.58m wingspan, the Boeing 344 was the largest twin-engined plane ever built.

10. The North American PBJ-1 was the version of the Mitchell B-25 intended for the Navy.

The XPBB-1 (Boeing model 344) was the biggest twin-engined flying boat built in the United States. (AAHS/R. Wagner collection)

The list below is a brief summary of the careers of Pan American Airways' (PAA) 12 Boeing model 314s. The production series numbers and registration and military serial numbers are given in parentheses.

Honolulu Clipper (no. 1988) prototype (NX18601) >> First flight on 7 June 1938. Delivered to PAA (NC18601). Transferred to US Navy. On 3 November 1945, it came down in the sea 600 miles off Hawaii after an engine failure. Badly damaged, it was towed then sunk by gunfire.

California Clipper (no. 1989) >> First flight on 13 January 1939. Delivered to PAA (NC18602). Transferred to USAAF on 18 December 1941. Transferred to US Navy. Returned to PAA. Bought by World Airways and cannibalised for parts.

Yankee Clipper (no. 1990) >> First flight on 24 January 1939. Delivered to PAA on 3 March 1939 (NC18603). Transferred to US Navy. On 22 February 1943, at the end of its 241st Atlantic crossing, it was damaged on touching down in the sea at Lisbon and sank, killing 24 people.

Atlantic Clipper (no. 1991) >> First flight on 6 March 1939. Delivered to PAA on 25 April 1939 (NC18604). Transferred to US Navy. Returned to PAA. Withdrawn from service in 1946 and cannibalised.

Dixie Clipper (no. 1992) >> First flight on 24 April 1939. Delivered to PAA on 28 June 1939 (NC18605). Transferred to US Navy. Returned to Pan Am. Withdrawn from service in 1946 and cut up.

American Clipper (no. 1993) >> First flight on 9 June 1939. Delivered to PAA (NC18606). Transferred to USAAF (serial number 42-88631). Transferred to US Navy (serial number 99083). Sold to World Airways in 1948. Fate unknown.

Bristol (no. 2081) >> First flight on 20 March 1941. Intended for PAA (NC18607). Sold to BOAC (G-AGBZ). Sold to World Airways (NC18607). Withdrawn from service in 1948 and sold to General Phoenix Corp.

Berwick (no. 2082) >> First flight on 19 April 1941. Intended for PAA (NC18608). Sold to BOAC (G-AGCA). Sold to World Airways (NC18608). Withdrawn from service in 1948 and sold to General Phoenix Corp.

Pacific Clipper (no. 2083) >> First flight on 11 May 1941. Delivered to PAA (NC18609). Transferred to USAAF (serial number 42-88632). Transferred to US Navy (serial number 99084). Returned to Pan Am. Sold to Universal Airlines. Damaged in a storm at San Diego and cannibalised in 1946.

Bangor (no. 2084) >> First flight on 6 June 1941. Intended for PAA (NC18610). Sold to BOAC (G-AGCB). Sold to World Airways (NC18609). Withdrawn from service in 1948 and sold to General Phoenix Corp.

Anzac* Clipper (no. 2085) >> First flight on 30 June 1941. Delivered to PAA (NC18611). Transferred to USAAF (serial number 42-88630). Transferred to US Navy (serial number 99082). Returned to PAA. Sold to World Airways. Withdrawn from service in 1948.

Capetown Clipper (no. 2084) >> First flight 28 July 1941. Delivered to PAA (NC18612). Transferred to USAAF (serial number 42-88622). Transferred to US Navy. Returned to PAA. Sold to American International Airways and renamed *Bermuda Sky Queen*. In October 1947, it was caught in a storm and went down in the Atlantic. Passengers and crew were saved but the aircraft was shelled and sunk.

* ANZAC is the acronym for 'Australian and New Zealand Army Corps'.

>> Down in Wichita

By 1941, the Stearman Aircraft Division, directed by Schaefer, had become the Wichita Division. In addition to the huge output of biplane trainers and before it became heavily involved in B-29 production, Stearman had participated unsuccessfully in several Army invitations to tender. The first was for a twin-engined attack aircraft for which Stearman had put forward its model X-100 whose prototype was delivered in September 1939, receiving the designation XA-21. This plane was Stearman's first twin-engined, first single-winged and first all-metal aircraft. Neither it nor its Martin competitor received any orders.

As for the Stearman X-90/X-91s and X-120s, these were trainers whose structure made as little use as possible of 'strategic' materials such as aluminium. In January 1942, the Army bought the X-91 with 400hp Pratt & Whitney R-985 engines, but did not order a production run. The X-120 might have won an order for 1,045 aircraft, but the Army gave preference to the Fairchild AT-21

To help with the rendezvous of B-17 formations over England, the Americans painted aircraft in bright colours. This B-17E (number 41-9100) from the 379th Bomb Group, photographed on 24 July 1944, was covered with broad red and white bands and nicknamed 'Birmingham Blitzkrieg'. (USAF)

>> The Flying Fortress: queen of the skies

With President Roosevelt's rearmament policy forging ahead, it seemed almost inconceivable that huge orders for the B-17 would not materialise. At the end of August 1939, Bill Allen persuaded 'Claire' Egtvedt to bring Phil Johnson back from his self-imposed exile in Canada following the dismantling of UATC (see page 46). As it happened, Johnson was an expert in industrial production and Boeing was going to need his talents. The first nine months of 1939 had seen a loss of $2.6 million and orders were not really flowing in. The prospect of taking up the post of president of the company persuaded Johnson to return.

At this point, the B-17 was very far from being perfect, needing substantial improvements before it was truly operational. Its deficiencies were not properly taken into account until the Royal Air Force started to use the aircraft operationally. The British took delivery of 20 B-17Cs that they christened 'Fortress B. Mark 1', the first of which arrived in Britain on 14 April 1941 after a stop-over in Newfoundland. The crews, however, were not ready to go into action until the beginning of July. On Monday 7 July, three of them carried out the first B-17 raid of the Second World War when the Wilhelmshaven submarine base was bombed. On the 23rd, other aircraft bombed Berlin and, on the 24th, it was the turn of Brest, where the German cruisers *Scharnhorst* and *Gneisenau* were at anchor.

The B-17E was the first USAAF bomber to go into action over Europe. (USAF)

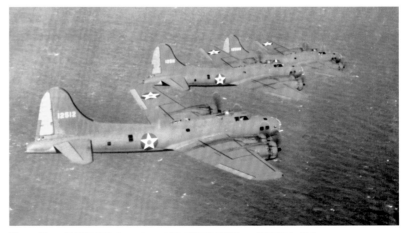

These three B-17E-BOs (numbered 41-25009, 2511 and 2512) built by Boeing, in Seattle, are on the way to their units. (USAF)

A B-17F from the 303rd Bomb Group flying over the English coast. It appears to be a B-17F-25-BO (numbered 42-24565) nicknamed 'Idaho Potato Peeler'. (USAF)

Externally, the B-17F was almost identical to the B-17E, but it had numerous improvements, especially in the fuel system, with its larger-capacity tanks. Here we see a B-17F-45-VE (numbered 42-6092) apparently attached to a training unit. (USAF)

Edward Wells

Boise, Idaho, 26 August 1910–1986

A native of Boise, Idaho, Edward Wells studied at the University of Willamette, then Stanford, from where he graduated in 1931 and immediately joined Boeing's engineering team. In 1936, he became manager of pilot studies, then, in 1938, engineer in charge of military projects. The following year, Ed Wells was appointed assistant chief engineer and, in 1943, chief engineer. After the Second World War, he became vice-president and chief engineer (May 1948) and, two months later, vice-president in charge of design studies. From April 1958 to August 1959, he was general manager of the Systems Management department. It was under his direction that Boeing won the development contracts for the Dyna-Soar and the Minuteman strategic ballistic missile.

In 1961, Wells became vice-president and managing director of the brand-new Military Aircraft Systems Division that merged, two years later, with the Transport Division to form the Aircraft Division. Wells was appointed vice-

(Boeing)

president of the division in January 1965 and, the following year, became vice-president of the Product Development Division. During his remarkable career with Boeing, Ed Wells was responsible for the design and development of such iconic planes as the Boeing B-17, B-29, C-97, 377, B-47, B-52 and 707. After his retirement on 1 January 1972, Wells remained active and became special adviser to Boeing's chairman of the board, T. A. Wilson.

On 16 August, the first B-17 was shot down by Messerschmitt Bf109s. To this must be added five aircraft already lost in various accidents. Further losses would follow – to the extent that by January 1942 half of the planes had been lost. The conclusions were clear: at high altitude the engines, though supercharged, were not delivering enough power, the machine guns were freezing up, and the lack of firepower aft was creating a dead spot that enemy fighters had not been slow to discover. In two months of operations, the British Flying Fortresses had carried out only 22 missions and, according to official statistics, less than a ton of bombs had hit the target.

During this time, Boeing's engineers had been looking to improve their aircraft, but the modifications they introduced, emerging in the B-17D (new electrical system, self-sealing tanks, engine covers fitted with cooling shutters, increased armour and armaments[11]), were little more than a stop-gap.

The majority of the B-17Ds produced were sent to the Pacific. On 21 May 1941, 21 B-17Ds arrived at Hickam Field, Hawaii, of which nine were transferred to Clark Field in the Philippines, to be joined by 26 others in November. On 7 December 1941, 12 B-17Ds, neatly lined up on the runway at Hickam Field, were taken by surprise and destroyed in the Japanese attack, while another 12 were preparing to land, one of which

was shot down. Nine hours later, the Japanese attacked Clark Field where 18 B-17s were reduced to smoking wrecks. Responding to the Japanese attacks, the other available B-17s led rearguard actions in

This B-17F, nicknamed 'Jack the Ripper II', is seen being handed over to its crew at Lockheed Vega. The previous 'Jack the Ripper' (from the 91st Bomb Group) had been shot down on 22 February 1944. (Lockheed)

---

11. The B-17Ds were armed with two ventral machine guns and two dorsal guns.

A Lockheed-Vega employee 'signs' this B-17G-75-VE, manufacturing number 8028, nicknamed 'March of Dimes' and serialled 44-8628. (Lockheed)

was now possible to install a tail-gunner's turret with two machine guns, and the new fin, twice the size of the previous one, brought improved stability. Motorised turrets were fitted on the back and under the belly. Now with a total of nine machine guns, the B-17E was better able to defend itself and justify its name.

Getting the B-17E into production, however, took a long time. This was mainly due to delays in the delivery of raw materials and fittings, but also to a chronic shortage of skilled workers. By the end of 1940, the situation had become so critical that Boeing was obliged to close some of its workshops and temporarily lay off workers; a disaster, bearing in mind the circumstances! By spring 1941, the situation had improved a little and the B-17E finally entered production. It was not until 17 September 1941, nearly 150 days later than originally intended, that the first B-17E left the Seattle plant to make its maiden flight. Fortunately, the speed of production picked up quickly, to the extent that the 512th and final B-17E emerged from the factory 49 days early.

The first B-17Es were delivered at the beginning of 1942 to the 7th Air Force, deployed to India, and went into action on 2 April over the Andaman Islands in the Bay of Bengal. Those destined for the 8th Air Force

which the weakness of their defensive armament constituted a serious handicap.

The first real improvements appeared with the B-17E. The team led by Ed Wells gave the plane such a profound rethink as to completely change its appearance. The rear end of the fuselage and the tailplane, in particular, were completely redesigned. With more space available in this part of the aircraft, it

The B-17G was the version produced in the greatest numbers, and its distinguishing features included its Bendix nose turret developed for the XB-40. After January 1944, the B-17s had no camouflage. (Lockheed)

arrived in England during the summer of 1942 and went into action over Europe on Monday 17 August, when 12 of them bombed the marshalling yards at Rouen-Sotteville in broad daylight. Despite the losses already sustained by RAF bombers in daylight raids, the American command remained convinced that the B-17s were capable of defending themselves unaided in daylight against Luftwaffe fighters and would bomb with much greater precision than by night. Unfortunately, both of these claims were soon to be revealed as false.

Although the B-17Es' performance had shown a significant improvement, a programme to improve it still further was put in place. In May 1943, a B-17E was experimentally fitted with V12 Allison V-1710 engines to test their effect on performance. The programme was cut short as the unique prototype (designated XB-38) was destroyed in a fire in June 1943 and the production of Allison engines was monopolised by the P-38 and P-40 fighters. Already, a new version, the B-17F, had gone into production several weeks earlier. Just 48 hours separated the production of the last B-17E and the first B-17F. The latter was the first version to be turned out in huge quantities, with a total of 3,405 planes being produced, not only by Boeing (with 2,300), but also by Douglas from its Long Beach factory (605) and by Lockheed-Vega from its Burbank plant (500). Compared with the previous model, the B-17F benefited from over 400 modifications ranging from details to significant items such as a monobloc, Plexiglas nose without glazing bars, thus improving visibility, and new propellers with broader blades coupled with the latest version of the Wright Cyclone R-1820-97 engine with a maximum power output of 1,380hp. In addition, extra 4,163-litre fuel tanks, dubbed 'Tokyo Tanks', were fitted in the outer section of the wings to take the ferry range up to 3,800 miles. The layout of the armament was also improved and

Crews were inclined to personalise aircraft with their own artwork. This B-17G-40-BO (number 42-97061) has been nicknamed 'Ike' after General Dwight D. Eisenhower. (USAF)

the last 76 aircraft produced by Douglas[12] were fitted with a new nose turret designed by Bendix to resist head-on attacks by German fighter planes. The B-17F would remain in production for 15 months.

While the B-17Es and Fs were swelling the ranks of the 8th Air Force ready for the Combined Bomber Offensive, the Allies decided to split up their roles. The

12. These were planes in the following batches: B-17F-70-DL, B-17F-75-DL and B-17F-80-DL, which were listed as B-17Gs by the 8th Air Force.

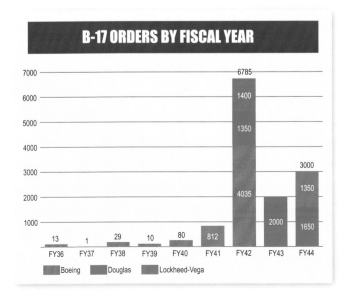

B-17 ORDERS BY FISCAL YEAR

	FY36	FY37	FY38	FY39	FY40	FY41	FY42	FY43	FY44
Boeing	13	1	29	10	80	812	4035	2000	1650
Douglas							1350		1350
Lockheed-Vega							1400		3000

Total FY42: 6785

INCREASE IN THE B-17's LADEN WEIGHT

299	Y1B-17	YB-17A	B-17B	B-17C	B-17D	B-17E	B-17F	B-17G
17,260	19,278	20,185	20,639	22,000	22,000	23,134	25,628	29,711

Building the B-17

A total of 12,731 B-17s were built, not only by Boeing, but also by Douglas and Lockheed. Having received a B-17E to work from, the Vega Airplane Company began production of the B-17F in its new A-1 plant situated next to the Burbank Lockheed Air Terminal in California, with a requirement to build 500 aircraft.

1. Assembly of the first formers and stringers on the front-left section of the fuselage. In the background is the front right section.

2. The skin is riveted to the stringers from the central part of the fuselage using a pneumatic riveter.

3. Final fitting of components before the glazed nose is added.

4. Fuselage front sections await the next stage.

5. An employee works on an access hatch for a Flying Fortress from the second batch of B-17Fs built by Lockheed-Vega (B-17F-3-VE), which has had only its fin painted.

6. Lines of B-17Fs from the seventh batch (B-17F-30-VE) build up before going into the final-assembly shop.

7. Fitting of a B-17F's outside-starboard Wright R-1820-97 engine.

8. An employee works on the right-hand wheel from one of the numerous suppliers involved in the production.

9. Workers gather to watch the roll-out of first B-17F built by Lockheed-Vega. This plane made its first flight on 4 May 1942, six months ahead of the schedule set by the USAAF.

10. Perched several metres off the ground, a worker polishes a B-17's Plexiglas nose.

(All photos Lockheed)

Because of its heavier laden weight, the B-17G flew lower and slower than previous versions. It took 37 minutes to get to 6,000 metres. (Lockheed)

Above and below: B-17Gs from the 381st Bomb Group escorted by a P-51B on a training mission over England, in the summer of 1944. By this time, American aircraft no longer wore camouflage. (USAF)

Americans would undertake daylight precision-bombing raids, while RAF Bomber Command would carry out night-time area bombing. Under these arrangements, it soon became apparent that, though bristling with machine guns, the B-17s were in urgent need of fighter escort. While awaiting the arrival of long-range fighter aircraft, an interim solution was tried out. The armament of a certain number of B-17s was virtually doubled, resulting in the creation of a real 'Flying Fortress' – in the true sense of the term – with 30 or so machine guns and cannon, designated XB-40. The prototype of this monster was followed by a short series of 20 pre-production YB-40s, the first of which were used in action on 29 May 1943 along with 147 B-17s attacking the submarine base at St Nazaire. It soon became clear that while the YB-40s were able to accompany the B-17s on the way over, it was certainly not the case on the return, where they struggled to keep up with the bombers now freed of their bomb load. The programme went no further...

The Boeing B-17G, of which 8,680 were produced (twice as many as all the other versions put together), was externally distinguished by its Bendix nose turret and a few other modifications to armament. For Boeing, it represented not so much a development as a

completely new version[13]. To turn out and deliver such numbers of aircraft in the time required, production continued to be spread between Boeing, Douglas and Lockheed-Vega. From 60 aircraft a month at the time of Pearl Harbor, the rate climbed steadily to reach four

13. The builder identified the B-17E, F and G by the same model number: 299-O.

Nicknamed 'The Queen' by their crews, the Flying Fortress was one of the chief protagonists in the air offensive against Nazi Germany. Despite their legendary strength, they paid a heavy price.

1. The first Fortress to have achieved 25 missions was B-17F Memphis Belle (serial number 41-24485). It is seen here on its return to the United States, at Patterson Field, Ohio. (USAF)

2. B-17G Pist'l Packin' Mama from the 324th BS, part of the 91st Bombardment Group. (USAF)

3. A B-17F crippled by flak. (USAF)

4. B-17F named Idiot's Delight (serial number 42-30301) from the 332nd Bombardment Squadron, part of the 94th Bombardment Group, is prepared for its next mission.

5. A 'Box' of Fortresses from the 398th Bombardment Group heads for its target (Neumünster) on 13 April 1945. (USAF)

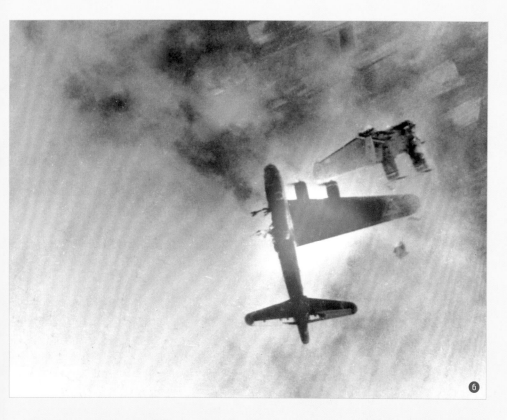

6. This dramatic picture shows B-17F Wee Willies of the 91st Bombardment Group with its left wing shot off by a Messerschmitt Me262 over Crantenburg on 8 April 1945. (USAF)

7. Flying at high altitude, American bomber formations could be picked out by their contrails. (USAF)

8. On 1 February 1943, this B-17F, nicknamed All American III (serial number 41-24406) was hit by a Messerschmitt Me109. Despite the damage, it managed to get back to base. (USAF)

9. Returning from a mission on 7 December 1944, this B-17G, nicknamed Mercy's Madhouse, from the 358th Bombardment Squadron (303rd Bombardment Group) was forced to make a belly landing. (USAF)

10. B-17G Duchess's Daughter (serial number 42-97272) from the 359th Bombardment Squadron (303rd Bombardment Group) after a belly landing. (USAF)

11. An anti-aircraft shell completely destroyed the nose of this B-17G of the 398th Bombardment Squadron piloted by 1st Lieutenant M. Delancey. (USAF)

To celebrate the completion of the 5,000th B-17 built at Seattle, each member of the workforce put his/her signature on the plane. (Boeing)

times as many 18 months later, culminating in a total of 578 planes during March 1944.

During this period, the strength of the 8th Air Force was increasing daily. The raids on Germany began on Wednesday 17 January 1943 with an attack on the port of Wilhelmshaven. Missions followed with steadily increasing rhythm, yet despite the significant damage inflicted on German industry by the B-17s, the air defences grew more precise and effective, and American losses rose to a level where they were no longer tolerable. On 17 August, attacks on factories at Regensburg and Schweinfurt ended in the loss of 60 planes, taking that week's total losses to more than 100 aircraft – at this rate the 8th Air Force would have ceased to exist within a matter of days. It was a grave lesson.

In the ensuing weeks, the Americans chose their targets carefully and it was not until new aircraft and crews arrived that the 8th Air Force resumed the offensive. This happened in October with the famous 'Big Week', but, on 14 October, 60 B-17s out of the 291 sent over Schweinfurt were shot down and numerous others damaged. These figures again put a

stop to the American offensive, for the time being, at least. For several months, the 8th Air Force's bombers were reduced to attacking less distant targets. They would have to wait for the introduction of the long-range North American P-51 Mustang fighter at the end of 1943, and the arrival of replacement B-17Gs, before they again ventured over the territory of the Third Reich. From then on, increasingly large formations of Fortresses dropped massive quantities of bombs over German industrial and communications centres. Their last large-scale mission took place on 25 April 1945, when 307 B-17s bombed the Skoda works in Pilsen. By the end of the war in Europe, Flying Fortresses had dropped more than 640,000 tonnes of bombs, or 41% of the total tonnage dropped in the European campaign[14].

But the B-17s were far from being confined to Europe. They were also very active in the Mediterranean (12th Air Force), the Pacific and in south-east Asia, even though the B-24s had been preferred. In addition, a few specialised versions made their appearance, such as the B-17Gs equipped with the British H2X bombing radar, those with a lifeboat that could be dropped for air-sea rescue (SB-17G) and those converted into radio-controlled missiles under the Aphrodite programme[15]. The 'sky queen's' career would not end with this. After the war, many of them were used in a whole range of roles. The very last ones were used to drop water in firefighting operations until the 1980s.

>> 'Grand Pappy'

Meanwhile, the XB-15 was following its discreet career. On 23 March 1943, it was transferred to the 6th Air Force Service Command (AFSC) and taken to Howard Field, in the Panama Canal Zone, where it was allocated to the 20th TCS (Troop Carrier Squadron). On 6 May 1943, the Engineering Division re-designated it as a transport plane: XC-105. Henceforth known as 'Grand Pappy', the giant former bomber carried 5,530 passengers, 22.6 tonnes of mail and 45.3 tonnes of cargo in 18 months of service. The plane that had been called the 'Leviathan of the Skies' had survived. The only one of its type, it had above all been an instrument of American propaganda. It had represented the high point of the 'biggest and furthest'[16] policy, but had not, in truth, been cut out for battle and had never achieved the performance expected by the ambitious Project A.

To supply fuel for the first B-29s operating out of China, a few planes were converted into tankers with their armament removed. (USAF)

>> B-29: the plane of all the superlatives

Back in late 1938, there had been an intention to design the biggest, heaviest and most powerful bomber of its time – and also the most complex. The boldness of the design was matched by the unprecedented industrial effort needed to produce the 9,000 examples ordered[17], to train the crews and mechanics, and to construct the bases capable of taking them. Unlike the B-17, the B-29 – the Superfortress – was not the result of progressive development, the production aircraft being very close to the prototypes. The bulk of this plane's development

---

14. The Americans dropped exactly 1,556,088 tonnes of bombs over Europe: 640,036 tonnes by the B-17s, 452,508 tonnes by all other aircraft types combined.

15. With their armour and now unneeded armament removed, these planes could carry a ton of explosive and were guided to their target from another plane. Five B-17Gs were thus modified.

16. Quoted by Harold Mansfield in *Vision*, page 81.

17. Precisely 9,052 B-29s were ordered and 3,960 were actually built.

The Boeing XB-15 while it was with the 49th Bombardment Squadron, identifiable by its 'BB' lettering. (USAF)

The many guises of the B-17

A major player in the Second World War, the Boeing B-17 was noted for its strength, longevity and versatility. Iconic plane though it was, the Flying Fortress was certainly not confined to the bomber role for which it had originally been designed. Over the years, it has taken on other roles...some quite unexpected.

1. Converted to a remote-controlled target plane, this QB-17L was used in the IM-99 Bomarc missile programme. It is seen here at the Cape Canaveral auxiliary base, on 30 January 1956. (USAF)

2. This B-17G, converted into a water-bomber, was still in use by Aero Union at Fresno Municipal Airport, California, in the summer of 1976. (A. Pelletier)

3. In its air-sea rescue version, the SB-17G carried an A-1 life raft under its belly. About 130 aircraft were converted in this way. (USAF)

4. Converted to a transport plane, this B-17 served with the Danish military from Kastrup air base. (DR)

5. In 1943, Boeing converted four B-17s into transport aircraft, which were designated XC-108 and YC-108. (Boeing)

6. After the war, several B-17Fs like this one were converted for crop spraying. The pesticide tank can be seen under the fuselage. (P.M. Bowers)

7. This JB-17G with five engines was used as a test bed for different types of engine, including the Wright R-3350 (shown here) and the Wright XT-35. (P.M. Bowers)

8. The B-40 was a heavily armed escort version. Seen here is the prototype, built by Lockheed-Vega, on 14 November 1942. (USAF)

9. In 1949, this B-17H belonged to the USAF's Air Rescue Service. (DR)

10. After the war, TWA used this Boeing model 299AB to reconnoitre near-east airline routes in 1947. (P.M. Bowers collection)

The B-29's cockpit was notable for its glazed nose, giving a clear forward view. (USAF)

took place on paper, even before the first parts had been manufactured.

It had all started in March 1938, when Boeing's engineers began to consider how to improve the XB-15 as well as to respond to the Air Corps' interest in an 'improved B-17' with a pressurised fuselage and tricycle undercarriage. The design work on the 'improved XB-15' had culminated in the model 316, a

four-engined aircraft with a high wing and powered by 2,000hp Wright Duplex Cyclone engines, whereas the 'improved B-17' had taken shape as the model 322, a sort of hybrid between the B-17 and the Stratoliner.

While design work was proceeding at Boeing, a report prepared at the request of General Martin Craig had been sent to the Chief of Staff of the Air Corps, General George C. Marshall. The report had concluded that the defensive capability provided by the Navy and coastal artillery was no longer sufficient to guarantee the security of the nation. Colonel Oliver Echols, the head of Materiel Command, had encouraged Boeing to continue its development work: 'Continue working on this big bomber. We will soon be in a position to launch a new programme that will mobilise all your resources.'[18] Indeed, in May 1939, the Air Corps had set up the Kilner Committee (named after the chairman, General Walter Kilner) charged with producing a specification for an extra-long-range bomber. This was finalised in November 1939. Colonel Echols and Colonel Bob Olds had in mind an aircraft capable of attacking enemy aircraft carriers at a distance of two days' from the US coast[19]. Meanwhile, at Boeing, the engineers were making progress: they had moved on to the model 333 (fitted with

Mass production was one of the big problems to be overcome with the B-29. This was shared among numerous sub-contractors and three final-assembly lines. Here, the forward sections of the fuselage are under construction at Lockheed-Vega. (Lockheed)

12-cylinder Allison V engines in tandem) and to the model 334 (fitted with Pratt & Whitney radial engines built into the wings).

The Air Corps' specifications required that the plane be capable of carrying a 900kg bomb load a distance of 5,333 miles at a speed of 400mph. It is interesting to note that while this performance was quite demanding for the time, the bomb load remained very modest, being no better than that of First World War bombers! Whatever the case, on 5 February 1940, the Army sent the R-40-B specifications to a variety of manufacturers who were asked to respond within one month[20]. A life-sized mock-up was to be ready for the following 5 August, with the first aircraft due to be delivered on 1 July 1941. Boeing, Consolidated, Douglas and Lockheed put forward proposals, Boeing offering two improved versions of the model 334 – the 334A and the 341. The latter had four 2,000hp engines and a wing load of 312kg/m², almost double what was normally considered acceptable. Eddie Allen

The B-29's pressurised rear compartment was equipped with bunks so that crew members could get some rest during long flights. Unable to pressurise the whole fuselage, Boeing's engineers chose to pressurise certain sections only. (USAF)

18. Quoted by Harold Mansfield in *Vision*, page 86.

19. Fully laden, the B-17 could intercept ships one day out from the coast.

20. At the same time, the Air Corps laid down specification R-40-C for a new-generation fighter.

Those B-29s selected for night operations had all their under-surfaces painted black, as with this final B-29 to be built by Martin at its Omaha, Nebraska, plant, seen ready to leave on 19 July 1945. (Martin)

decide to deal with this problem by fitting enormous Fowler flaps[21], which, when deployed, increased the wing surface by a good third. In addition, the presence of bomb bays made pressurisation of the fuselage difficult. It was therefore decided to pressurise only the front and rear parts of the fuselage and to link the two compartments by a narrow tubular corridor, also pressurised.

In view of the course of military events in Europe, the authorities decided that none of the bids was acceptable and asked the manufacturers to make substantial improvements in crew and fuel-tank protection, defensive armament, bomb load and operating ceiling, without any loss of performance. Faced with these military demands, Ed Wells was supposed to have told Colonel Echols: 'We can put in a lot of armament and cut down on performance, or we can keep performance up and stay out of range of fighter planes. Which do you prefer?' Echols replied 'We've got to have both[22].' Boeing thus revised its design and came back, on 11 May 1940, with plans for the model 345. The plane had now grown appreciably, with the laden weight increasing from 38 to 50 tonnes, the wing span from 38 to 43 metres and

the engine power from 2,000 to 2,200hp (the Pratt & Whitneys had been replaced by new Wright R-3350s). After a careful study of the different plans, Boeing's bid won the day.

On 17 June 1940, the USAAC agreed an $85,652 contract for development and wind-tunnel tests. On 27 June, a contract was signed for the construction of a full-scale model 345, and on 6 September a further contract for $3,615,095 was agreed for the building of two prototypes designated XB-29 and a static-test airframe[23], while the Air Corps placed a similar contract with Consolidated for the XB-32, so as to avoid putting all their eggs in one basket[24].

Boeing worked on the project's development and, by April 1941, had built another full-sized mock-up, while the Army had put in an order for a production batch of 264 B-29s. This was still 15 months from the date of the prototype's maiden flight! The order was increased to 500 in January 1942, with various amendments over the ensuing weeks taking the total up to 1,600 planes before the prototype had even flown. This situation was almost without precedent[25]. The risk was all the greater in that the B-29 was far from being a conventional design. While it followed

Edmund T. 'Eddie' Allen

*Chicago, Illinois, 4 January 1896 –
Seattle, Washington, 18 February 1943*

A native of Chicago, Edmund T. Allen, nicknamed 'Eddie', lost his father when he was still in his teens. As the family's means of support, he was obliged to go out to work for a few years before taking a place at the University of Illinois. In 1917, at the age of 21, he joined the US Army Air Service, where he learned to fly and became an instructor. The Army soon sent him to Britain to study British methods of flight testing. He was back at McCook Field before the Armistice and became the first NACA test pilot. In 1919, he returned to the University of Illinois for a year, followed by two years at MIT. From 1923 to 1925, he was an independent test pilot and often worked as such at McCook Field. From July 1925 to mid-1927, he was a pilot for the Postal Service and carried mail on the Cheyenne–Salt Lake City route.

From 1 September 1927, he worked for Boeing Air Transport, piloting 40As. From 1928 to 1943 he carried out maiden flights with 30-odd aircraft, including some very significant ones (DC-1, XB-15, B-17, etc). On April 26th 1939, he was hired by Boeing as director of aerodynamic research and flight testing, none of which stopped him from flying other manufacturers' aircraft prototypes, such as the Lockheed Constellation. However, Eddie

(Boeing)

was no tearaway. He thought of himself as an engineer as much as a pilot and was convinced that the test pilot should be involved in a plane's design from the beginning and not be content merely to fly it.

On 6 September 1940, the Army Air Corps ordered prototypes of the XB-29 heavy bomber from Boeing and Allen gathered an unprecedented test team around him. The first XB-29's maiden flight took place on 21 September 1942 and the second plane flew on 30 December of the same year. During the latter's ninth flight, on 18 February 1943, one of its engines caught fire and the aircraft crashed, killing Allen, the seven other crew members, and 20 people on the ground.

standard construction methods, it featured a number of innovations such as a pressurised cabin, remotely operated turrets and a bomb load ten times greater than in the original specification. A generator, known as an APU (Auxiliary Power Unit), provided electricity for the 150-odd systems and components, among which were two fuel systems and the new Wright Duplex Cyclone R-3350 turbo-compressor engines turning propellers of 5.18-metre diameter.

Aerodynamically, the B-29's wing (Boeing model 117), designed by George Schairer, was to a new profile with a very high aspect ratio (particularly advantageous for high-altitude flight). There was a ten-man crew: pilot, co-pilot, bomb-aimer, navigator, engineer, radio operator and four gunners. The various modifications took the laden weight up to 54 tonnes and the wing load to $337kg/m^2$. The cost of a single B-29 was calculated to be \$639,188[26]. As might have been expected, development problems were numerous, but it was the engines that gave the engineers the biggest headache.

Production was spread over three factories and hundreds of sub-contractors: the new Boeing no 2 plant at Wichita (on which work had begun on 24 June 1941 and which was owned entirely by the government); the new Bell Aircraft factory in Marietta, Georgia; and the new Glenn L. Martin Company plant in Omaha, Nebraska. To these was shortly to be added the Renton factory after the Navy handed it back.

The first XB-29 flew on Monday 21 September 1942, with Eddie Allen at the controls, accompanied by Al Reed as co-pilot. Allen took the aircraft up to 1,800 metres, assessing its stability as well as its responsiveness to the controls. The flight lasted 75 minutes and was adjudged entirely satisfactory. Tests continued, but the number of technical problems and engine failures began to mount, forcing Allen to cut short several flights[27]. One flight, on 28 December 1942, was intended to test the plane's practical flight ceiling, but again one of the engines failed and the

Large-scale production of an aircraft as complex as the B-29 ran into numerous difficulties. (Martin)

flight lasted just 26 minutes. With the aircraft back on the ground, it was discovered that a second engine had been on the point of cutting out. By 30 December, the second XB-29 was ready for its maiden flight. This lasted only 32 minutes: one of the engines caught fire but cool-headed Eddie Allen brought the plane back. It was then noticed that fire had started in another engine and a third was on

21. The invention of Harland D. Fowler, the flaps were mounted on rails. They both increased the wing surface area and created a gap through which non-turbulent air flowed.

22. Quoted by Mary Wells in *Boeing's Ed Wells*, page 93.

23. An amendment to this contract for a third prototype was added on 14 December.

24. The XB-32 spawned a small run of the B-32 Dominator, which saw service in the Pacific during the final weeks of the war.

25. The other case had been with the Martin B-26, of which 200 had been ordered before the prototype's maiden flight.

26. This amount was made up of \$399,541 for the airframe, \$98 567 for the engines, \$10,537 for the propellers, \$34,783 for fittings and \$95,715 for armament.

27. Only 27 flying hours were achieved over the first 23 flights.

B-29A-1-BA (serial number 42-63353), nicknamed Belle Bottom, was with the 468th Bomb Group based in China, late 1944. (R.J. Francillon collection)

Almost impossible to distinguish from the B-29, the B-29A nonetheless had a very different structure, especially in the central section of the wings and the engine nacelles. Pictured is a B-29A-30-BN (serial number 42-94106) fresh out of the factory. (AFFTC)

Superfortresses in action. The aircraft in the foreground is a B-29-25-BA (serial number 42-63529) from the 468th Bomb Group. (USAF)

The first of three XB-29-BO prototypes. (USAF)

the point of cutting out. The aircraft could be put back into flying order only by borrowing the engines from the first prototype (at that time undergoing modification). In order to keep down the engine's weight, the crankcase had been made out of magnesium, which, though it was certainly light, was liable to catch fire.

By 17 February, the second XB-29 had managed a total of only 7 hours 27 minutes of flying time over eight flights. At this point, Eddie Allen expressed grave doubt about the usefulness of continuing with the test programme while the engine problems remained unresolved. On the other hand, increasing the number of flights while trying out

various adjustments might bring about a solution. But now Eddie faced a real dilemma, according to Robert Robbins[28]. 'The B-29 was potentially a fine airplane. It was urgently needed in the Pacific. It was committed to production — 1,600 B-29s were now on order at four separate plants. Flight test was way behind its expected schedule and the data was badly needed to: prove the airplane; quickly find and correct the problems; minimize production disruptions' develop training and operating procedures and manuals. But it was currently a dangerous airplane. Major improvements were badly needed. Temporary grounding would be normal, prudent thing to do. But they were not normal times. The sooner the B-29 could be used in combat, the sooner the war would end and the sooner the casualties and carnage would stop. Eddie concluded that he must continue flight testing as rapidly as possible.' The flights continued.

The following day, 18 February, Allen took off in the XB-29 at 12.09. Eight minutes later, a fire broke out in the outboard port engine. The propeller was immediately feathered and an extinguisher triggered. Taking no chances, Allen began an immediate descent towards Boeing Field. At 12.24, the navigator announced that the plane was at an altitude of 450 metres, four miles north-east of the runway. The situation seemed to be back under control when, a minute later, witnesses on the ground

Named Enola Gay, *this B-29-45-MO gained the sombre distinction of having been the aircraft that dropped the first atomic bomb on Hiroshima. (USAF)*

heard a violent explosion and saw a large piece of the plane break away. At 12.26, the prototype crashed onto a meat-processing plant while still more than three miles from the runway. The eight men on board and 20 others on the ground were killed outright.

The programme continued regardless. On 15 April 1943, the first production B-29 emerged from the Wichita plant, but, despite all the efforts made, the B-29 remained a very complex aircraft and, in January 1944, not one of the 97 planes produced was combat-ready and only 16 planes were fit to fly. All the others required a good 50 modifications at the very least.

In July 1943, Boeing commenced delivery of the B-29s to the 58th Bombardment Wing based at Smoky Hill Army Air Field, Kansas and under the command of Brigadier-General Kenneth Wolfe[29]. During March 1944, General Arnold visited the 58th BW to discover that the group was confronted not only with problems of a technical nature, but numerous logistical ones too. 'Hap' Arnold, who had hoped to send 150 of the bombers to India, launched a troubleshooting operation on 10 March 1944. Named the 'Battle of Kansas', it aimed to mobilise the whole of the Wichita workforce in building 175 B-29s to a strict schedule. In spite of harsh winter weather, work went on

24 hours a day for four weeks, farm labourers, housewives and shopkeepers working ten-hour shifts, day and night. A month later, the B-29s were ready for action in Asia.

Hap Arnold had originally planned to use three Bomber Commands to encircle Japan: one in India and China, a second in the Pacific and a third in the Philippines. In the event, only two were deployed: the

Close up of Bockscar, *the B-29 that dropped the second atomic bomb, on Nagasaki. (USAF)*

28. Quoted by Robert Robbins in *The Global Twentieth*.
29. The 58th Bombardment Wing became active on 1 June 1943 at Marietta, Georgia.

20th BC in Asia and the 21st BC in the Pacific (subsequently these were integrated). The 20th Air Force was created and 58th BW's B-29s left Kansas for India on 26 March 1944. The first B-29 touched down in India on 7 April 1944 and the 20th Air Force was allocated to four airfields in the Calcutta area[30]. The B-29s received their baptism of fire on 5 June 1944 when they attacked the Makasan marshalling yards near Bangkok. Ten days later, 50 B-29s bombed Yawata in Japan. It was the first time the Japanese archipelago had been targeted since General Doolittle's famous raid in April 1942. In June 1944, the B-29s were sent to five bases on the Marianne Islands (two on Guam, two on Tinian and one on Saipan). Located about 1,500 miles from Japan, the B-29s could now undertake significant attacks on the mainland. The first one was launched against Tokyo on 24 November 1944 when 111 Superfortresses bombed the Musashino engine plant.

Meanwhile, a drama had taken place back at Boeing. On 14 September 1944, during a visit to the Wichita plant, Boeing's president, Philip Johnson, suffered a heart attack and died. The shock was felt not only at Boeing, but throughout the country. Aviation workers observed a minute's silence in his memory.

On 20 January 1945, Major-General Curtis LeMay established himself on Guam at the head of 21st Bomber Command. He decided upon a change of tactics, with the main effort directed towards Japanese industrial cities, which were to be attacked by night with incendiary bombs. The first of these raids was made against Tokyo during the night of 9–10 March 1945. It reduced more than 15 square miles of the Japanese capital to ashes. Over the following ten days, Nagoya, Osaka and Kobe received the same treatment from the B-29s, causing substantial damage.

But this was nothing compared with the fate that awaited two other Japanese cities. On 6 August 1945, a B-29 named *Enola Gay*, piloted by Colonel Paul W. Tibbets, dropped the first atomic bomb on Hiroshima. Three days later, the B-29 *Bockscar*, piloted by Major Charles W. Sweeney, dropped a second bomb over Nagasaki, bringing the immediate surrender of Japan and the end of the Second World War. There was suddenly no further need for the incredible industrial effort of recent times and the orders for 5,092 B-29s were simply cancelled.

---

30. Chakulia, Charra, Piardoba and Kharagpur.

B-29 production

For B-29 production, the Wichita plant used the 'multi-line assembly system', developed by Boeing's production manager, Oliver West. Instead of a single production line along which the aircraft steadily took shape, six sub-assembly lines fed four final-assembly lines. The sub-assemblies included the front, centre and rear fuselage/tailplane sections, the wing mid-sections, engines and housings and the outer and leading edges of the wings.

There were 55,000 parts in a B-29, put together using 600,000 rivets. It required the factory's 15,000 workers to put in around 57,000 hours to produce one aircraft. The staff worked seven days out of seven, in two ten-hour shifts (06.00–16.45 and 16.45–03.30) with a break of 45 minutes for lunch.

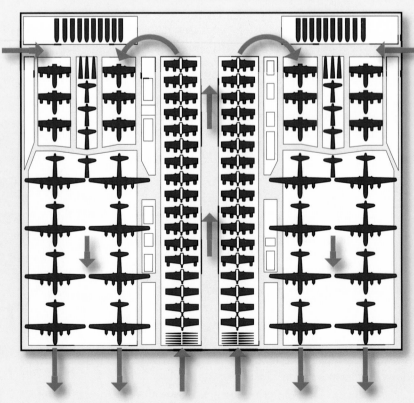

Diagram of the B-29's production line. (A. Pelletier)

>> Sixteen planes a day!

Even today, we remain in awe of the huge outputs achieved at this time. It must be pointed out, however, that none of this was achieved without problems and firms had to keep pace with the huge explosion in workers with a sustained social policy in order to deal with absenteeism, turn-over and the risk of strikes. In addition to a huge training programme, workers were able to avail themselves of an increasing number of social services (crèches, entertainment, etc), salary changes and bonuses, and – later on – a reduction in working hours. At one point working hours reached 80 hours a week over six days out of seven, but were eventually reduced to 45 hours over five days.

The number of workers in the Seattle plants had stood at 1,755 in January 1938 and rose to 2,960 by the end of that year. The number reached 8,714 by

August 1940, climbed to 28,840 at the time of the Japanese attack on Pearl Harbor, and culminated at 44,754 by January 1945. As so many men were away on active service, Boeing, just like other industrial sectors, resorted to a substantial female workforce, which was embodied in the quasi-mythical figure of 'Rosie the Riveter'.

Factory size underwent the same kind of growth. Boeing obtained $5.5 million from the Reconstruction Finance Corporation for the expansion of its plants. To fulfil orders, production was constantly growing. The Seattle shops were turning out some 60 aircraft a month in 1942, and by March 1944 this had grown to 362 – and at one point the plant was producing 16 planes a day!

Work was organised in three shifts, day and night, in conditions of the utmost security. Badges allowed access to the various shops and the whole area was

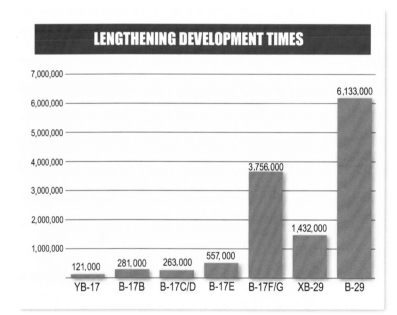

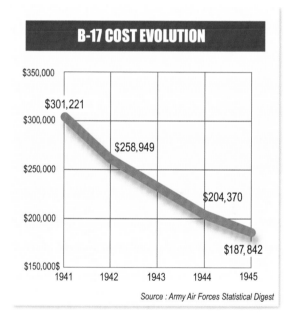

Source : Army Air Forces Statistical Digest

Boeing placed a YB-29 at the disposal of General Motors for use as a test bed for the 24-cylinder Allison V-3420 engine. This aircraft, which was named XB-39 Spirit of Lincoln, *did not go into production. (General Motors)*

The XF8B-1 marked Boeing's short-lived return to building fighter aircraft. (Boeing)

camouflaged against potential Japanese air attacks. However, in the autumn of 1945, everything changed. After the surrender of Germany and then Japan, contraction bit deep. Boeing's Seattle workforce declined from 35,000 to 6,000 and in Wichita from 16,000 to 1,500. The aeronautics giant that Boeing had become had to readapt to civilian life.

» From bombers to cargo planes

While Boeing's activities were based on just two types of aircraft, the Seattle research department devoted some resources to designing new planes. One, the model 367, was a heavy transport aircraft derived from the B-29. The tailplane, wings, landing gear and power plant were the same, but the fuselage was entirely new. So as to achieve the desired capacity while mitigating the constraints imposed by pressurisation, the Boeing engineers opted for a double-lobe fuselage section (formed by the intersection of two circles), with the floor of the hold at the point where the fuselage narrowed. The lower lobe had the same diameter as the B-29's fuselage, while the upper section was broader so as to accommodate 134 armed troops, three lorries or two light tanks. Wide doors with loading ramps were fitted at the rear of the fuselage.

Three prototypes of the model 367-1-1 were ordered in January 1942 under the XC-97 designation and the first one flew out of Seattle on 9 November 1944. On the 9 January 1945, the XC-97 established a transcontinental record by taking a payload of nine tonnes a distance of 3,323 miles between Seattle and Washington in 6 hours and 3 minutes, at an average

Along with the rest of American industry in the Second World War, Boeing employed an increasing proportion of female workers to keep its factories going. In 1940, about 10% of Boeing's workers were women; in 1940, it was up to 15%. By 1944, the proportion was over 40%. None of this happened by chance. To encourage women to take factory jobs, the government launched an unprecedented recruitment campaign. In 1942, the graphic designer J. Howard Miller created a poster for Westinghouse depicting a female worker flexing her biceps with the slogan 'We can do it'. The poster, which had used Geraldine Doyle as its model, soon became a national icon.

Early in 1943, Redd Evans and John Jacob Loeb wrote the song 'Rosie the Riveter', eulogising female industrial workers. Finally, the *Saturday Evening Post* of 29 May 1943 published on its cover a picture by Norman Rockwell of Rosie eating a sandwich while crushing under her feet a copy of *Mein Kampf*. 'Rosie the Riveter' was born. She would become a symbol for the six million women who went to work in the factories. To make things easier, Boeing set up a car-sharing and bus service to bring them to work. Work schedules were adjusted so that mothers could be at home for most of the day. Cafeterias were built and leisure activities were organised to help them combat stress.

One of the numerous riveters employed in the aeronautical industry during the war. (Lockheed)

The Stearman X-120 used a large proportion of non-strategic material, such as wood, in its construction. (Boeing)

speed of 383mph. Thanks to the pressurised cabin, it was able to cruise at an altitude of 9,000 metres and take advantage of the prevailing winds. Satisfied with the new plane's performance, the military authorities placed an order in July 1945 for a pre-production run of ten aircraft (YC-97), which were very similar to the prototypes. The first one made its maiden flight on 11 March 1947.

» The last fighter

At the Navy's request, a team of engineers started work on a long-range carrier-borne fighter-bomber. Designated XF8B-1 under Navy classification, but known to Boeing as the model 400, it was the first fighter that the Seattle firm had designed for some time. A contract was signed on 4 May 1943 for the construction and

testing of three prototypes, the first of which flew on 27 November 1944. Weighing 9.3 tonnes when full, it was the biggest piston-engined fighter ever designed in the United States.

It was a response to the Navy's requirement to carry out missions flown from aircraft carriers against the islands of the Japanese archipelago. To do this, the engineers had worked around the 3,500hp Pratt & Whitney XR-4360-10 to design an aircraft capable of fulfilling interdiction, escort, dive-bombing, conventional bombing and torpedo missions with equal ease. Its armament comprised six heavy machine guns or cannon and 2,900kg of bombs. With the end of hostilities in the Pacific, the need for such a plane disappeared and, although the other two prototypes were built, the XF8F-1 was never put into production. It would be a long time before Boeing would design another fighter.

The first of three prototype model 367-1-1s (XC-97) flew on 9 November 1944. Note the retractable skid at the rear of the fuselage. (USAF)

The Stearman X-100 was the only aircraft to be given 1,150hp Pratt & Whitney R-2180 Twin Hornet engines. The shape of the fuselage front was later modified. (DR)

Find the factory!

The Japanese attack on Pearl Harbor stunned America. The shock was so great as to encourage the military to believe that national territory itself was threatened by enemy air power. It was deemed an urgent task to hide large industrial installations on the west coast from the prying eyes of Japanese bomber crews. Camouflage experts were given free rein to indulge themselves and their masterpiece was indisputably Boeing's Factory no. 2 in Seattle. Located on the banks of the Green River, the enormous site was laid out as if it was a housing estate.

Camouflage experts displayed their sense of humour in naming the mock village's streets. An employee is seen here at the intersection of 'Synthetic Street' and 'Burlap Boulevard'. (Boeing)

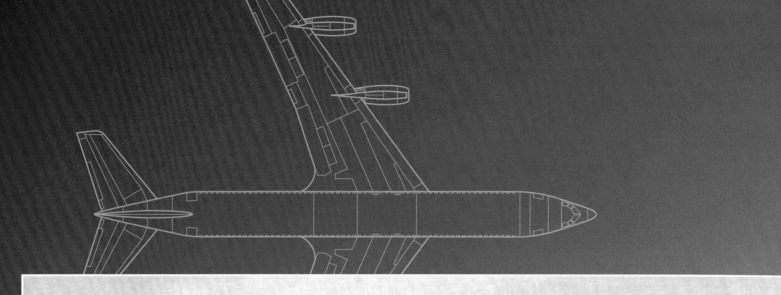

The last of the three YC-97As
(model 367-4-6) was brought up to
the standard of the production
C-97As and later converted to a
C-97D. (DR)

CHAPTER 4

The dawn of a new era

>> For the American aviation industry, the return to peacetime conditions was more brutal than gearing up for war had been. Between 1945 and 1946, military aircraft production plummeted from 46,865 to just 1,417 and the workforce declined from 1,684,000 to 192,000. At the same time, civil aircraft production had risen from 2,047 to 35,001, although most of these were light aircraft. At Boeing, in a period of 60 days, $1.5 million-worth of contracts were cancelled. By the end of 1945, 38,000 workers were to find themselves without a job.

I n 1943, when Allied victory appeared inevitable, some planning was undertaken on the restructuring of American industry that would be needed at the end of the war[1]. The future looked grim for manufacturers given the scale of cancellations and the gloomy outlook for the market. On 10 July 1944, the Chamber of Commerce for Aeronautics presented the Senate Military Affairs Committee with a report entitled *The Aircraft Industry Prepares for the Future* that argued in favour of a national aviation policy. A law on 'War mobilisation and Restructuring' was passed on 3 October 1944. As expected, the first contract-cancellation letters were sent out to companies from 17 August 1945.

The increase in passenger aircraft orders was not immediately felt. There were still numerous manufacturers and some kind of rationalisation appeared inevitable; indeed, talks about mergers between certain companies had already begun. Thus it was considered that Consolidated-Vultee might merge with Lockheed, or North American, or perhaps Northrop; Fairchild with Martin, Boeing with Curtiss-Wright – but nothing came of it. On 1 September 1945, the same day as the USAAF asked for a reduction in B-29 production to just 50 a month, William Allen, after much hesitation, accepted the post of president of the Boeing Airplane Company and was unanimously elected by the board five days later.

Until then, Allen had been in charge of the legal department. 'I'm a lawyer. I've always been a lawyer,

---

1. The first of these studies was led by professors Lynn Bollinger and Thomas Lilley of the Harvard Business School, in 1943.

United Airlines ordered seven model 377-10-34s that were used on the Hawaii route. One of them was wrecked in an accident and the other six were sold to BOAC. (UAL)

Northwest Airlines received ten model 377-10-30s that differed from the others by their rectangular portholes and the fitting of weather radar in the nose. (DR)

and now I have to run an enterprise dominated by engineers,' was his comment[2]. He was 45 years old and had built a reputation in the field of aeronautics as a man of integrity. A cautious man, he undertook to start taking on staff again as soon as the airline companies bought the Stratocruiser, a luxury airliner derived from the four-engined C-97 military transport plane, which had first flown in November 1944. The success of tests on the XC-97 had led to an order for ten pre-production YC-97s (six YC-97s, three YC-97As and one YC-97B) that were built in Seattle's plant no. 2 using the space made available by the cessation of B-17 production. While the YC-97s differed little from the prototypes, the YB-97As and Bs benefited from a number of improvements, the chief of which was the use of 3,500hp (2,710kW) Pratt & Whitney R-4360 Double Wasp engines mounted in new housings. The YC-97Bs were distinguished by having porthole windows and a cabin layout similar to that of an airliner. Although it had flown after the civil version's prototype, it was this aircraft that could be considered the true prototype of the model 377 Stratocruiser.

Starting with the military transport's airframe, the design department developed a civil version that allowed Boeing to make its return to the passenger aviation market. Designated model 377-10-19 and christened the 'Stratocruiser', the prototype made its first flight on 8 July 1947.

Little did Bill Allen realise how truly he spoke when he had said: 'Our difficulties are all ahead of us.' While still engaged in a battle to keep the company going, Allen found himself facing a strike that would last nearly six months. Called by the Aeronautical Machinists' Union, its origins lay in the desire of Boeing's management to redefine the rules relating to seniority. The union was opposed and demanded an across-the-board increase in salaries. Talks began on 16 March 1947, but the management refused to budge. The union called workers out on 22 April 1948. After 144 days, during which a local union was formed to recruit strike-breakers, the strikers decided to return to work. The strike had cost the company $2 million and significantly slowed production of the B-50s.

In the meantime, Boeing had been talking up the

The last production-series C-97A-BO (serial number 48-423) in the livery of the Continental Division of the Military Air Transport Service. (DR)

The first of 14 C-97Cs (number 50-690). These aircraft differed from the earlier versions only by their reinforced cabin floor and their radio equipment. (P.M. Bowers collection)

BOAC's first model 377-10-32 was registered as G-AKGH and named Caledonia. *It was sold on to the Californian Transocean Airlines in 1958. (P.M. Bowers collection)*

Stratocruiser with all the big airlines, with the result that six of them ordered a total of 55 aircraft to be delivered between January 1949 and March 1950. They were: Pan American Airways (twenty planes), Scandinavian Airlines Systems (four planes), American Overseas Airlines [a transatlantic subsidiary of American Airlines] (eight planes), Northwest Airlines (ten planes), British Overseas Airways Corporation (six planes) and United Airlines (seven planes). Unfortunately for Boeing, the Stratocruiser did not make the hoped-for commercial breakthrough. No further orders were forthcoming.

PanAm took delivery of its aircraft from 31 January 1949, putting them into service on intercontinental routes. In the summer of 1950, the company bought six Stratocruisers from American Overseas Airlines and increased the fuel capacity of some of its planes so as to be able to offer non-stop services between New York, London and Paris. By the time they were retired from service in 1961, some of these aircraft had accumulated over 30,000 hours' flying time. BOAC's first Stratocruiser touched down at London-Heathrow on Friday 28 October 1949 after a non-stop flight from New York and the British company's first commercial flights started in December of that year.

BOAC bought six Stratocruisers from United Airlines, including this one, registered G-ANUA and named Cameronian. *(H. Kofoed)*

For the time, these aircraft offered the wealthy traveller an exceptional degree of luxury, worthy of an ocean liner. Depending on how it was fitted out, the main cabin could accommodate between 55 and 100 seated passengers, or 28 Pullman couchettes for

---

2. Quoted by Robert J. Serling in *Legend & Legacy*, page 69.

Pan American World Airways ordered model 377-10-26 Stratocruisers in November 1945. Some of them had their fuel capacity increased by 1,700 litres, allowing them to fly non-stop between New York and Paris. (Boeing)

For night flights, Stratocruiser cabins were fitted with couchettes. (R.J. Francillon collection)

Companies using the Stratocruiser took every opportunity to organise public relations events to show off the aircraft's comfort. Here, we see a fashion parade aboard a Pan Am plane. (DR)

overnight flights. On the same deck were cloakrooms, toilets and an office. A spiral staircase led down to the lower deck where 14 passengers could be seated, although a bar more often occupied this area. The airlines presented the Stratocruiser as the last word in air travel. Thus in a BOAC leaflet on the so-called 'Monarch' service one could read: 'The Monarch is the last word in luxury air travel… the last word in speed, comfort and spaciousness. You fly overnight, above the weather in a pressurized Stratocruiser Speedbird – the largest, fastest, most luxurious airliner in the world.'

Already made obsolete by the Douglas DC-7C and the Lockheed Starliner, both of them faster and with greater range, the Stratocruiser finally disappeared with the arrival of jet airliners. Airlines got rid of them as soon as the Boeing 707 and Douglas DC-8 became available, whereupon they entered the second-hand market. The Californian Transocean Airlines bought ten planes from BOAC, while the Venezuelan company Rutas Aereas Nacionales SA (RANSA) used six of them as cargo planes[3] and five others were acquired by Israel Airlines[4]. Finally, two of them would have an unusual end to their career when they were transformed into 'Guppies' for NASA's Apollo moon programme (see page 162).

Sadly, the Stratocruiser was far from being a profitable project for Boeing, losing them $15 million.

It was quite a different story for its military alter ego, the C-97 Stratofreighter. Indeed, by the time production ended in 1956, no fewer than 888 aircraft had been built. The first contract was signed on 24 March 1947 for 27 C-97As (model 367-4-19) powered by three 500hp (2,600kW) Pratt & Whitney R-4360-27 engines and capable of carrying 24 tonnes of cargo or 134 troops. This order was increased to 50 aircraft in December 1948 and the first one flew on 16 June 1949 and was delivered on 15 October.

With the Seattle no. 2 plant being fully occupied building the B-50, Boeing had the Renton plant reopened for production of the C-97A. These planes differed from the pre-production series by the installation of radar in the nose[5], the fitting of a large cargo door on the forward starboard side and an increase in fuel capacity to 29,485 litres. They were ordered on 24 March 1947 and were followed by 14 C-97Cs intended for humanitarian evacuation missions (the C-97B version was never built). As the C-97D was the same as the C-97B plus five C-97As converted to passenger configuration, the next production series

3. The aircraft acquired by RANSA were nos. 15922, 15926, 15928, 15929, 15931, 15934, 15935, 15936, 15941, 15953 and 15961. Some of these planes were cannibalised for spares..

4. The aircraft acquired by Israel Airlines were nos. 15925, 15930, 15962, 15963 and 15964.

5. This was the Bendix AN/APS-42 airborne radar that was also installed in the C-54, C-97, C-118, C-119, C-121, C-124, C-130 and C-131.

≫ 377 Stratocruiser cabin layout

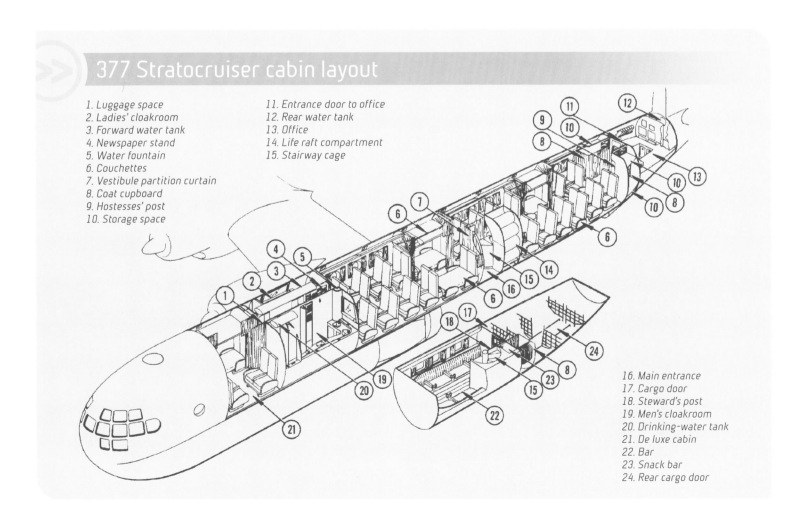

1. Luggage space
2. Ladies' cloakroom
3. Forward water tank
4. Newspaper stand
5. Water fountain
6. Couchettes
7. Vestibule partition curtain
8. Coat cupboard
9. Hostesses' post
10. Storage space
11. Entrance door to office
12. Rear water tank
13. Office
14. Life raft compartment
15. Stairway cage
16. Main entrance
17. Cargo door
18. Steward's post
19. Men's cloakroom
20. Drinking-water tank
21. De luxe cabin
22. Bar
23. Snack bar
24. Rear cargo door

In 1963, 135 KC-97Gs in use with National Air Guard units were modified to C-97Gs by the removal of their in-flight refuelling equipment. One such aircraft is shown here (serial number 53-106) in March 1975 at Davis Monthan AFB. (B. Knowles)

was the KC-97E, 30 of which were built at Renton in 1951 and 1952, with the first one being delivered on 14 July 1951. These aircraft were equipped for in-flight refuelling, but could also be used as cargo planes.

The change to 3,800hp R-4360-59B engines gave birth to the KC-97F, of which 159 were built at Renton. The aircraft's development culminated in the KC-97G, which was produced in the greatest numbers of all (592 aircraft), the first being delivered to the USAF on 29 May 1953. Three years later, on 18 July 1956, the last KC-97 left the Renton plant. Until the arrival of the KC-135 in 1957, these planes formed the backbone of the Air Force's in-flight refuelling fleet. Other versions did appear later, as the result of modifications to existing aircraft. Among these were the 92 KC-97s powered by two General Electric J47-GE-25A auxiliary jet engines of 2,720kg thrust (26.7kN) as well as the 28 HC-97Gs search and rescue aircraft.

≫A super Superfortress

On 21 March 1946, the USAAF underwent a profound reorganisation resulting in the creation of three operational commands: the Strategic Air Command (SAC), the Tactical Air Command (TAC) and the Air Defense Command (ADC). The SAC had to be able to carry out long-range offensive missions anywhere around the world, either alone, or acting in concert with land or naval forces. To fulfil this task, it needed to have the most modern equipment capable of carrying out large-scale operations, in particular long-range strategic bombers. This reorganisation was just the first step in a process that was to lead to the passing of the National Security Act, on 26 July 1947, and the creation of an independent US Air Force.

B-29 production ended in 1946. There was no doubt that it had been the most complex and sophisticated production aircraft built during the Second World War. Far from being satisfied, in 1944, the AMC had started working on improved versions,

Northwest Airlines traded in its model 377-10-30s as part of a deal for Lockheed Electras; Lockheed then sold them on to Aero Spacelines in 1963. This one (serial number N74603) was still in quite good condition when it was photographed at Tucson in August 1976. (A. Pelletier)

Some KC-97s found themselves on the civil market, like this KC-97G (serial number 52-2698), which was used by Hawkins & Powers Aviation Incorporated in the battle against forest fires. It is seen here at Fairbanks, Alaska, in the summer of 2002. (A. Pelletier)

A KC-97G (serial number 52-883) of the Utah National Guard at Hill AFB, in March 1974. (B. Knowles)

The Arizona National Guard was the last to use KC-97Gs. Here is one of them (serial number 52-2695), based at Phoenix International Airport, in 1976. (A. Pelletier)

notably in terms of bomb load; hence the XB-44 programme (known by Boeing as model number 345-2). This was a B-52 that had been given 3,500hp Pratt & Whitney R-4360-35 Wasp Major engines, while another avenue of development saw a weight reduction through the use of new light alloys. Despite this, the aircraft that emerged turned out to be significantly heavier than the standard B-52. Defensive armament remained unchanged, while the bomb load

went up to more than 9 tonnes (with an extra 3.6 tonnes of external payload available).

A substantial production run for the aircraft seemed assured when the USAAF ordered 200 B29Ds (in the meantime, the XB-44 designation had been altered to XB-29D even before construction had been completed), but necessary post-war economies reduced this figure to just 60 planes, which were given the designation of B-50A. In the event, 69 B-50As

The many guises of the B-29

Superfortresses were built in just two basic versions: the B-29 and B-29A. However, because of its size and the height at which it could operate, the plane was an ideal platform for a variety of specialised types, such as in-flight refuelling tankers, photo reconnaissance, launch vehicle for experimental aircraft, etc.

1. The experimental Douglas D-558-2 Skyrocket is launched from a Boeing P2B-1S (serial number 84029) in summer 1951. The Skyrocket was the first aircraft to exceed Mach 2 in level flight, on 20 November 1953. (NASA)

2. In July 1951, three B-29s were given AN/APS-20C radar as part of the development work on an early-warning system. (USAF)

3. This weather reconnaissance WB-29 (serial number 45-21717) was used by the 308th Weather Group based at Fairfield-Suisun, in September 1948. (W.T. Larkins)

4. Hydraulic jacks were used to raise the Bell X-1E to its attachment point under the B-29. (NASA/GRIN)

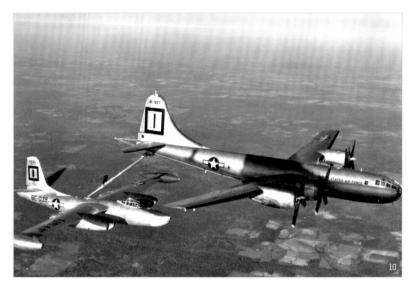

5. The XB-44 was the prototype of a more powerful version of the B-29, fitted with Pratt & Whitney R-4360-33 Wasp engines of 3,000hp (2,235kW). (Boeing)

6. Two Republic EF-84B Thunderjets were experimentally attached to the wings of an EB-29A to increase their range. (USAF)

7. This B-29 (serial number 45-21748) was modified to carry the 5,440kg Tarzon guided bomb. It can be seen under the fuselage, behind the AN/APQ-13 radome. (USAF)

8. Eight B-29s were converted to carry out search and rescue missions and were fitted with an A-3 life raft that could be dropped from the plane. Pictured is an SB-29 belonging to the 5th Air Rescue Squadron. (USAF)

9. In 1948–9, the Glenn L. Martin Company and Westinghouse Corporation used this B-29 (serial number 44-84121) to test a high-altitude airborne television booster system named 'Stratovision'. The aircraft was fitted with radio and video transmitters for the purpose, as well as an 8.5-metre folding aerial. (Martin)

10. A total of 116 B-29s were converted into KB-29Ps for in-flight refuelling duties. Pictured here is an aircraft (serial number 44-83927) from the 9th Air Refuelling Squadron refuelling a North American RB-45C from the 9th Strategic Reconnaissance Wing. (USAF)

A total of 112 B-50s were converted into KB-50Js for in-flight refuelling and fitted with two supplementary General Electric jet engines. Pictured is an aircraft (serial number 48-0088) from the 421st Air Refuelling Squadron. (USAF)

A number of B-50s were converted to do reconnaissance. Fourteen RB-50Bs were modified to RB-50Fs and equipped with SHORAN navigational radar to undertake special missions. Pictured here is an RB-50F (serial number 47-144). (USAF)

were constructed, the first of which flew on 25 June 1947[6], although it was not until February 1948 that the SAC took delivery of its first B-50As[7].

In the course of the ensuing months, the B-50s demonstrated their strategic capability with two exceptional flights. Towards the end of 1948, a B-50A completed a return flight from Carswell AFB, Texas, to Hawaii (9,870 miles) in 41 hours 40 minutes, during which it was refuelled three times by KB-29Ms. Following this, on 6 February 1949, a B-50A named *Lucky Lady II* achieved the first non-stop round-the-world flight. Taking off from Fort Worth, Texas, in an easterly direction, it completed the circumnavigation of 23,452 miles in 94 hours 1 minute, with three in-flight refuellings.

Production of the B-50A ended in January 1949 just as the first examples of the next version, a batch of 45 B-50Bs, were starting to be delivered. These aircraft, which were later converted to carry out strategic reconnaissance missions (RB-50B), were heavier than their predecessors. They were fitted with bombing radar and could be refuelled in flight. Later modifications gave birth to the RB-50E (14 aircraft), RB-50F (14 aircraft) and RB-50G (15 aircraft). The bomber version was the B-50D, which was delivered from May 1949, and reached a total of 222 aircraft by

---

6. 59 B-50As were ordered in the 1946 fiscal year and 20 in the 1947 fiscal year; the 60th aircraft from the first batch was reserved as a prototype for the B-50C, a project that never came to fruition.

7. The first unit to be supplied with the B-50A was the 43rd Bomb Group based at Davis-Monthan, Arizona.

the end of 1950. To these aircraft were to be added 24 trainer TB-50Hs in 1952 and 1953.

It was at this time that the SAC possessed the largest number of B-50As and B-50Ds with 220 of each. However, this was not to last as the SAC was already entering the jet bomber era and would transfer its B-50s to other commands for use as in-flight refuelling aircraft (KB-50D, KB-50J and KB-50K) or for other subsidiary missions (WB-50D and WB-50H for weather reconnaissance, JB-50D as test-beds) where they would remain in service until the mid-1960s[8].

8. The last WB-50 was withdrawn from service with the 56th Weather Reconnaissance Squadron on 14 September 1965.

The B-50D (model 345-9-6) differed considerably from its predecessors, most noticeably by its in-flight refuelling receptacle. Some of them, including the one pictured (serial number 49-310), were converted into weather-reconnaissance planes. (USAF)

>> Tupolev's carbon copy

Stealing others' designs is not a modern phenomenon. Over 60 years ago, the Boeing B-29 was the victim of one of the most remarkable examples of pirating of all time, helping the USSR to make up for its backwardness in strategic bomber design.

In mid-1944, when the B-29s were sent over Japan, crews of damaged aircraft were instructed that in an exceptional emergency they could make a landing at Vladivostok. Over the ensuing months, three B-29s made emergency landings at the Russian airfield (on 29 July, 11 November and 24 November). Both crews and aircraft were interned by the Soviets and it soon became clear that Stalin was not in a hurry to send them back. Quite the opposite...

At the time, Russian engineers estimated that it would take a good five years to design and build a strategic bomber. This opportunity gave them a way to catch up. All they had to do was make an exact copy of the B-29 down to its last detail. Stalin gave them two years to do it.

The best engineers and technicians were brought in to check over and measure each of American bomber's 55,000 parts. To achieve this, one of the B-29s was completely dismantled, while another was used as a master and the third was used for pilot training. Very soon the Russian engineers realised that this was wishful thinking. It was not just a question of copying the plane itself, but also its engines, weapons and fuel systems, navigation equipment, etc. To

get this to work, Tupolev was chosen to copy the airframe, while Shetsov was to do the same for the engines. This 'carbon copy' of the B-29 was designated the Tu-4.

By 1945, despite enormous difficulties, the Tu-4 project was well advanced. So much so that, on 3 August 1947, Tu-4s took part in the Tushino Air Show near Moscow. The Americans were astounded to discover that the Russians had a bomber that could reach any US city. For the Western powers this came as a major shock. The Tu-4 was given the NATO codename 'Bull'. However, there were still some major technical problems to be overcome, particularly with the firing control system, pressurisation and the engines. It was not, therefore, until 1949 that the Tu-4 became fully operational. It is estimated that about 850 of the Tupolev aircraft were built and they remained in service until the early 1960s, when they were replaced by more modern aircraft. In addition, a number were delivered to China, who used some of them until 1968.

Apart from the red stars, the Tu-4s were perfect clones of the B-29. (H. Leonard collection)

>> Stratojet: the first modern bomber

At the beginning of June 1943, the AMC (Air Materiel Command) had approached several manufacturers to carry out preliminary design work on a jet-engined bomber and reconnaissance aircraft. This took concrete form when, on 17 November 1944, an invitation to tender was sent out. The design specification was for a jet-engined medium bomber with a speed of 550mph, a range of 3,500 miles and a service ceiling of 13,700 metres. During the course of December 1944, four manufacturers submitted their plans: Boeing, Convair, Martin and North American[9].

Boeing had already been working on a jet bomber for some time. The Seattle design department had initially gone for a reconnaissance aircraft that could be converted into a bomber (the model 413), followed by the model 424, a four-engined jet with a straight wing, whose airframe made use of sub-assemblies from the B-29. However, wind-tunnel tests on the planes had not been very satisfactory.

To match the specification, the engineers designed a new aircraft, the model 432, with a straight wing and four General Electric TG-180 (J35) jet engines of 2,180kg thrust (21.4kN) mounted in the upper part of the fuselage, their large air intakes forming bulges on each side of the cockpit. The exhaust nozzles were located in the upper part of the fuselage. It was this curious aircraft that the USAAF asked Boeing to develop, under the XB-47 designation. However, it was not to keep its unusual shape for very long.

Quite soon, under pressure from George Schairer, the Boeing team changed direction. Schairer and the engineer George Martin had been in the design teams who went to Germany to inspect research centres

The prototype XB-47 takes off under full throttle aided by 18 solid-fuel rockets of 450kg thrust each. In the background can be seen a Lockheed T-33 chase plane. (AFFTC)

(notably the Aeronautical Research Institute in Brunswick), where they had been able to question the engineers and study the various documents that had been seized. The work on the swept-back wing had been the main preoccupation of the group led by Dr Theodor von Kármán of the California Institute of Technology. On 10 May 1945, Schairer informed Seattle that this group's findings confirmed his own calculations and, on 13 September 1945, George Martin sent a report to the AMC proposing a four-engined jet bomber with swept-back wings. Schairer's information was carefully scrutinised and wind-tunnel tests soon confirmed the German studies. Indeed the results were so convincing that design work on the straight-wing model 432 was halted.

Retaining the model 432's fuselage, the Seattle

---

9. The plans submitted by the other three firms were the Convair model 109 (future XB-46), the Martin model 223 (future XB-48) and the North American NA-130 (future XB-45).

A KB-29P refuels an F-86A Sabre fighter using its flying boom. To keep down to the four-engined tanker's speed, the fighter's pilot has had to lower the flaps and the undercarriage. (AFFTC)

On continuous alert, these three Strategic Air Command B-47Bs are ready for take-off. The plane in the foreground is a B-47B-50-BW (serial number 51-2335). (USAF)

A B-47B Stratojet from the 11th production series (B-47B-50-BW). With its General Electric J-47-GE-23 jet engines, this version could fly at 616mph. (USAF)

team got down to work on models 446 and 448. Both featured a thin wing set back at an angle of 35°, but differed in the number of engines. The model 446 had six jet engines in the fuselage (four at the front behind the cockpit and two at the rear under the tailplane), while the model 448 had just four mounted side-by-side at the rear of the fuselage. The engineers at Wright Field considered this layout to be vulnerable, unsafe and likely to make maintenance very difficult. In October 1945, new design work started on the model 450-1-1[10], powered by six engines (four in pairs housed in pods under the wing and one at each wing tip). Gradually, the XB-47 began to take on its final form. The estimated performance figures gave it a speed of 560mph at 7,600 metres and a range in the region of about 4,000 miles. The military approved this pilot-study with the proviso that fuel capacity be increased, which was achieved by increasing the wing span (from 30.48 metres to 35.36 metres). This development became the model 450-2-2, all of whose engines were now to be mounted in pods under the wings. The use of wing pods meant that the airframe's integrity was not compromised in the event of a fire or explosion in one of the engines.

Another of the military authorities' requirements was that the XB-47 be able to carry a 10-tonne 'Grand Slam'-type[11] bomb in its bomb bay. This forced the engineers to completely revise the undercarriage into the tandem type, with two sets of wheels, located one behind the other, folding into the fuselage, while two stabilising wheels retracted into the engine pods.

The US Navy used two NB-47Es modified by Douglas to be used in electronic warfare and simulation of Soviet bombers. This is the second example (serial number 53-2104) seen in November 1974. (B. Knowles)

10. From this time, the model numbering changed so as to reflect the variants and sub-variants of each model. Thus the model 450 started with 450-1-1 and eventually ended up at 450-171-51.

11. This bomb had been designed during the war by the British and, in the United States, Bell had developed a guided version named 'Tarzon'.

A Boeing B-47 makes a spectacular JATO-rocket-assisted take-off on 15 April 1954. (USAF)

Finally, in April 1946, two prototypes were ordered while the mock-up was inspected. The first XB-47 was to be powered by six General Electric J35-GE-2 engines of 1,700kg thrust (16.7kN). The second was fitted with General Electric J47-GE-3 engines of 2,360kg thrust (23.1kN). However, to compensate for the slow acceleration of jet-engined aircraft, 18 auxiliary, solid-fuel JATO rockets were installed in the sides of the fuselage.

The first XB-47 emerged from the Seattle plant on 12 September 1947 and made its first flight at the hands of Bob Robbins on 17 December. It was the world's first bomber with a swept-back wing and opened the way for an even larger aircraft, the iconic B-52. The XB-47 commenced its test programme, in the course of which, on 8 February 1949, it unofficially broke the transcontinental speed record by flying the 2,289 miles separating Moses Lake AFB from Andrews AFB in 3 hours 46 minutes. In November 1949, when tests were well advanced, the USAF signed the first contract for ten pre-production B-47As to be built at the big Wichita factory where the B-29s had been made, even though the prototypes had been constructed in plant no. 2 at Seattle.

During this period, the international situation was worsening and the Cold War was in full swing. On 24 July 1948, Berlin was subjected to a total blockade, forcing the Western Allies into undertaking an unprecedented airlift, which would last until 12 May 1949. In the meantime, on 18 March, the United States, Canada, France, Great Britain and the Benelux countries had concluded a 20-year treaty with the aim of defending their democratic freedom. The coordination of these countries' military forces was henceforth to be ensured by the North Atlantic Treaty Organisation (NATO). A few months later, on 14 July 1949, the Soviets exploded their first atomic bomb. The mission entrusted to the SAC now took on even greater significance.

In November 1949, the Air Force took delivery of the first 88 B-47Bs for the SAC. In 1950, with the outbreak of the Korean War and the rising threat of Soviet nuclear power, the USAF began a programme of expansion, particularly in its fleet of strategic bombers. Thus orders for the B-47B rose from 88 to 399. These aircraft were substantially heavier than the prototypes, a handicap for which the provision of more powerful jet engines (the 2,360kg thrust – 23.1kN – J47-GE-11) did not fully compensate. The more powerful engines were installed from the 87th aircraft of the series onwards.

As with the B-17 and B-29, the need to get the B-47 into service rapidly obliged the Department of Defense to involve other manufacturers. While the majority of the 399 B-47Bs were produced at Wichita, eight were built by Lockheed at Marietta, Georgia, and ten by Douglas at Tulsa, Oklahoma. This distribution of work proved to be something of a rehearsal for the B-47E's production, of which 386 were built by Lockheed, 274 by Douglas and 931 B-47Es, as well as 240 RB-47E reconnaissance aircraft by Boeing Wichita. The B-47E, which made its first flight on Friday 30 January 1953, was distinguished by its two 20mm tail cannon, a pack of 33 jettisonable JATO rockets and auxiliary external fuel tanks with a capacity of 6,416 litres. It was powered by six General Electric J47-GE-25 engines of 3,365kg thrust (32kN). As for the RB-47E, it had a lengthened fuselage, cameras and integral JATO rockets. Later, many B-47Es were upgraded or converted for experimental work or various missions. Among these, it is worth mentioning the B-47 launch vehicles for the Bell GAM-63 Rascal, the Radioplane GAM-67 Crossbow, Martin ALBM-199B Bold Orion and the McDonnell GAM-72 Quail.

With the B-47C designation having been reserved for a potential four-engined version fitted with Allison 450-EL (J35-A-23) jet engines[12], the next in the series was the XB-47D, two of which were experimentally fitted with YT49-W-1 turboprops of 10,000hp (7,450kW). Following this there were 35 B-47Es that as electronic communications aircraft became EB-47L; then three B-47Bs converted respectively into YB-47F, KB-47G and YB-47J for the evaluation of in-flight refuelling systems. The final production aircraft were built at Wichita for electronic reconnaissance, namely 32 RB-47Hs and 15 RB-47Ks.

The first B-47s went into service from 23 October 1951[13] and, in January 1953, the first detachment of Stratojets was sent to Great Britain. By the end of that year, the SAC had 329 B-47s, a figure that had risen to 795 by the end of 1954, 1,086 by the end of 1955 and 1,306 by the end of 1956.

In total, more than 2,000 B-47s were built, the last of which rolled off the production line in February 1957. Withdrawal began in the same year. By December 1961, their number was down to 889 and the last B-47Es were withdrawn from service on 11 February 1966. In the event, none of the bomber versions was used in active service, although some of the reconnaissance versions were exposed to enemy fire whilst carrying out missions on the edge of Soviet airspace. The RB-47 fleet remained operational until December 1967.

12. The initial plan (model 450-19-10) was to use Allison 450-EL jet engines, but other types of engine were considered such as J40-WE-6, TG-190X3, XJ57 and TJ-14.
13. The first B-47B was sent to the 306th Bombardment Wing, stationed at MacDill AFB.

A B-47 Stratojet being refuelled. It has 5,675-litre auxiliary tanks under the wings. (USAF)

The RB-47E version was assigned to strategic reconnaissance missions. Bombing equipment was removed and 11 cameras fitted. Flares were also supplied for night photography. (USAF)

Armourers work on the 12.7mm machine guns of a B-47B from the 306th Bombardment Wing based at MacDill AFB, Florida, in June 1953. (USAF)

The many guises of the B-47

With over 2,000 aircraft built in the space of ten years, the B-47 underwent numerous modifications, some barely visible, others much more extensive, without counting the plethora of projects considered by the Seattle design teams.

1. Two YDB-47Es were specially converted to carry the large Bell GAM-63 Rascal air-to-ground missile. (Boeing via P.M. Bowers)

2. The TB-47B was the trainer version. (DR)

3. The EB-47E was an electronic warfare version fitted with Tee Town pods. Pictured is an aircraft from the 301st Bombardment Wing. (Al Lloyd)

4. Boeing modified two B-47s to test the British in-flight refuelling system. The KB-47G (upper) was the tanker and the YB-47F (lower) the plane to be refuelled. (Boeing)

5. A B-47B was lent to the Royal Canadian Air Force as a test bed for the Orenda Iroquois engine intended for the Avro CF-105 fighter. (Boeing)

6. An XB-47B was modified to evaluate the possibility of a version powered by Wright YT-49-W-1 turboprops. (Boeing)

7. One of the two NRB-47Hs hired by Hughes Electronics to test different radar and navigation systems. (R.J. Francillon)

8. The RB-47E was a reconnaissance version distinguished by its extended nose. (USAF)

9. The QB-47Es were used as targets in missile tests. Pictured is an aircraft from the 3,205th Drone Group. (B. Miller)

The B-47E's undersides were painted white to reflect radiation heat from nuclear explosions. This was also applied retrospectively to some B-47Bs. (USAF)

The SAC's purpose was to be capable of military intervention anywhere on the globe. Hence, in January 1948, while the XB-47 was undergoing initial testing, the USAF asked Boeing to look at different systems of in-flight refuelling. Tests of the 'flying boom' system began in September 1948 using a modified B-29 (KB-29P – see page 107). The tests were deemed satisfactory and the Wichita no. 2 plant was reactivated to modify the B-29s, and later on B-50s, for in-flight refuelling duties. The first of the 116 KB-29Ps were put into service with the SAC from September 1950.

Starting in January 1952, similar tests were conducted with a KC-97E, KB-47G and KB-47F. Most of the B-47Bs were fitted with a receptacle for use with the flying boom and the USAF would eventually acquire a total of 814 KC-97s, the first of which entered service in 1951.

The XL-15-BW Scout was Stearman's last creation. This multi-role aircraft could be easily dismantled and moved around on its wheels. (Boeing)

The use of the KC-97 posed the problem of the considerable disparity in performance between the refuelling aircraft and the aircraft being refuelled. In practice, refuelling could take place only during a shallow dive; consequently, when refuelling was complete, the bomber would have to consume some of the fuel it had just taken on as it climbed back to altitude. As a solution to this problem, the fitting of auxiliary jet engines on the KC-97 was never more than a stop-gap measure. Indeed, this drawback would not really be overcome until the KC-135A Stratotankers entered service in October 1958.

» Diversifying and enlarging the range

While Boeing was pushing ahead with the C-97, B-50 and B-47 programmes, they were also working on other, less spectacular plans with the intention of broadening their range and keeping their factories going. In the civil aviation field, design work was underway on two such projects for small- to medium-sized aircraft: models 417 and 431 for 30 to 40 passengers. Like many other projects at the time, these were intended to be successors to the 'indestructible' DC-3, but, with no takers, they were soon abandoned.

In the military sphere, J. E. Schaefer, the director of Stearman, sustained his company's activity by convincing Boeing's directors to work on a design for a new observer plane, even though the military authorities had not expressed any need for such an aircraft. Nevertheless, two prototypes of the Stearman model 200 (or Boeing model 451) were ordered under the name of 'XL-15 Scout', the first of which flew on 13 July 1947. After a pre-production run of ten aircraft (YL-15) and the prospect of an order for 47 production aircraft, the US Army lost interest, putting an end to the programme. After this, in the military field, the Seattle firm found itself confined to strategic bombers and refuelling aircraft. It was, of course, a high-priority area, but also one whose viability depended upon day-to-day decisions by the USAF, who might easily put an end to any of the programmes.

After the Second World War, besides its purely aeronautical activities, Boeing began to take an interest in missiles. Wanting to ensure protection against possible air attacks, the AMC asked Boeing to design an anti-aircraft missile christened GAPA (Ground-to-Air Pilotless Aircraft), able to intercept aircraft flying at up to 700mph at between 2,500 and 18,000 metres altitude. The result was a two-stage supersonic missile that had its first firing on 13 January 1946, but development was abandoned in 1949 after 112 launches.

However, the tests had not been in vain. A few months later the United States made the decision to acquire a full defence system against a possible Soviet attack, and Boeing was given the task of developing a

The Bomarc missile was originally conceived as a pilotless interceptor and ordered under the F-99 designation. It was then re-designated as an interceptor missile (IM-99). Seen here is one of the XIM-99 prototypes (serial number 54-3079) next to an Atlas ICBM and a Nike rocket. (Author's collection)

long-range supersonic missile in collaboration with the Michigan Aeronautical Research Center. Named Bomarc (BOeing and Michigan Aeronautical Research Center), the missile was to be powered by two ramjets. Provided with small wings, this impressive, seven-tonne missile was initially classed as a fighter (F-98), then later as an interceptor missile (IM-99). After a first firing at Cape Canaveral, on 10 September 1952, the test programme went on until 1961 with some 70 firings. In November 1957, the Air Force signed an order for a first production batch of 23 IM-99As to be constructed by Boeing's Pilotless Aircraft Division in Seattle. Allocated to ten sites[14] in the eastern United States and Canada, the first Bomarcs were declared operational in September 1959. The 269 production IM-99As were followed by 36 XIM-99Bs and 301 Super Bomarc IM-99Bs whose operational deployment began in June 1961 at the Kincheloe base[15].

>> The birth pangs of the B-52

Even as a team of engineers was concentrating all its efforts on getting the XB-47 ready as soon as possible, the AMC announced that Boeing had won the bid to design and build the next of the Air Force's strategic bombers, the XB-52. This aircraft was intended to supersede the Convair B-36, even though the latter had not yet flown[16]. On 23 November 1945, the AMC had sent out invitations to tender for a bomber capable of achieving 300mph at an altitude of 10,000 metres with a range of 5,000 miles carrying a 4.5-tonne bomb load. Three manufacturers had responded with bids: Martin, Convair (Consolidated Vultee) and, of course, Boeing, the undisputed specialist in heavy bombers. On 5 June, Boeing was declared the winner and victory was confirmed by the signing of a contract, on 28 June, to design and build a full-sized mock-up of an experimental bomber designated XB-52.

The aircraft, allotted model number 462 by Boeing, could not deny its ancestry. Following the B-29's

A Boeing CQM-10A Bomarc missile is fired from the US Air Force's Vandenberg base in California. (DoD/F.J. Hooker)

general structure, it differed in its power plant, which consisted of six 5,500hp Wright XT-35W Typhoon engines driving six-bladed propellers. With a span of 67 metres, it weighed 165 tonnes on take-off. On paper at least, it could fly at over 435mph at an altitude of 10,000 metres and carry a 4.8-tonne bomb load over 3,575 miles. Although these performance figures met some of the specification requirements, they fell short on range and did not represent much of an advance over those of the B-36. The model 462 was clearly some way from achieving the required 5,000-mile range. The engineers therefore moved on to the model 464, notable for its moderate dimensions and needing only four engines. However, the problem of operational range remained crucial and could only be overcome by using external fuel tanks and in-flight refuelling.

At this time, General Curtis LeMay, assistant chief of staff in charge of research and development in the Air Force, had increased his demands, with the aircraft now required to be capable of covering 11,800 miles. To achieve this, the model 464's size was again increased and new variants were considered: model

The XB-52 was distinguished chiefly by its five-man crew and two-seater cockpit canopy. (USAF)

14. The bases were at Dow (Maine), Duluth (Minnesota), Kincheloe (Michigan), Langley (Virginia), McGuire (New Jersey), Niagara Falls (New York), Otis (Massachusetts), and Suffolk County (New York) in the United States, and La Macaza (Quebec) and North Bay (Ontario) in Canada.

15. The Bomarcs were withdrawn from service in 1965 and the Super Bomarcs in 1972. Subsequently, some were used as target drones.

16. The B-36 programme had been launched in the early months of the war when it was feared that Britain might be invaded by the Germans and there would be a need for an aircraft capable of bombing Europe from the United States. The XB-36 made its first flight on 8 August 1946.

464-16 (long-range nuclear bomber) and model 464-17 (medium-range conventional bomber). The swept-back wing made its first appearance on model 464-29, thus permitting an increase in speed to a projected 445mph, further increased in January 1948 to 500mph with the XT35-turboprop-powered model 464-35.

Aware that they had reached the limit of what they could expect from turboprop performance, the engineers began to look at the use of jet engines, as a result of which the model 464-40 appeared on the drawing boards. Making use of the 464-35's airframe, the 464-40 was to have eight Westinghouse XJ40-WE-12 jet engines mounted in pairs on under-wing pods; but there was little increase in the projected speed (505mph).

Boeing's engineers presented the results of their deliberations to Henry Warden, the Air Force's officer in charge of the project. He, too, came to the same conclusions. However, when the Air Force ordered two XB-52s, in July 1948, both were powered by turboprops, although design work on other versions proceeded and the model 464-40 continued to develop. Variants with six Westinghouse J40s (model 464-46) and six Pratt & Whitney jet engines (model 464-47) were also presented to the Air Force.

Subsequent events were to enter into legend with the B-52 joining the club of aircraft allegedly 'designed in a few hours in a hotel room'[17]. On Thursday 21 October 1948, George Schairer, Art Carlsen and Vaughn Blumenthal[18] went to Wright Field to show the model 464-35 design to Colonel Peter Warden, who was in charge of bomber development at the Wright Air Development Center (WADC). Warden could not hide his disappointment at the plane's performance and asked Schairer to produce a design for a jet-engined version as quickly as possible. Schairer asked Ed Wells to drop everything and join him. Wells arrived that evening at the hotel and, using the files on jet engines that they had brought with them, the four men drew up the basis of a plan for a jet bomber that they took to Colonel Warden the next morning.

Warden was not over-enthusiastic: 'I don't think you've gone far enough,' he told them. 'I think you need to use a faster, more swept-back wing, like the B-47's.'

'Let's see what we can do', replied Wells. 'We'll be back on Monday morning.' Bringing in the skills of Robert Withington and Maynard Pennell, two Boeing engineers who happened to be in Dayton on other business[19], the small team worked relentlessly to come up with another design. They had just 72 hours. The aircraft that emerged was a bomber with a span of 56 metres and a negative-dihedral, swept-back wing with four pairs of JT3 engines mounted beneath the wing.

17. A similar legend is attached to the story of the Douglas AD Skyraider attack aircraft.

18. Art Carlsen was in charge of weight calculations and Vaughn Blumenthal was director of preliminary studies.

19. Robert Withington was vice-president in charge of engineering and Maynard Pennell was project director.

One of the prototype B-52's faults lay in the cockpit canopy, which gave no downward visibility. This photo gives a good impression of the overall shape of the aircraft. (USAF)

The first B-52D-1-BW (serial number 55-0049) built at Wichita, Kansas. (USAF)

A B-52G with all its flaps down prepares to carry out a touch-and-go landing on the runway at Mather AFB, California, on 11 August 1976. (A. Pelletier)

The B-52G could carry 84 227kg bombs in its bomb bay, as well as a further 24 bombs under the wings. (USAF)

A Boeing NB-52 launching an experimental North American X-15 rocket plane in 1959. (NASA/DFRC)

The total weight was estimated at 150 tonnes and the range around 11,500 miles – a performance only possible because the Boeing team hoped to have available the new Pratt & Whitney X-176 (future J57) jet engine. A typist was hurriedly recruited to type up the 33 pages of the report, while Schairer made a balsa model of the plane. On Monday morning, as agreed, Schairer was back in Warden's office and this time he was won over by the design.

By January 1949, design work on the turboprop versions was halted, as was construction of the model 464-35 mock-up. Designated model 464-49, the jet-engined version underwent continued development with a view to increasing its range. By January 1950, the design department had got as far as model 464-67 with a 35° swept-back wing, eight jet engines and a take-off weight of 176 tonnes. The wing used profiles specially worked out by Boeing (Boeing 236 and 237). The engines were Pratt & Whitney YJ57-P-3 of 3,940kg thrust (38.7kN). The undercarriage, consisting of four moveable dollies, retracted into the fuselage. Finally, the defensive armament consisted of four 12.7mm machine guns in the tail. Like the B-47, the XB-52 and the YB-52 had tandem cockpits under a narrow cover. However, at the express request of Commander-in-Chief of the SAC, General Curtis LeMay, this layout was shelved on the production run, in favour of side-by-side cockpit seats.

By March 1951, wind-tunnel tests had been sufficiently convincing for the Air Force to send Boeing a letter of intention for the construction of three aircraft designated B-52A (model 464-201-0) and the preparation of tooling needed for a production run. As for the two prototypes, they were built in a restricted area of the no. 2 plant. The XB-52 emerged from the shops on 29 November 1951, hidden under large tarpaulins, to be taken to the hangar where it was to be prepared for its maiden flight. This process took ten long months during which the aircraft was damaged when the pneumatic systems were pressurised, thus explaining why the second prototype (YB-52) took to the skies first, on Tuesday 15 April 1952; XB-52 did not take off until 2 October.

The B-52As differed from the prototypes not only in their substantially modified nose end, but also in their Pratt & Whitney J57-P-9W water-injection engines and jettisonable, 3,785-litre, external fuel tanks located under the wing tips. Fully laden, the B-52A weighed 177 tonnes. The first one flew on 5 August 1954 and, with the other two, was used in the development programme.

The first proper production version was thus the B-52B (model 464-201-3), 50 of which were built (including 27 delivered as RB-52B). Delivery into service did not begin until 29 June 1955 when the first planes were sent to 93rd Bombardment Wing based at Castle AFB, in California. The 35 B-52Cs (model 464-201-6) were the first to receive J57-P-29W water-injection engines. Like all the earlier aircraft, the B-52Cs were built at Seattle. With the B-52D (model 464-201-7), production was shared between Seattle and Wichita. Seattle produced 101 B-52Ds, 42 B-52Es and 44

B-52Fs (which were to be the last B-52s built there). For its part, Wichita built, respectively, 69, 58 and 41. Apart from their more modern electronics and other equipment, these three versions were similar to the B-52C, although the B-52F was supplied with J57-P-43W engines with 6,237kg thrust (61.2kN). The first B-52D flew on 28 September 1956 and went into service at the end of that year with the 42nd Bombardment Wing. The first B-52E flew on 3 October 1957 and entered service with the 6th Bombardment Wing the following December. Finally, the B-52Fs were delivered to the 93rd Bombardment Wing from June 1958.

For Boeing, the B-52 programme was without any doubt the most important of the post-war period. A few figures will give an idea of its size. Even before the first flight, 3,042,207 hours of development were devoted to the programme, to which can be added the 1,313,528 hours for the test-flight programme. By January 1955, around 34,500 technical drawings had been traced and 11,529,544 hours had been devoted to the entire programme.

The final two variants of the B-52 (B-52G and H) differed substantially from all of their predecessors. The most obvious differences were in the tail fin, which was 2.5 metres lower, and the engines, which were Pratt & Whitney J57-P-43WA on the B-52G and Pratt & Whitney TF33-P3 on the B-52H. Additional internal fuel tanks extended the range by 1,850 miles compared with the early B-52s. The tail guns were

A B-52G from 1,708th Bombardment Wing takes off on a mission during Operation Desert Storm, on 2 September 2005. (USAF)

A B-52H (serial number 60-3) uses its parachute brake on landing at Barksdale AFB in October 2004. (USAF)

now remotely controlled and the B-52G could carry two North American Aviation Hound Dog AGM-28 supersonic missiles with a 600-mile range[20]. All the B-52Gs and B-52Hs (193 and 102 aircraft respectively) were built at Wichita. The first one flew on 27 October 1958 and the last left the production line in 1963. The 5th Bombardment Wing was the first unit to receive them. The first B-52H flew on 16 March 1961. This version was originally intended to be armed with Douglas Skybolt AGM-87A missiles with a 900-mile

range, but the Skybolt was cancelled and they were armed instead with Hound Dogs. Throughout their long career, the B-52Gs and Hs would benefit from various modernisation programmes, the most important being the fitting to the B-52H of TF33 dual-flow engines, 20mm rotating cannon (in place of machine guns) in the tail, and improvements to the electronic equipment.

20. In 1970, the USAF decided to replace the NAA AGM-28s with Boeing AGM-69A SRAMs.

B-52 production timeline

13 February 1946 >>	The USAAF issues a specification for a new heavy, long-range bomber.
28 June 1946 >>	Boeing gets a contract for preliminary studies on a turboprop bomber.
25 October 1948 >>	Boeing proposes a bomber with eight jet engines to the USAF.
26 January 1949 >>	The USAF asks Boeing to build two prototypes.
15 April 1952 >>	YB-52's first flight at Seattle.
2 October 1952 >>	XB-52's first flight at Seattle.
28 September 1953 >>	Wichita is chosen as the second production site.
5 August 1954 >>	B-52A's first flight.
25 January 1955 >>	B-52B's first flight.
29 June 1955 >>	First delivery of a B-52B to the SAC.
9 March 1956 >>	B-52C's first flight.
14 March 1956 >>	First flight of the first B-52D built at Wichita.
28 September 1956 >>	First flight of the first B-52D built at Seattle.
3 October 1957 >>	First flight of the first B-52E built at Seattle.
17 October 1957 >>	First flight of the first B-52E built at Wichita.
6 May 1958 >>	First flight of the first B-52F built at Seattle.
14 May 1958 >>	First flight of the first B-52F built at Wichita.
27 October 1958 >>	First flight of the first B-52G built at Wichita.
25 February 1959 >>	Delivery of the last B-52 built at Seattle.
16 March 1961 >>	B-52H's first flight at Wichita.
26 October 1962 >>	Delivery of the last B-52H built at Wichita.

Seen from a KC-135 refuelling tanker, this B-52H from the 2nd Bombardment Wing prepares for in-flight refuelling, in February 2006. The bulges on each side house the ALQ-117 warning radar. (USAF)

Boeing's two legendary bombers, the B-17 and the B-52, are caught for a moment flying in formation at the 'Defenders of Liberty' air show at Barksdale AFB, California, on 13 May 2006. (USAF)

>> The 707: icon of air travel

In August 1952, Douglas, having almost lost its way developing a turboprop version of its four-engined DC-7, announced its intention to put a jet-engined airliner, designated DC-8, on the market[21]. Three weeks later, Boeing followed suit. This was an important moment at which these two big manufacturers made crucial choices about their futures. Drawing confidence from experience, Boeing immediately set about building a test aircraft, or 'demonstrator' to use the now-established expression, while Douglas took the cautious approach and waited for the airlines to put out tenders before constructing a prototype.

Boeing had not made its announcement lightly. Ever since late 1946, the design department had worked on 60 or so pilot studies, including an outline for a four-engined jet aircraft with a high, swept-back wing designed by Robert E. Hage and very much influenced by work on the B-47[22]. These pilot studies had been filed under the generic name of 'model 473'. The first, model 473-1, was a 22-tonne, 27-seat, twin-engined jet. It also had a swept-back high wing and Rolls-Royce Nene engines of 2,720kg thrust (26.7kN) mounted in wing pods. However, its 1,200-mile range restricted it to internal flights. With the range extended to 1,500 miles, the model 473-11 was a little better, but was still not suitable for intercontinental flights. Model 473-25, of May 1949, with its six Pratt & Whitney

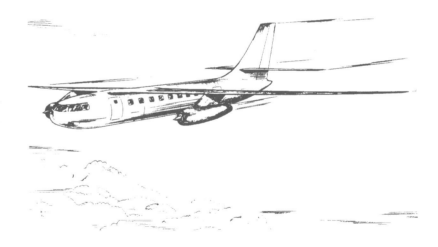

The Boeing model 473-11 was a high-wing, twin-jet-engine aircraft with Rolls-Royce Nene engines of 26.7kN. (R.J. Francillon)

4,500kg-thrust (44.5kN) J57 engines was much inspired by the B-52's outline and marked a substantial improvement, as – on paper at least – it laid claims to transatlantic capability, and had room for 98 passengers. With model 473-47, Boeing returned to the medium-haul, twin-engined option. As for the final manifestation of this group, the model 473-57 of April 1950, this was a three-engined aircraft with a 50-passenger capacity.

Faced with so many pilot schemes, all different from

---

21. This was actually the second DC-8, Douglas having worked on an identically named airliner inspired by the experimental XB-42 bomber.

22. No model number appears to have been allocated to this early draft.

The Boeing model 367-80, more commonly known as the 'Dash 80', is towed past a B-52C. (Boeing)

With flaps and undercarriage lowered, a 367-80 poses for the photographer on its first flight, on 15 July 1954. (Boeing)

one another, it is understandable that Boeing's management remained somewhat dubious. Simultaneously, another team of engineers was working on the development of the C-97 (model 367) in both transport and refuelling-tanker versions. With its conventional power plant and consequent moderate performance, the C-97 turned out to be unsuited to the task of refuelling the B-47. Boeing therefore looked at the possibility of designing a C-97 derivative

fitted with turboprops or jet engines. In April 1948, model 367-15-23 made its appearance on the drawing board. Significantly bigger, it had four Allison T38 turboprop engines of 2,900hp (3,890kW). Once again, one design followed another, ending in January 1951 with model 367-64 using Pratt & Whitney J57 engines. As was to be expected, the first tests, in March 1951, of B-47s being refuelled from KC-97s confirmed the unsuitability of the latter for this purpose. The

The Dash 80 in its final configuration, after being restored for donation to the National Air & Space Museum, in May 1972. (Boeing)

engineers persevered and proposed further derivatives such as models 367-68 and 376-70 with Bristol Olympus jet engines, as well as models 367-69 and 367-71 with Pratt & Whitney J57 engines. Models 367-70 and 367-71 had 18° swept-back wings. All this, however, was wasted effort as the Air Force did not at the time have the means to equip itself with a fleet of jet-engined refuelling tankers.

In the autumn of 1951, in the absence of any consensus about which of these pilot studies to choose, the design department started from a clean sheet and began work on plans for an aircraft that could be used either as an airliner or a refuelling tanker. It was allocated the model number 707. Once again, various configurations were tried, with four or six jet or turboprop engines, but all with 35° swept-back wings. By spring 1952, these designs had culminated in the model 707-6, which, according to the engineers, best matched the airlines' needs. The aircraft had space for 76 passengers and was to be powered by four Pratt & Whitney JT3P engines of 4,300kg thrust (42.3kN).

For Bill Allen, the moment had arrived for a decision – the decision. He brought his principal colleagues together and handed them a questionnaire concerning different aspects of jet aircraft construction, in terms of feasibility, costs, organisation, etc. 'I want you to take the time needed to answer these questions,' he

An American Airlines model 707-123B landing at Los Angeles International Airport in 1968. The airline was to acquire 25 of these aircraft. (R.J. Francillon)

told them. 'We mustn't get this wrong.' On 21 April 1952, six days after the B-52's first flight, Allen convened another meeting to look at the answers to the questionnaire. Jim Burton, the finance director, informed them that it would cost $16 million to construct a prototype. Maynard Pennell explained that the aircraft would meet the military's need for a cargo/refuelling plane. Al Jacobsen claimed that he had the necessary manpower and factory space. These

Built at the Renton plant, the 707s had to cross the Cedar River bridge to get to the runway. Seen here is a Continental Airlines 707-124 with the small fin used on the first production aircraft. (P.M. Bowers collection)

The transition from one era to another is represented by the model 377 Stratocruiser giving way to the 707, the latter being Pan Am's first 707-121. Just six of this version were delivered to this airline. (Pan Am)

After it had bought two 720-062s, Pacific Northern was itself bought by Western Airlines in June 1967. (Boeing)

responses were sent to the executive committee who, on 22 April, took the decision to allocate a budget of $16 million to the construction of a demonstrator. For Boeing, this represented a considerable risk as this sum was more than twice the previous year's profits.

So that competitors would not think that the aircraft was just a derivative of the C-97, it was given the model 367-80 designation rather than the logical 707-6, and came to be generally known as the 'Dash 80'. Construction of the 367-80 was completed two weeks ahead of the initial schedule. It left the Renton works on 14 May 1954 and was named by Mrs William E. Boeing, but it did not make its maiden flight until 15 July in the expert hands of Alvin M. 'Tex' Johnston (and Richard L. 'Dick' Loesch as co-pilot). This is a date to be remembered in the history of post-war civil aviation. While the flight passed off quietly enough, it sealed the fate of piston-engined aircraft by rendering them obsolete at a stroke. More than this, it swept aside the British aeronautical industry in the long-haul jet market.

The first phase of the test programme came to an end on 29 September 1954 with the 26th flight, at which point the prototype had accumulated more than 43 hours of flying time. The way was thus clear to begin demonstration flights for the airline companies and, on 13 October, Pan American Airways announced its intention to purchase 45 jet airliners: 20 Boeing 707s and 25 Douglas DC-8s. The cut-throat battle for market share had begun.

The Israeli airline El Al ordered two 707-458s in March 1960. The first one, seen here, was named Shehecheyanu. (Boeing)

A TWA model 707-331B (registered N8730) takes off from Fresno Airport, California, in June 1973. (Boeing)

(Boeing)

Alvin M. 'Tex' Johnston

Admine, 18 August 1914–
Mount Vernon, 30 October 1998

From his first flight, at the age of 11, Alvin Johnston was hooked by aeroplanes. By the time he was 16, he had started flying lessons, paid for by doing 'odd jobs', and he later attended the Spartan School of Aeronautics to study mechanics.

He then joined Inman's Flying Circus, which gave him the opportunity to build up his flying hours. Eventually, he acquired an aircraft of his own, a Command-Air biplane. After Pearl Harbor, Johnston flew on escort duties for the USAAF until 1942 when he joined Bell to take up test flights on the P-39, XP-63 and XP-59, as well as taking part in races with a modified P-39.

He oversaw testing of the Bell X-1 until 1947, when he moved to Boeing to carry out testing on the XB-47, YB-52 and, especially, the Boeing 707. In the early 1960s, Johnston became deputy director of the X-20 Dyna-Soar programme.

Without further ado, on 7 June 1955, Douglas announced the decision to build its DC-8 and fit it with Pratt & Whitney JT4A engines, which were more powerful than the JT3Ps used by Boeing. It would also have a wider fuselage giving room for six rows of seats. Boeing counter-attacked with a proposal for a wider-bodied variant also fitted with JT4A engines. In the meantime, the Dash 80 continued its tests and demonstrator flights. On 7 August 1955, Tex Johnston put it through two hesitation flick rolls at the Lake Washington Naval Show in Seattle. On 16 October 1955, it flew non-stop from Seattle to Washington DC and back, beating all records for transcontinental flights by civil aircraft at an average speed of 592mph outward and 558mph on the return. By the end of 1955, it had made 281 flights, to which it added 237 in the following year. By the end of its career, in 1970, the Dash 80 had no fewer than 1,691 flights on its record, giving a total of 2,350 hours' flying time.

Yet Douglas, with its DC-8, was a serious rival to Boeing. It had a number of significant advantages, including profound knowledge of the airline companies' requirements gathered from its sales of DC-4, DC-6 and DC-7 aircraft. In particular, Douglas knew that on the North Atlantic route competitive advantage would go to the aircraft that could complete the journey without any stop-offs, whatever the weather conditions. It was for this reason that range had been one of the engineers' primary

NASA carried out test crashes using a real model 720 to assess the strength of the aircraft's construction. (NASA/DFRC)

considerations when designing the DC-8.

But Douglas was not Boeing's only competitor. There was a third party eyeing up its slice of the cake: Convair. Based in San Diego, California, Convair had announced, in January 1946, its intention to develop a four-engined jet designated the model 22 Skylark (the future Convair 880). By putting speed above range, Convair was clearly targeting internal traffic and short international routes. The Dash 80 found itself caught in something of a pincer movement and Boeing felt obliged to fight on two fronts simultaneously: on the one hand by developing larger versions with JT4A engines and, on the other, by working on a medium-haul version, the model 720.

The initial order for 20 Boeings was confirmed by PanAm on 13 October 1955 and amended in December to reduce the number of aircraft with JT3C engines to six (model 707-121) and to increase the number with JT4A engines (model 707-321) to 14; both types were to have wider cabins (3.76 metres as against 3.66 originally). The Boeing 707-121 first flew on Friday 20 December and delivery to PanAm began on 15 August of the following year. Commercial service started on 26 October 1958 with a flight from New York to Paris, including service stops at Gander on the outward trip and at Keflavik on the return.

Faced with Douglas's merciless competition, Boeing's directors took the decision to provide 'made-to-measure' planes to all its new customers. Although popular with the airlines, this policy turned out in the long run to be very costly and made the 707 programme a rather unprofitable operation, with margins being eroded by the difficulty in keeping costs down on limited production runs. Boeing offered no fewer than four fuselage lengths, two internal cabin widths and three wing types, not to mention the different engines (Pratt & Whitney JT3C and JT4A, Rolls-Royce R.Co.12, etc).

Several companies committed themselves to the model 707-120 with JT3C engines: Pan American Airways, American Airlines, Continental Airlines, TWA, Qantas (in the shorter-fuselage version to gain greater range, albeit with a smaller payload) and Western Airlines. This model, however, was not particularly well-suited to the transatlantic route. Operating at the extreme edge of their range, the PanAm 707s were obliged to make stops at Gander and Shannon or Prestwick to refuel. The first true transatlantic versions appeared with the 707-320s and 420s. Fitted with JT4A engines of more than 7 tonnes thrust and a greater wing span, the model 707-320 was able to cross the Atlantic without stop-offs. It also benefited from a 58% increase in fuel capacity (80,500 litres instead of 51,000) and improved lift augmentation devices. Thus its maximum take-off weight was increased to 143 tonnes, compared with the 707-120's 117 tonnes.

The 707-320 made its first flight on 11 January

The KC-97 soon showed its limitations when asked to refuel the new jet-engine bombers. Here, a KC-97G refuels an RB-47E. (USAF)

In 1951, during the development stages of the C-97, Boeing's engineers imagined a swept-back-wing, four-jet model 367-64. (Boeing)

Between June and August 1955, the Dash 80 was equipped with a boom to demonstrate refuelling a B-52. (Boeing)

The first KC-135A (Boeing model 717) taking off from Boeing Field. It was fitted with an anemometer on the nose, later removed. (USAF)

The last of the 45 C-135 Stratolifters ordered by the US Air Force was delivered to the Military Air Transport Service on 29 August 1962. (USAF)

Crew training on KC-135s was undertaken by the 93rd AREFS based at Castle AFB, California. (USAF)

France ordered 12 C-135Fs for in-flight refuelling of its Mirage IVA strategic bomber fleet. (DR)

1958 and delivery to the airlines began on 20 August of the same year. PanAm put its planes into service on 26 August 1959, with Air France, Sabena, TWA and South African Airways close on its heels. With the introduction of the new Rolls-Royce R.Co.12 fan-jet engine, the Seattle engineers saw the chance to offer a more powerful but less thirsty version. Identical to the 707-320 apart from its engines, the 707-420 made its first flight on 20 May 1959. However, the arrival of the Pratt & Whitney JT3D fan-jet limited the 707-420's production run to just 37 planes[23].

While the 707-220, 320 and 420 had been designed to compete with Douglas's various DC-8 models, Boeing's engineers had not forgotten about Convair and its model 880. After various configurations had been considered, the definitive form of the 707-020 (which would become the 720) was settled upon in November 1957. It was a shorter, lighter aircraft, powered by JT3C jet engines and carried up to 149 passengers on short-haul routes. Although it was an almost exact copy of the 707-120, the 720 was considered a separate model. It made its first flight on Monday 23 November 1959 and only 64 were

delivered to seven companies, but this total nevertheless matched, to within one aircraft, the number of Convair 880s built. Against the Convair 990 with its fan-jet engines, Boeing put up the 720B with JT3D fan-jet engines, of which 89 were built. These would not be the only Boeing models with fan-jet engines as there were also models 707-120B, 707-320B and 707-320C fitted with them (the last named being a so-called 'convertible' model with a large loading door and a reinforced floor for cargo).

Including aircraft built for military use, a total of 1,010 Boeing 707/720s was produced between 1959 and 1991, the year in which the last of the line left the Seattle plant (an E3D for the RAF). The 707s started to disappear at the beginning of the 1970s as the first large-capacity planes made their appearance. They nonetheless continued to fly all over the globe on behalf of secondary operators. Indeed, the second-hand market flourished to the extent that specialist firms sprung up to modernise the 707 by changing the

23. The 707-420 was used by BOAC, BOAC-Cunard, Cunard Eagle Airways, Lufthansa, Air India, Varig and El Al. BOAC put its 707-420s into service in May 1960.

The KC-135 entered service with the Strategic Air Command from June 1957, a year in which 24 of the aircraft were delivered. (Boeing)

engines, refurbishing the cabins and even fitting silencers to bring them into line with the latest FAA noise regulations.

>> The flying petrol station

By the end of 1953, the Air Force, which had accumulated 18 months' experience of in-flight refuelling, was well aware of the piston-engined KC-97's limitations when refuelling jet bombers. With the signing of the first production contracts for the B-52, the need for a fleet of jet-engined refuelling tankers had become clear. With this in mind, on 18 June 1954, the Air Research & Development Command (ARDC) put out a tender to the principal manufacturers (Boeing, Convair, Douglas, Fairchild, Lockheed and Martin) for a transport and tanker aircraft, provisionally designated KC-X, and indicated that there would be a need for around 800 planes.

With the experience acquired from the KB-29, KB-50 and KC-97, as well as the launch of the Dash 80, there was little doubt that Boeing had a considerable advantage over their rivals. In a bid to

short-circuit the competition, Boeing flew a B-52A and a Dash 80 in refuelling formation, even though the latter was not equipped with a boom. On 5 August 1954, before the Dash 80 had been able to demonstrate its capability as a tanker, the Air Force announced that it would acquire 29 Boeing model 717s under the KC-135A designation as an interim measure. A few weeks later, it ordered a further 88 KC-135As. For the Air Force, this was indeed an interim order, as six months later, Lockheed, with its CL-321 project, was declared the winning KC-X bidder and a prototype was ordered. The latter was never built, while Boeing received yet another order for 169 KC-135As, followed, on 27 March 1958, by a fourth order for 157 aircraft. Production of the KC-135A Stratotanker began at Renton on 1 September 1954, but nearly two years passed before the first KC-135A emerged from the factory on 18 July 1956[24] and made its first flight on 31 August.

Although similar in appearance, the model 707 and the KC-135 (model 717) were very different aircraft so,

---

24. On the same day, the last KC-97 emerged from the production line.

Some civil 707s were converted into tankers for foreign governments. Seen here is a 707-370C that was sold to Iran and fitted with Beech 1800 refuelling booms at each wing tip. (Beech)

During the Vietnam War, the KC-135 gave fighter-bombers a considerably greater range. Here, Republic F-105D Thunderchiefs head for their target, on 1 January 1967. (USAF)

contrary to what Boeing had hoped, the same tooling could not be used. Their structures were different and made use of different materials; the KC-135 was made according to 'safe-life' standards, which were less restrictive than the usual 'fail-safe' standards imposed on civil aircraft. One consequence of this was that costly modifications were later required to prolong the planes' useful life.

Delivery to the Air Force began on 30 April 1957 and the SAC put its new tankers into service from 28 June, with the 93rd Air Refuelling Squadron (ARS) based at Castle AFB, California. At that date, 215 KC-135s had been ordered, added to which would be an additional 130 aircraft in April 1958. Later orders and continuing development of new versions eventually brought the total production up to 820 aircraft divided as follows:

- 732 KC-135As for the SAC
- 17 KC-135Bs for the SAC
- 10 RC-135Bs for the SAC
- 15 C-135As for the MATS
- 30 C-135Bs for the MATS
- 4 RC-135As for the MATS
- 12 C-135Fs for the French Air Force

To these aircraft may be added 36 model 707s and a model 720 built for the US Air Force and various foreign governments, as well as 93 other specialised aircraft built using 707-320 airframes. By autumn 1956, Boeing was thus committed to several major programmes that would provide the company with work for some years to come. Quite a road travelled in under 40 years! That autumn was also marked by the loss of the founder of this aeronautical giant. On Friday 28 September 1956, William Boeing passed away on board his yacht, *Taconite*.

A B-52 from the 5th Bombardment Wing waits to join the take-off runway at Minot Air Force Base, North Dakota. (USAF/MSgt L. Cheung)

CHAPTER 5

1957–1969

Changing times

>> Boeing entered 1957 with a full order book. Within the space of a few months, sales were being won with numerous major airlines: Pan American, American, Braniff, Air France, Continental, Sabena, TWA, Lufthansa, Air India, Qantas, British Overseas ... B-52 production was in full swing. But appearances were deceptive. Over the course of the next few years, the Seattle firm would endure several successive setbacks that would gradually see it losing its grip in the military aircraft field.

As the year 1957 dawned, there were some 300 Stratofortresses in service with SAC units. Five years later, the number of B-52s in operational service would peak at 650 aircraft. In the meantime, on 18 January 1957, three B-52s had flown around the world, a distance of 24,320 miles, in 45 hours 19 minutes at an average speed of 534mph, halving the record time set in 1949 by the B-50, *Lucky Lady II*. New versions of the B-52 had appeared and the last one (a B-52H built at Wichita) would be delivered on 26 October 1962.

>> The search for the B-52's successor

Quite early on, Boeing began some initial design work on a B-52 replacement. This was happening at a time when engineers thought that they could sufficiently tame nuclear energy for it to be used to power aircraft. Design work started in August 1954 with model 713-1 using conventional power and 713-2 using nuclear power. The latter was renamed model

722 in July 1955 and separate teams worked on each of the projects until the abandonment of the 722. Model 713-1 passed through a multitude of different configurations until model 713-1-169 was shown to the US Air Force in April 1955. It was a swept-back-wing aircraft with a 36-metre span, powered by four turbojets and capable of carrying a 4.5-tonne bomb load. It could fly over its target at Mach 3 and at an altitude of 18,000 metres.

In December 1955, with the object of significantly increasing the range, the engineers turned to the model 724. Though quite similar to the 713, it differed by having two 20-metre-long external fuel tanks and 'floating' wing tips. In January 1956, design work on model 725 also began. This would continue into December 1957 and generate 143 configurations. For Bill Allen, this was a battle that Boeing had to win at any cost, and he decided to construct a $30-million test centre so that the company would be the best equipped to build the new bomber.

The Air Force, however, rejected all these 'paper aeroplanes'. There were simply no runways capable of

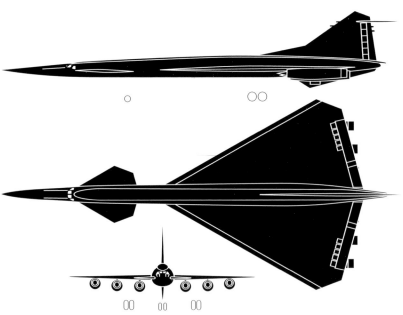

Model 804-4 was just one of the many configurations of the 804 considered under the WS-110 Weapons System. It was put before the evaluation committee on 4 November 1957. Power was to be six General Electric X279J jet engines.

taking these monsters, some of which weighed 340 tonnes! In September 1956, the Air Force asked Boeing and its competitor, North American, to completely revise their plans and announced that they would shortly reveal their choice after a competitive tender. On 18 September 1956, they put out a tender for an aircraft with a Mach 3–Mach 3.2 cruising speed at between 21,000 and 23,000 metres and a range of 7,000 to 12,000 miles. Total weight on take-off was

not to exceed 220 tonnes. The two manufacturers had to respond within 45 days. Known as the 'weapons system WS-110A', the programme gave birth to another derivative of the 725, the model 804, whose design work was led by H. W. 'Bob' Withington and Lloyd Goodmanson. Around ten configurations were looked at, with the fourth one (model 804-4) being chosen for submission. This aircraft, 63 metres long and with a wing-span of 29 metres, the aircraft would be powered by six General Electric X279J engines in separate pods.

However, the WS-110A project faced competition from other areas, notably from intercontinental ballistic missiles (ICBM). George Schairer realised that the future for conventional bombers was limited. He expressed this point to Bill Allen: 'It's clear that the ballistic missile is about to replace the manned bomber as a vector for nuclear weapons[1].' The plans were assessed in October and November with the result that North American's proposal was considered superior to Boeing's, the choice being confirmed on 23 December 1957[2]. For Boeing's directors, this came as a shock. Three days later, Bill Allen convened a meeting of his closest colleagues to decide how they should proceed. The situation was summed up in two fundamental questions. Did Boeing want to retain its leading position? If so, did this mean that they had to enter the field of ballistic missile design?

Boeing's divisions were not all in the same situation. With orders for the 707 and the C-135, the Transport Division had guaranteed work and it was much the

William McPherson Allen

LOL, Montana, 1 September 1900–Seattle, Washington, 29 October 1985

(Boeing)

Graduating from the University of Montana and Harvard Law School, Allen joined Boeing in 1925 to take charge of the company's legal affairs. Two years later, he married the daughter of the Governor of Montana, Dorothy Dixon, with whom he had two children.

'Bill' Allen was just 31 when he was appointed to Boeing's board of directors. During the war years he worked in close collaboration with the president of the time, P.G. Johnson and, on 5 September 1945, he took over the reins at the critical moment when military aircraft orders were in free fall. He was to hold the post for 23 years. His first major decision was to put the model 377 Stratoliner into

production so that the company could stake its claim in the civil airliner market, while maintaining its position as a leading producer of bomber aircraft. His biggest gamble was to invest $16 million in the design and construction of a jet transport that would go on to carve out an illustrious career, the model 707.

Several major military programmes were also launched under his direction, notably the B-47, B-52 and the Minuteman intercontinental ballistic missile. In the civil field, Allen was instrumental in the development of the 727, 737 and 747 families. On 29 April 1968, he was appointed chairman of the board and chief executive. Four years later, in September 1972, William McPherson Allen took a well-deserved retirement after 47 years of service with Boeing. In recognition, he was given the distinction of honorary president in 1978.

same, even if on a smaller scale, in the Wichita Division with its B-52s and in the Pilotless Aircraft Division with the Bomarc. By contrast, the Seattle Division, under George Martin, was about to find itself without work, as it had fully expected to be producing the new bomber.

» The Space Shuttle's forerunner

Since the mid-1950s, a number of advanced design programmes had been under study, such as the Bell SR-118P BoMi (Bomber Missile), the RS-459L Brass Bell, the RoBo (Robot Bomber), and the SR-121 Hywards hypersonic weapons system, but they had all been undertaken without any proper coordination. On 4 October 1957, the announcement of the launch of Sputnik 1, the world's first artificial satellite, provoked a crisis of conscience in the upper echelons of the Air Force. To take up the challenge, a concentration of effort in a single programme was needed. By November 1957, the choice had been made to go for a suborbital aircraft that would be able to glide in the upper layers of the stratosphere. This manoeuvre is known as dynamic soaring, a term that gave its name to the programme itself: Dyna-Soar.

In June 1958, the Air Force put a tender out to ten manufacturers[3], but later reduced this to just two competitors: Martin and Boeing[4]. However, a discussion soon arose over what use the Dyna-Soar might be put to. Indeed, it proved difficult to define precisely which military missions it might fulfil. After a few months, the purpose of the programme was redefined. It was now to be a hypersonic, piloted, manoeuvrable craft capable of landing at a pre-determined base. It was Boeing's proposal that was accepted, on 9 November 1959, while development of the Titan I launcher was entrusted to Martin. A few days later, the Dyna-Soar programme was given the designation of 'Weapons System WS-620A' to indicate its military vocation. Yet the arguments persisted and the project's viability continued to be questioned. After taking another look at the programme, at the end of April 1960, the Air Force's scientific committee gave Boeing's project a favourable review, subject to a few changes.

The full-size mock-up of the Dyna-Soar as exhibited in Seattle. (Boeing)

For three and a half years the programme made progress. With a length of 10.6 metres and a span of 6 metres, the Dyna-Soar was a single-seater, delta-wing craft made from a nickel alloy with a columbium heat-shield and weighed around 4.5 tonnes. On 11 September the Air Force inspected a life-sized model, but in mid-1961 Robert S. McNamara, the new Secretary of State for Defense, asked the Air Force to justify the programme's military value. Unconvinced by the response, McNamara decided to turn it into a research programme[5]. Renamed X-20 (26 June 1962), the programme continued for a further 18 months

1. Quoted in *Vision, the Story of Boeing*, page 226.

2. For further details, and especially drawings of the various configurations, the reader should refer to the article by Dennis R. Jenkins devoted to the Boeing WS-110A, in no. 6, volume V of *Aerospace Projects Review*, November/December 2003.

3. These ten manufacturers were Bell, Boeing, Convair, Douglas, General Electric, Lockheed, Martin, North American, Vought and Western Electric. Later, McDonnell, Northrop and Republic were also consulted.

4. The group led by Boeing comprised Aerojet, General Electric, Ramo-Wooldridge, North American and Chance Vought, while the Martin group comprised Bell, American Machine & Foundry, Bendix, Goodyear and Minneapolis-Honeywell.

5. McNamara proposed focusing the programme on the tricky technical problem of sending a manned craft into space and returning it to a precise location.

The Dyna-Soar underwent numerous wind-tunnel tests. (AEDC)

The Australian airline Qantas used 707-138s and 138Bs with shortened fuselages. The aircraft seen here, named City of Geelong *and registered VH-EBL, was delivered on 19 August 1964. (Boeing)*

until, on 10 December 1963, McNamara decided to scrap it[6]. By this time, work was already well advanced and there were plans for a small run of ten X-20s. The loss of the programme, which had cost the American taxpayer the not-inconsequential sum of $410 million, put 5,000 Boeing employees out of work. However, the development work had not been a complete waste of time; it would prove to be of use nearly 20 years later in the design of the space shuttle.

The VC-137s were designated 'Air Force One' when the president was on board. This one is awaiting President Ronald Reagan for a flight to Rome, on 28 May 1987. (DoD/GSgt Hernandez)

» The 707 family

The first 707s entered service in the autumn of 1958. There had been a satisfactory number of orders, but production costs had far exceeded expectations, thanks to the numerous modifications requested by the airlines. On 28 October 1958, the first 707-120 emerged from the Renton factory and made its first flight on 20 December. On 15 August 1958, four months ahead of schedule, Pan American took delivery of its first jet airliner, putting it into service over the North Atlantic on 26 October.

In the meantime, on 15 May 1958, the Air Force had ordered three 707-120s for use by the president and Army VIPs. Designated VC-137A, the planes were christened 'Air Force One' (when the president was on board). The following year, President Dwight D. Eisenhower became the first American president to fly on a VC-137A. In 1962, two 707-320B airframes were specially adapted for presidential use. Designated VC-137C, they served as presidential aircraft until 1990, when they were replaced by two new Air Force One planes (designated VC-25A) using 747-200 airframes.

6. At the same time, McNamara announced that all efforts would henceforth be directed towards the Manned Orbiting Laboratory (MOL), which was itself scrapped in 1969.

This former American Airlines 707-023B was used by Ecuatoriana in this striking decor. It is seen at Quito Airport in 1975. (R.J. Francillon)

As mentioned earlier, to attract orders from companies that had previously been customers of Douglas, Boeing indulged in a complex and expensive diversification of its range. The base model was the 707-120, from which the model 707-120B was derived specifically for American Airlines. Ordered by the airline in October 1959, it followed the 55 707-120s already ordered (30 in November 1955 and 25 in July 1958) and put into service on the New York–Los Angeles route on 25 January 1959. The 707-120B, which first flew on 22 June 1960 and entered service on 12 March 1961, featured fan-jet JT3D-1 engines of 7,700kg thrust (75.6kN) and a total of 78 planes were built. Model 707-220 was a version designed to operate out of airports located at altitude or in very hot climates; to achieve this, it had JT4A-3 engines of 7,160kg thrust (70.3kN). Ordered by Braniff in November 1955 and put into service on 20 December 1959, the 707-220 had a very small market and just five of them were sold (one of which crashed before delivery). Version 707-320 made its first flight on 11 January 1959, having been ordered by Pan American three years earlier. This was fitted with JT4A engines for intercontinental use and take-off weight had risen to 143 tonnes.

It could cross the North Atlantic without stop-offs, whatever the weather. Sixty-nine were built, the first one entering service on 26 August 1959. Boeing developed a fan-jet-engined version, model 707-320B, with 8,165kg-thrust JT3D engines and a different wing shape[7]. Production reached 167 aircraft, the first one flying on 31 January 1962 and entering service with Pan American on 1 June of the following year. The next along was the 707-320C in February 1963 when

A 707-321B (registered HK-2015) owned by the Colombian airline Avianca, at Rio de Janeiro in February 1991. (R.J. Francillon collection)

7. The span and consequently the wing surface area were increased; the lift augmenters were modified.

One of Royal Australian Air Force's four 707 tankers refuelling an F/A-18C Hornet from the US Navy's VFA-131 squadron in April 2002. These aircraft were equipped with two FRL Mk.32 systems beneath the wings. (US Navy)

The KC-135s changed livery several times during their careers. Seen here is a KC-135E (serial number 59-1447) of the 72 ARS at Abbotsford, British Columbia, on 8 August 1991. (J.G. Handelman)

the first of 304 of this model made its maiden flight, remaining in production until 1978. Using fan-jet JT3D engines, it was produced in two variants, one for cargo and the other convertible. Finally, 707-420 was a 'made-to-measure' version for the British, whose government had just cancelled the ambitious Vickers 1000 military transport project (which was also to have a civil derivative, the VC-7). It was powered by fan-jet Rolls-Royce R.Co.12 Conway engines of 7,940kg thrust (77.8kN) and could carry 141 passengers over more than 4,900 miles. Curiously, Lufthansa was the first to acquire this version. It first flew on 20 May 1959 and entered service in March 1960, with a total of 37 planes being produced.

While models 707-220, 320 and 420 had been developed to compete with the various DC-8 models produced by Douglas, Boeing could not ignore the competition from Convair with its model 880 (former model 22 Skylark). After a dozen configurations had been considered, the definitive model 707-020 (which would become known as the 720 at the express request of United Airlines) was settled upon in November 1957. It was a shorter, lighter aircraft, fitted with Pratt & Whitney JT3Cs and carried less fuel.

While being very similar to the 707-120, model 720 was considered a distinct model, able to carry up to 149 passengers on short-haul routes. This version made its first flight on 23 November 1959 and was put into service by United on 5 July of the following year

The Italians use four 707-320Cs converted to refuelling tankers. (R.J. Francillon collection)

on the Chicago–Los Angeles route. Just 64 aircraft were delivered to six airlines (Aer Lingus, American Airlines, Braniff, Eastern Airlines, Pacific Northern and United), which is within one aircraft of the number of 880s built by Convair. However, to compete with the Convair 990 with its fan-jet engines, Boeing offered a fan-jet version of the 720, the 720B, which made its first flight on 6 October 1960; 89 720Bs were built.

At the same time, KC-135A production was in full swing. The first KC-135A emerged from the Renton plant on 18 July 1956 and flew three days later. Deliveries to the SAC began on 28 June 1957 when

Why always '7'?

Since 1955, Boeing's jet transport aircraft have been identified by a number beginning and ending with 7. Why? Is it to do with the favourable significance attributed to the number 7 (the seven colours of the rainbow, seven notes on the musical scale...)? Not at all; the number 7's origin is far more prosaic.

Ever since the 1920s, the Seattle design department has allocated a model number to its aircraft. At the end of the Second World War, with the diversification of the company's activities, the model-numbering system was rationalised with batches of 100 numbers being allocated to different product lines. Thus the 300-series (already in use) and the 400-series were reserved for aircraft, the 500-series for turboprops, the 600-series for rockets and missiles and the 700s for jet transport planes. At the time, design work had already begun on a plane of the latter category based on the model 367 (C-97) military transport aircraft. Successive designs appeared on the drawing board, ending with the model 367-80.

When the time came to market the aircraft, in adherence to the new system, the number 700 was allocated, but the sales department didn't like the sound of 'seven hundred', feeling that 707 – 'Seven-O-Seven' – had a better ring to it. By the same logic, 717 was allotted to the military variant (KC-135). Thereafter, airliners followed in a natural sequence: 727, 737, 747, 757, 767, 777 and, most recently, 787.

In 1965, the supersonic transport competitor to Concorde was named 2707, at a time when the year 2000 was still something of a futuristic dream. At the time of the McDonnell Douglas takeover, the number 717, which had never really been in the public domain, was re-used for the MD-95. The one exception to the number 7 rule was the model 720. This designation was arrived at by a contraction of 707-020 to comply with a specific request by United Airlines, who, for commercial reasons, did not want it to appear that they had acquired Boeing 707s when they had just bought DC-8s.

The many guises of the C-135

By 2008, the C-135, the military version of the Dash 80, had seen half a century of service. Over the years, the basic plane had given rise to 43 variants (which included 13 EC-135 variants, 12 RC-135 variants and seven variants of the KC-135). What follows is just a selection.

1. This KC-135A was used by NASA in 1979 and 1980 to carry out wind-tunnel tests with a full size aircraft on the 'winglets' that had been invented by Richard Whitcomb. (NASA/DFRC)

2. The EC-135G variant serves as a flying radio communications relay station. Here one of the four comes in to land at Mather AFB in California. (Jim Dunn)

3. During Operation Iraqi Freedom, a KC-135R from the 380th Air Refuelling Wing has just refuelled an F/A-18 Hornet from the carrier USS Enterprise. (US Navy/Lt P. Solomon)

4. The 'Constant Phoenix' RC-135W version is used to collect radioactive particles from the atmosphere under the nuclear non-proliferation treaty. (USAF)

5. A strategic reconnaissance RC-135W seen being refuelled in flight by a KC-135R over Nebraska, in June 2006. (USAF/Sgt Doug Hayes)

6. One of the 14 NKC-135As was used by the 4,950th Test Wing to test an airborne laser. (USAF)

7. Six aircraft were converted into EC-135Ps to carry out missions in the Pacific. They were based in Hawaii. (J.G. Handelmann)

8. This NKC-135A was used by the Aeronautical Systems Division (ASD) to measure atmospheric radiation. (DR)

9. The EC-135N was equipped with a large nose antenna to follow the trajectory of the Apollo spacecraft. (DR)

10. The second C-135F delivered to the French Air Force, at Istres in September 1969. It has since been re-engined with CFM56s. (A. Pelletier)

This spectacular shot shows a Lockheed C-5A Galaxy being refuelled by a KC-135R. (USAF)

the 93rd Air Refuelling Squadron, based at Castle AFB, California, received its first planes. By the end of 1957, 24 aircraft had been delivered and subsequent years would see the fleet of KC-135As grow rapidly to reach 674 aircraft by 1964. The 732nd and last KC-135A would be accepted by the Air Force on 12 January 1965. At this time, Boeing also delivered 12 KC-135As to the French Air Force and various specialised versions began to appear (EC-135C aerial command posts, C-135A transports, VC-135B for special missions, WC-135B for meteorological reconnaissance, RC-135A and RC-135B for electronic reconnaissance, etc).

In addition to these purely military models, there were dozens of civil aircraft modified to meet the requirements of foreign governments: South Africa, Germany, Saudi Arabia, Argentina, Australia, Brazil, Canada, Chile, Colombia, Egypt, Spain, Iran, Israel, Italy Libya, Morocco, Peru, Portugal, Qatar and Venezuela.

» Big changes

In 1959, Boeing's workforce fell from 100,000 to 80,000. Bill Allen was very clear about the changes that were on their way in the aeronautical industry. 'We have to recognise that the era of big production runs, particularly in the military sphere, is coming to an end. From now on, programmes like the B-52 will be few and far between. In their place, there will be products costing infinitely more to develop, which will be produced in much smaller quantities and whose production will require far fewer personnel. [...] To remain competitive, we have to have better products to sell. To develop and offer better products, we have to design these products better and show our ability to keep costs under control. [...] If we want to be the best in these fields, we have to invest to help our design teams and put our capital into research. And we either have to get capital from our profits, or attract investors[8].' Allen applied these

A General Dynamics FB-111 variable-geometry bomber launching one of four short-range Boeing AGM-69 SRAM missiles with which it is armed. (USAF)

principles by reinvesting 80% of the profits in research and new facilities, including a new hypersonic Mach 20 wind tunnel (the most up-to-date of its type). Elsewhere, the Pilotless Aircraft Division, the Seattle Division and the Systems Management Office were regrouped into a single entity, the Aerospace Group, confirming Boeing's change of course.

On 3 May 1961, the Boeing Airplane Company changed its name to the Boeing Company, thus indicating that its activities were no longer limited to aviation. The firm was now composed of six operational sections: the Aerospace Group, the Commercial Airplane Division, the Turbine Division, the Vertol Division, the Wichita Division and Boeing Associated Products.

» Missiles to the fore

As far as missiles were concerned, the situation rapidly became critical. The launch of Sputnik 1 had been like a bomb going off in American military circles, where it was suddenly realised how far the Soviets had come in the field of technology. On 14 August 1958, Senator J.F. Kennedy declared: 'Our nation could have afforded, and can afford now, the steps necessary to close the missile gap.' The issue of the 'missile gap' fuelled the controversy that was developing around the

A Minuteman LGM-30 intercontinental ballistic missile on its transport vehicle. (USAF)

question of conventional bombers and ICBMs. The XB-70 programme soon found itself targeted and, at Boeing, they began to think that it would be better to lose this contract and land the Minuteman contract instead.

On 10 October 1958, after production had begun on the Bomarc, Boeing was chosen by the Air Force to develop and produce the Minuteman LGM-30 intercontinental ballistic missile system (weapons system WS-133A), on which preliminary work had started in 1957. This weapons system was to form the backbone of the SAC's missile arsenal. It had been planned to go into service in mid-1963, but in view of the urgency of the situation it was brought forward to July 1962. This meant that testing and the start of production would have to be virtually simultaneous. There were to be 100 missiles operational by mid-1963 and 400 by 1964. It was to have a nuclear warhead and a range of over 6,000 miles, and would be fired from underground silos or specially equipped railway wagons[9]. The first test firing took place on 1 February

AGM-69 missiles sit on a trailer waiting to be attached under the wings of an FB-111 at Pease AFB, on 4 October 1989. (DoD/MSgt K. Hammond)

8. Quoted by H.Mansfield in *Vision*, page 256.
9. The railway option was finally abandoned on 7 December 1961.

1961 from Cape Canaveral, Florida and work on the first silos began on 16 March of the same year, at Malmstrom AFB, Montana. Delivery of the first production missiles began in July and the first firing from a silo took place on 17 November. A few months later, in March 1962, Boeing started development work on the Minuteman II, which was distinguished by its greater range (7,000 miles), improved guidance system and its two-megaton nuclear warhead. Over a period of three years, around 800 Minuteman I missiles were deployed at SAC bases. Their replacement by Minuteman II, and later III, began in 1964, with Minuteman II becoming operational in August 1964 and Minuteman III in April 1970. The latter was distinguished by its three independent nuclear warheads and 8,000-mile range.

After the Douglas AGM-48 Skybolt air-launched ballistic missile system was scrapped in December 1962, the Air Force had to find a way of bringing the B-52's armament up to date. In March 1964, it launched the Short Range Attack Missile (SRAM) programme, awarding the development contract to Boeing on 31 October 1966. The missile, designated AGM-69A, had its first firing in July 1969 and, after completion of tests, production began in January 1971. Eighteen months later, the SRAM was declared operational and replaced the AGM-28 Hound Dog missiles. Armed with a 200-kiloton nuclear warhead, the missile could fly at speeds above Mach 3. The B-52 could carry eight of them in its bomb bay and another 12 under the wings. It would remain in service until June 1990, after a production run of more than 1,500[10].

» TFX: the myth of the common-user aircraft

In 1959, the Tactical Air Command (TAC) started to consider a replacement for the Republic F-105 Thunderchief, 833 of which had been built. General F.F. Everest, commander of the TAC, drew up a specification for an aircraft that would out-perform any supposed Soviet equivalent and with a range sufficient to allow the Air Force to do without its European bases. It would have to be capable of flying supersonically at sea level, crossing the Atlantic without refuelling, carrying tactical nuclear weapons and was to have a variable-geometry wing[11].

A Minuteman I ICBM is fired from its silo at Vandenberg base, California, on 18 February 1981. (DoD/F.J. Hooker)

>> The numbering jungle

With the 707's launch, Boeing introduced a new numbering system to designate its aircraft. As the 707-120's first customer, Pan Am had its aircraft designated, naturally enough, 707-121. Following this logic, other models acquired by Pan Am retained the '21' in their designation. In this way, each customer had its own number. The system was followed all the way up to 99, when new customers were allocated numbers between 01 and 19 that had not been used up. Number 20 was reserved for Boeing's own aircraft.

The manufacturer also introduced an alphanumeric system, which began with A0 to A9, followed by B0 to B9, and so on. When this system was, in turn, exhausted, a further alphanumeric system took its place, in which the letter and the number were reversed. In theory, the system ran from 1A to 9Z, but in practice not all the possibilities were used. More recently, a two-letter system has been introduced, but it seems to follow no particular logic. Finally, it should be pointed out that although the designations are customer-specific, they do not change when the aircraft is sold on to another company.

The specification was not to everybody's liking and the SAC in particular felt that its strategic role was threatened. Despite this, in July 1960, Specific Operational Requirement SOR-183 was sent to the manufacturers. The size of the programme, as well as its technological and financial risks, drove some of the manufacturers to work together: General Dynamics joined up with Grumman, Republic with Vought and McDonnell with Douglas; Boeing, Lockheed and North American preferred to go it alone. Concurrently with the Air Force's SOR-183, the Navy set up a programme for a new Fleet Air Defense Fighter (FADF).

The 1960 elections saw the arrival of a new Secretary of State for Defense, Robert S. McNamara, who put at the heart of his policy value for money, the use of equipment in common, centralisation of procurement and the avoidance of duplication (at the time, the Air Force had six types of supersonic fighter[12]). He re-examined the TFX specification to see if it could be made to fulfil three roles: the original TAC role, the close support required by the Navy and the Marines, and the air defence needed by the Navy. But the Navy did not see things this way. For close support, it opted for a smaller and simpler aircraft[13] and, for aerial defence, launched the F6D Missileer[14] programme. Despite numerous meetings, the Air Force and the Navy could not reach agreement on a common specification. On 1 September 1961, McNamara decided to take matters into his own hands and lay down the TFX's characteristics himself: it was to be a fighter/interceptor using SOR-183 as the design basis. Suffice to say that this decision did not go down well with the Navy. On 1 October, an invitation to tender was issued to the manufacturers, of whom six responded: Boeing, Lockheed, McDonnell, North American, Republic and the pairing of General Dynamics and Grumman.

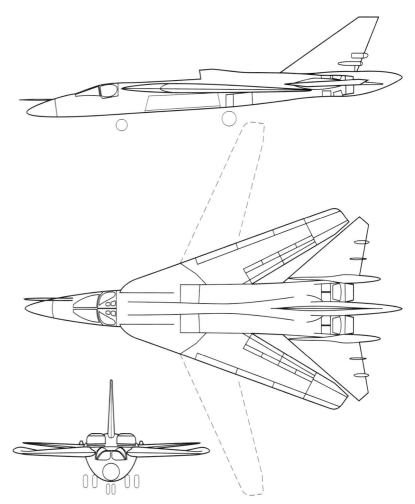

Under the TFX programme, Boeing proposed the model 818 side-by-side twin-seater aircraft powered by two Pratt & Whitney TF30 fan-jet engines developing 8,390kg thrust with afterburner.

10. The SRAM was fully deployed by 1975, by which time 1,451 were in service. By 1990, the year of its withdrawal, there were still 1,048 in service.

11. NASA had conducted very promising studies on variable-geometry wings, particularly with the experimental Bell X-5.

12. North American F-100, McDonnell F-101, Convair F-102, Lockheed F-104, Republic F-105 and Convair F-106.

13. This was the May 1961 VAX programme that led to the designing of the LTV A-7 Corsair II.

14. The Douglas F6D Missileer programme was launched on 21 July 1960 and scrapped in April 1961.

Two months later, the Air Force/Navy selection committee decided to retain just the Boeing and General Dynamics/Grumman bids, even though these were not completely satisfactory. Boeing was obliged to drop its choice of General Electric engines in favour of the Pratt & Whitney TF30, which, though less up to date, was at a more advanced stage of development. A second bidding round was launched in April 1962, but, yet again, the proposals from General Dynamics/Grumman and Boeing were deemed unacceptable, although Boeing's was judged superior. A third round took place in June 1962, when Boeing's bid was again considered better. A fourth round in September produced the same result. McNamara, however, thought otherwise. He favoured the superior structure and the greater number of elements in common of the General Dynamics/Grumman aircraft over the better performance of the Boeing plane. Thus on 24 November 1962, the Department of Defense announced that General Dynamics/Grumman were the winners of the TFX bidding contest (the aircraft would later develop into the F-111).

The announcement had caught everyone by surprise, as throughout the contest, Boeing's proposals had been thought superior. With a maximum 31-tonne take-off weight, the Boeing model 818 would have been able to fly at Mach 2.35. Aside from its variable geometry, it featured two dorsal air intakes and thrust invertors. A very controversial programme, TFX was a text-book case of the complexities of procurement procedures, where military doctrine, inter-service rivalry, technological innovation, budgetary constraints and, of course, politics were all mixed. If military versions of civil aircraft are excluded, the loss of the TFX contract marked Boeing's exit from the military aircraft domain.

» The gamble with the 727

The prospect of substantial financial losses on the 707 programme threw a shadow over Boeing's future civil aircraft projects, notably the short/medium-haul 727. The Seattle firm learned from its European office that Douglas was planning to launch a four-engined derivative of its DC-8 (the model 2067). Bruce Connelly, director of the Transport Division, authorised feasibility studies for a competitor aircraft. At a meeting in San Francisco, the representatives from United Air Lines made it clear that they were not much interested in a two-engined solution, citing the fact that passengers preferred four engines. It appears that Douglas had encountered the same reaction, as they now turned toward a small four-engined plane. For Boeing, there was the risk that a four-engined 727 would be in competition with their own 720, not even taking into account the cost of such an aircraft, estimated at $3.25 to $3.5 million, compared with $1.27 million for the Vickers Viscount, $2.1 million for the Lockheed Electra and $3.5 million for the Boeing 720.

In the spring of 1959, market research for the 727 was no longer a top priority. The Renton plant was fully committed to 707/720 production. With the plethora of versions, the deficit was deepening by the day. There was no question of launching a new plane into an uncertain market. Yet if Douglas brought out its DC-9, not only would the 727 be still-born, but the 720 would be faced with severe competition. The years 1963–64 were promising to be difficult...

The stakes were huge. Short-haul aircraft design was running into a contradiction: to maximise performance, a small, sharply swept-back wing was needed, but to operate from short runways, a wing with a large surface area and moderate sweep back (a

A United Airlines 727-22C coming in to land at Los Angeles International Airport in 1968. With Eastern Air Lines, United was one of the first to order 727s, on 5 December 1960. (R.J. Francillon)

A Kitty Hawk Aircargo 727-223F landing at Sacramento on 29 August 1999. This former American Airlines plane had been converted to carry freight. (R.J. Francillon)

The Bolivian airline, Lloyd Aereo Boliviano, took delivery of this 727-1A0 on 17 February 1970. It is seen here at Cochabamba in May 1977 and is still in use today. (R.J. Francillon)

solution employed on the Caravelle) was required. A new wing design appeared to be what was needed, using both marginal-layer control systems and multi-slotted flaps, and it would be vital to verify the feasibility of such a wing before taking any decision.

By autumn 1959, the Transport Division's financial problems had reached a critical stage. In October, figures for the first year of the 707's production showed a loss of over $200 million, equivalent to Boeing's total capital. Douglas and Convair were in a similar position. Under these circumstances, did it make sense to launch the 727? Such a course of action would represent a much more significant risk than that taken with the launch of the 707. The same applied to the survival of the enterprise as a whole. While Boeing was perhaps lucky that profits from the military contracts largely compensated for the losses in the civil sector, this could not be relied upon to last forever.

After considering numerous configurations, Boeing decided to proceed with a three-engined aircraft, following the route taken by de Havilland with its Trident and, initially, by Sud Aviation with its Caravelle. Two types of fan-jet engine were considered: the Allison ARB.963 (derived from the Rolls-Royce Spey)

and the Pratt & Whitney JT8D, the latter eventually being chosen as it had greater potential for development. For the wings, the Dash 80 was used as a test bed for the development of triple-slot flaps and to evaluate the performance of the engines mounted at the rear of the fuselage. At this point, Boeing received its biggest-ever order for civil airliners when,

A Pluna Airline 727-30C at São Paulo-Congonhas in August 1980. (R.J. Francillon)

Thanks to the test results from the Dash 80, development of the 727 proceeded rapidly and the first aircraft was able to fly on 9 February 1963, at Renton. One of its principal features was the use of an augmented-lift system. (Boeing)

on 5 December 1960, United Air Lines and Eastern Air Lines each ordered 40 727s, to which were added a further 12 planes ordered by Lufthansa two months later. The 727's career was under way.

So as to gain time and money, Boeing decided to dispense with a prototype stage and the first production 727-100 emerged from the factory on 27 November 1960 and made its first flight, at Renton, on 9 February 1961. Carrying between 106 and 131 passengers over a distance of more than 1,700 miles, the 727 quickly took over the market. It benefited from several strong points, among which was a cabin width identical to that of the 707, which provided

passengers with a similar level of comfort to that experienced on long-haul flights. The 727-100 went into service with Eastern Air Lines on 1 February 1964 on the Philadelphia–Washington–Miami route.

The 727 was the first airliner to top the 1,000 mark in numbers manufactured, and production eventually totalled 1,832, making it the biggest-selling jet airliner of its time, even though it was offered in a limited number of versions. Indeed, Boeing marketed only two versions[15]. The base version, the 727-100, had Pratt & Whitney JT8D fan-jets with 6.3 tonnes thrust (62.3kN). Model 727-200, a mixed cargo/passenger 'combi' variant that appeared in 1967, had its fuselage lengthened by six metres and was supplied with the more-powerful JT8D-9 engines. Depending on whether it was fitted out for two classes or one, it could carry between 134 and 189 passengers and cover 2,500 miles; 164 were produced. Finally, the 727-200 Advanced, first delivered to All-Nippon Airways in June 1972, was supplied with JT8D-17R engines of 7.9 tonnes thrust (77.6kN). It also benefited from a fuel capacity increased to 39,800 litres and a complete updating of the passenger cabin.

≫ The race for a supersonic transport

On 9 January 1961, the FAA published a report on supersonic air travel that had been prepared jointly with NASA and the Department of Defense. The report concluded that American industry should build a Mach 3 airliner, although there was little to encourage manufacturers to rush into the task.

In June 1963, barely had Pan American expressed its intention to buy Concorde than John F. Kennedy gave the green light to the development of a competing supersonic aircraft, the SST. 'This Government should immediately commence a new program in partnership with private industry to develop at the earliest practical date the prototype of a commercially successful supersonic transport superior to that being built in any other country of the world[16].' A few months later, Congress released the first research funds and, on 15 August 1963, the FAA drew up a specification that would form the basis of the invitation to tender. On 10 September, three manufacturers (Boeing, Lockheed and North American) announced their intention to bid, as did three engine manufacturers (General Electric, Pratt & Whitney and Curtiss Wright). At Boeing, fortified by the experience gained in the WS-101A programme (see page 147), a team directed by Bill Cook had started to work on just this type of aircraft.

On 20 May 1964, President Lyndon Johnson gave the go-ahead for two plane makers (Boeing and Lockheed)[17] and two engine manufacturers (General Electric and Pratt & Whitney) to compete for construction of the aircraft. They were to take account of the experience gained in the Lockheed SR-71, North

A simulation of what a future supersonic transport might look like. (NASA/LaRC)

American XB-70 and General Dynamics F-111 projects so as to minimise risks and reduce the development costs. The president asked Congress for $140 million to undertake this first phase of the programme and, on 31 December 1966, the FAA chose Boeing's model 733 (which would be known to the public as model 2707) and General Electric's GE4/J5 engine.

Boeing's proposal was very ambitious. Model 2707-100 was to fly at Mach 3 at an altitude of 21,000 metres, carry 277 passengers[18] over a range of 4,000 miles, have a variable-geometry wing, an articulated droop nose to aid visibility during take-off and landing (like Concorde), and make extensive use of titanium alloys (unlike Concorde). Power was to come from four GE4/J5P engines of 28,677kg thrust (282kN). However, as development work progressed, Boeing's engineers gradually scaled down their ambitions. The 2707-200 saw its cruising speed reduced to Mach 2.7. Despite the obvious aerodynamic advantages, the variable-geometry wing carried a heavy weight penalty, to the detriment of the plane's payload. So it was that Boeing announced on 21 October 1968 that it was officially abandoning the programme. In its final version, the

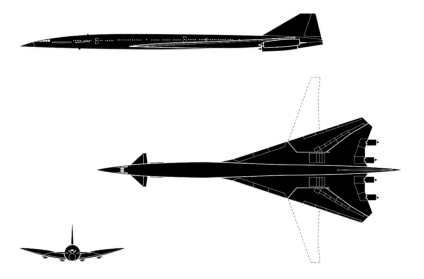

One of the model 2707-200's many configurations. It had a variable-geometry wing, allowing sweep-back of between 20° and 72°.

15. The last model 727 was delivered to Federal Express in 1984.

16. Speech given on 5 June 1963 at the US Air Force Academy.

17. North American's proposal was rejected. It was derived from the XB-70 bomber and could carry between 36 and 76 passengers depending on the layout.

18. This figure comprised 30 passengers in first class and 247 in tourist class.

The full-size mock-up of the model 2707-200 under construction at Seattle. Comparison with the workers gives an idea of the aircraft's size. (Boeing)

2707-300 with a delta wing could carry 290 passengers and had a fully laden weight of 290 tonnes. The savings in weight allowed an increase in range of 250 miles.

On 23 September 1969, President Nixon announced his intention to continue with the programme in order to maintain the American lead in air transport. Two 2707-300 prototypes were ordered and construction began immediately, two years behind the original schedule. The first flight was planned for early 1973. The aircraft was unveiled to the public in June 1970, by which time Boeing had received 122 firm orders from 26 companies. But in the context of the gloomy economic climate of the 1970s, Boeing's programme ran up against vehement opposition from environmentalists, as did its European equivalent. Another of the programme's enemies was its astronomical cost, which was not to the liking of many in American political circles. The SST drew more and more opposition and, on 24 March 1971, Congress voted against the allocation of further budgetary resources.

Despite this decision, Boeing was still free to carry on with the programme at its own expense, but things slowly fell behind schedule and the SST was eventually abandoned. Concorde suddenly found itself without any competition, which, contrary to what one might think, turned out to be a disadvantage. The relentless attacks of the anti-SST faction grew still stronger. Nonetheless, Boeing was not to suffer unduly from the abandonment of 2707-300, as the 747 project was looking promising.

>> CX-HLS: an HGV in the skies

In 1961, the Air Force began work on the features required of an aircraft that could eventually replace the Douglas C-133 Cargomaster and complement the fleet of Lockheed C-141 Starlifters. The MATS (Military Air Transport Service) hoped to have the plane available by 1967 and the quantity was expected to be 160 aircraft. The CX-4, as it was now called, had to have a fuselage large enough to house heavy tanks and troop-carrying helicopters.

Preliminary studies led to the drawing up of a specification for the Heavy Logistics System CX-HLS and an invitation to tender was issued on 17 April 1964. By this time, the requirement had been revised downwards to 115 planes. The new aircraft would have to be able to take off fully laden from a 2,440-metre runway, land on less-than-perfect airstrips of no longer than 1,220 metres, carry 56.7 tonnes over a distance of 8,000 miles and have a life span of 30,000

The supersonic transport underwent numerous experiments. Seen here is a model of the aircraft in NASA's Langley Research Center wind tunnel, in July 1973. (NASA/LaRC)

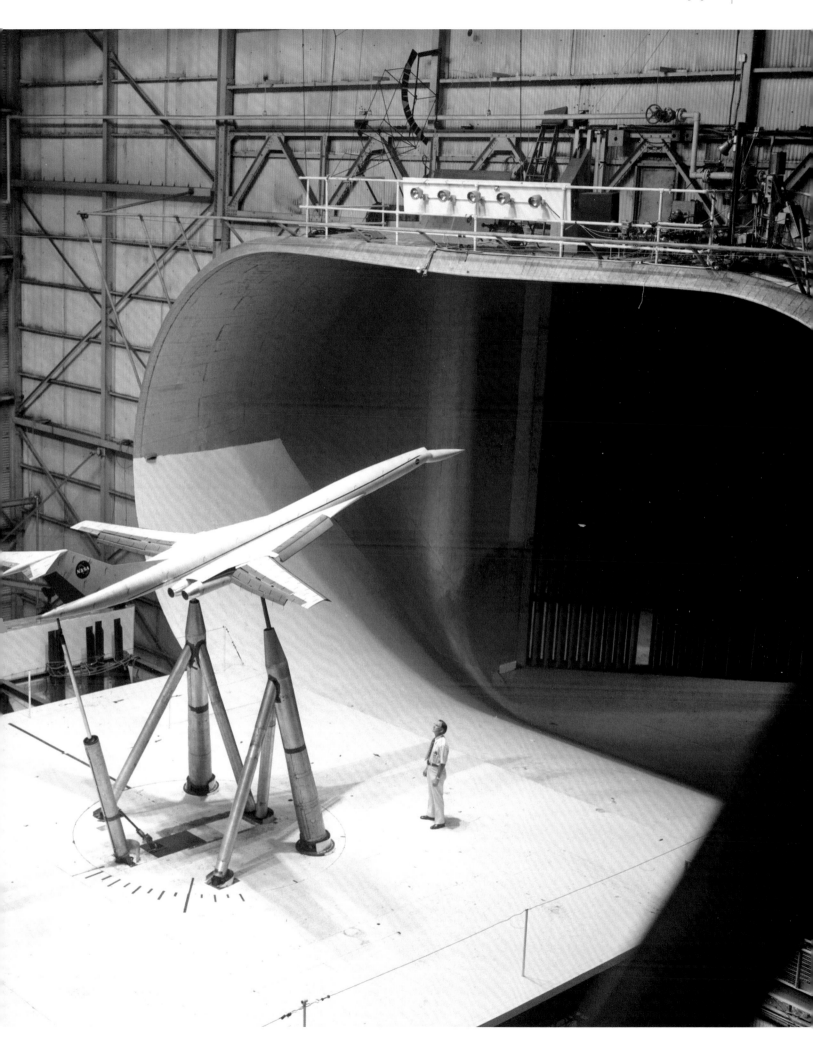

hours. A month later, on 18 May, Boeing, Douglas, General Dynamics, Lockheed Georgia and Martin-Marietta presented their respective proposals, while the engine manufacturers[19] submitted their suggestions for the power plant.

At the end of this first phase, Boeing, Douglas and Lockheed were chosen to undertake preliminary design work. The three proposals showed a number of similarities, such as a high wing, four fan-jet engines mounted in nacelles and ramps to both front and rear doors. The AFSC (Air Force Systems Command) declared Boeing the winner from the performance point of view, but for socio-economic reasons it was Lockheed's bid that was favoured by Robert McNamara[20].

>> Birth of a winner

At this time, the range of civil aircraft was about to widen. With its 737, Boeing was about to have the biggest-selling jet airliner of all time. Yet, at the time of its launch, it was far from evident that success was assured. Indeed, Boeing was late entering the small-airliner market, occupied as it was with 707 and 727 production. The model 737 flew a good two years after the Douglas DC-9 and some observers gave it

The prototype 737 on take-off. The aircraft entered a market already occupied by the Douglas DC-9, the Caravelle and the BAC 111. At the time, Boeing could hardly have imagined that it would become one of the most successful aircraft ever built. (Boeing)

little chance of a profitable career with so many other planes already established in the market (DC-9, Caravelle, BAC 111 and, to a certain degree, the Tupolev Tu-124).

The 737 programme was launched in November 1964, just after American Airlines had ordered 15 BAC 111-400s. Boeing needed to get moving. To keep costs down, the design department used the same width of

Lufthansa was the first customer and one of the 737's big users. This 737-330 (reg. D-ABXT) was delivered on 3 January 1989 and is still in use today. (Lufthansa)

fuselage as in the 727, allowing them to fit six seats abreast. The wings were similar to those on the 727, although smaller and with only a 25° sweep back (instead of 32°). The Pratt & Whitney JT8D-7 fan-jet engines with 6.3 tonnes thrust (62.3kN) were mounted just beneath the wings so that the undercarriage could be as short as possible. Up to 103 passengers could be accommodated and, as with the 727, there was no prototype.

The first customer turned out to be from outside America, namely Lufthansa, which ordered 21 737-100s on 15 February 1965. The first one flew on 9 April 1967 and was delivered to the German airline in the following February. At this point, Douglas had had orders for 502 DC-9s. Suffice to say that the 737 had to fight for its market share and was by no means an instant success.

By adding fuselage sections – a method that would be used extensively by most manufacturers – the 737 slowly grew in length over successive versions. The first was the 737-200, a version developed for United Air Lines. It was lengthened by 1.93 metres so as to accommodate 130 passengers in tourist class and its fuel capacity went up from 10,788 litres to 16,012 litres, increasing the range to 3,000 miles. The first aircraft of this version flew on 31 August 1967 and entered service on 28 April 1968. Model 737-300 was launched in 1981 with CFM-56 engines of 9 tonnes thrust (89kN) and a fuselage lengthened by 2.6 metres, increasing passenger accommodation to 149. With US Air as the first customer, this version made its first flight on 24 February 1984 and went into service on 7 December of the same year. These so-called 'first-generation' planes would be followed by a new generation of 737s, which, while retaining the same overall shape, would be virtually brand-new aircraft.

» The Jumbo and air travel for all

While supersonic airliners captured the headlines, ordinary air travel continued to evolve. By the early 1970s, subsonic airliners had reached their limits in terms of speed. Their maximum cruising speed had reached a ceiling of around 525mph and higher subsonic speeds (in the region of 600mph) appeared out of reach, both technically speaking, given the high costs of development, and economically because of the high fuel consumption of such planes. A profitable way forward in the development of air travel, for manufacturers as well as airlines, lay in reducing the cost per passenger per kilometre and the direct

19. General Electric Company, Curtiss-Wright Corporation and Pratt & Whitney Aircraft Division of UAC.

20. The respective costs of the three bids were as follows: $1.9 billion for the Lockheed L-500; $2 billion for the Douglas D-920; $2.3 billion for the Boeing.

Seen coming in to land at Oakland in November 2000, this Vanguard Airlines 737-2B7 was originally delivered to US Air on 1 December 1983. It is currently in service with Fresh Air, registered as 5N-BFQ. (R.J. Francillon)

This 737-2Y5 was originally delivered to Air Malta on 31 March 1983 and subsequently used by a number of airlines before being sold to Frontier Airlines in July 1999. In May 2004, it was sold again to Atlantic Airlines of Honduras. (C.E. Porter via R.J. Francillon)

A Southwest Airlines 737-3H4 coming in to land. The 300-series 737s were the first to be supplied with CFM56 high-by-pass-ratio engines. (R.J. Francillon)

This 747-123 began its career with American Airlines in 1971 and was converted to cargo use in 1976. It was sold on to UPS in August 1984. It is seen here landing at Portland, Oregon on 30 June 1994. (R.J. Francillon)

operating cost (DOC)[21]. To achieve this, high-capacity aircraft had to be designed and American manufacturers applied themselves to the task, with Boeing at the forefront.

Ever since 1957, Boeing's design department had considered this possibility, starting with a large, double-decker plane, model 707-320-101, with room for 250 seats, but at the time the airlines had considered it too big for their short-term needs. In the mid-1960s, when many people thought that the future of civil aviation lay in supersonic flight, Boeing's teams began work on what would eventually become the Boeing 747. Though disappointed by the failure to win the contract for the Air Force's cargo aircraft, Boeing's engineers had considered various designs for a large,

four-engined plane with a median wing capable of carrying up to 500 passengers spread over two decks – an aircraft, in other words, with twice the capacity of the Douglas series 61/63 DC-8. However, faced with the cool reaction from the airlines, Boeing went back to the drawing board and came up with a single-decker plane with a low wing.

By this time, airlines and manufacturers had started to realise the market potential of high-capacity aircraft to the point where Lockheed was proposing a civil version of its C-5, the L-500, and Douglas was working on various pilot schemes under the generic title of 'DC-10'. Boeing, who strongly believed in the worth of its project, now focused all its energy on looking for customers. On 13 April 1966, they announced the programme's launch and construction of the prototype began in June at the new Everett plant. Boeing assumed that a large proportion of 747 sales would be for the cargo version, which is why it was designed with the cockpit perched on top of the fuselage, so that there would be room for a nose door big enough to load 2.40m x 2.40m containers.

Pan American was the first company to put in an order for a batch of 25 Boeing 747-100 models (or, to be precise, 747-121, using the designation in force at the time). However, to meet PanAm's requirements, the aircraft was significantly modified (wing span and payload increased, sweep back reduced, etc) and Pratt & Whitney JT9D-3 fan jets of nearly 19 tonnes thrust (187kN) were fitted. By the end of 1966, Boeing had taken 83 orders and had acquired land at Everett, north-west of Seattle, to build a new assembly plant dedicated to the 747. In 1967, with a turnover of $2,879 million, Boeing was in second place in the ranks of aerospace manufacturers, just behind

---

21. The number of air travellers was rising inexorably: from 106,000 in 1960, it had exceeded 200,000 by 1966 and 300,000 by 1970.

A Japan Air Lines cargo 747-246F taxiing at Los Angeles International in November 2000. (R.J. Francillon)

The US Air Force has two VC-25s that are used by the 89th Airlift Wing based at Andrews AFB. The first of the two is seen flying over Mount Rushmore. (USAF)

This 737-260 was delivered to Ethiopian Airlines on 29 December 1987. On 15 September the following year it was wrecked after a bird strike at Bahar Dar, Ethiopia. (Boeing)

This 747-1D1 delivered to the Canadian company Wardair in April 1973 is still in use today with Saudi Arabian Airlines. (Boeing)

A Canadian Airlines 737-217 Classic at Oakland, California. This aircraft made its first flight on 19 May 1982 and was delivered to CP Air. (R.J. Francillon)

McDonnell Douglas[22]. With 142,700 employees, Boeing was the biggest employer in the whole of the aerospace industry[23].

The first 747-100 left the new Everett plant on 30 September 1968. By the year's end, there were 148 aircraft on the order books. On 9 February of the following year, Jack Waddell made the first flight in the new plane, which had been symbolically registered N7470. It was just three months behind on the original schedule. The delay had been due to development problems, particularly with the engines. The difficulties lasted right through 1969, such that the plane was not given approval until 30 December. The first commercial flight, by Pan American on the New York–London route did not take place until 22 January 1970, followed a month later by TWA's first commercial flight with a 747.

The base model (747-100) was soon improved by the provision of new JT9D-3A engines of 20.5 tonnes thrust (200.2kN), and the introduction of several sub-versions: the 747-100B, whose permitted maximum take-off weight was increased by nearly 7 tonnes; the 747-100 (SCD) combi; the 747-100SF cargo; and the short-haul 747SR, 747SR-100B and 747SR-100B (SUD) (SR for Short Range). In 1968, the model 747-200 made its appearance, with the Dutch airline, KLM, being the first user. Making its first flight on 11 October 1970, this was a long-haul version with a range of 6,000 miles (compared with the 747-100's

A 767-223 passes behind two Northwest Airlines 747-251Bs. The aircraft in the foreground, registered N636US, was delivered to Northwest on 6 May 1986. It has been mothballed at Mojave, California, since May 2003. (R.J. Francillon)

NASA used an old American Airlines 747-123 as a test bed. It is seen here, in 1974, undergoing vortex tests, accompanied by a Learjet and a Cessna T-37. (NASA/DFRC)

4,600 miles). It entered service in June 1971 and spawned several variants: the 747-200B with increased maximum permitted take-off weight; the 747-200B (SUD) and 747-200M (SUD) with lengthened upper deck; 747-200C convertible; the 747-200F and 200 (F) cargo; the combi 747-200M and 747-200 (SCD) with a side cargo door.

At Everett, the rate of production rose rapidly with deliveries going from four planes in 1969 to 92 in 1970, a year when the 747 made up almost half of the company's aircraft deliveries. In 1971, only 69 747s were delivered, as the design department was beginning work on new versions, notably the 747SP and 747-300.

A KLM 747-206B with an extended upper deck. In this configuration, the 747 could carry up to 598 passengers. The aircraft illustrated is registered PH-BUP and named Ganges. (R.J. Francillon)

22. Turnovers for competing companies were: $2,933 million for McDonnell Douglas, $2,438 million for North American, $2,335 million for Lockheed and $2,253 million for General Dynamics.

23. The size of the workforce at the other companies was as follows: 140,000 at McDonnell Douglas, 115,000 at North American, 103,000 at General Dynamics and 92,000 at Lockheed.

With its five rocket engines powering the Boeing S-1C first stage, a Saturn V lifts the Apollo 15 capsule on 26 July 1971. (NASA)

>> Boeing at the heart of the space programme

In 1961, President Kennedy challenged America to put a man on the moon before the end of the decade. The keystone of the Apollo programme, the Saturn V launcher, was to be the biggest rocket of all time. Standing 110 metres tall, it comprised three stages, the first of which, designated S-IC, was 42 metres tall and had a diameter of 10 metres. It weighed 136 tonnes empty and 2,270 tonnes with the tanks full. The five engines, firing for 2 minutes, provided 3,400 tonnes of thrust and would take the rocket to a speed of 6,000mph at 40 miles above the earth. On 15 December 1961, NASA announced that it had chosen Boeing as project manager for this first stage. Under the terms of the contract, Boeing was to build a batch of 15 S-ICs[24].

Furthermore, on 20 December 1963, NASA had also chosen Boeing to build eight Lunar Orbiter craft, whose mission would be to photograph the moon's surface accurately enough to select landing zones for the Apollo programme. Weighing 385kg, the probes had a life span of 800 days. Between 10 August 1966 and 1 August 1967, five Lunar Orbiters photographed 36 million square kilometres (13.9 million square miles) of the lunar surface, from which eight landing zones were chosen.

The Boeing model 939 Lunar Orbiter drew power from four solar panels, giving it a life span of about 800 days. (NASA/LaRC)

The first S-IC to be built left Boeing's Michoud plant, near New Orleans, on 15 March 1965. Too big to be transported by road, it was loaded aboard a barge to be taken to Cape Kennedy. After two unmanned launches (Apollo 4 on 9 November 1967 and Apollo 6 on 4 April 1968), the third S-IC (S-IC-3) was used to launch the Apollo 8 mission (Frank Borman, James Lovell and William Anders) on 21 December 1968, beginning a run of ten successive launches, including the one on 16 July 1969 that culminated in Neil Armstrong setting foot on the moon.

This was not Boeing's only contribution to the moon programme. In October 1969, Boeing was given the job of building the LRV (Lunar Roving Vehicle), more commonly called 'moon buggy', which the astronauts would use to explore the lunar landscape during the final three Apollo missions. After an invitation to tender, Boeing was awarded the contract over Bendix Corp. Boeing worked on a number of proposals, the most significant being MOLAB (Mobile Lunar Laboratory) and LSSM (Local Scientific Survey Module). The various studies led to the LRV, the first of which was delivered to NASA on 15 March 1971, less than 17 months from the signing of the contract.

Contrary to the impression given by their rather rustic appearance, the LRVs were high-tech masterpieces, particularly the wheels designed by Delco Electronics and the electricity supply by Eagle Picher Industries. The LRVs could manage 9mph and cover 55 miles. The first one was used by the crew of Apollo 15, in July 1971, and allowed them to collect twice as many samples as on the previous missions. In April 1972, it was the turn of John Young and Charles Duke to explore the moon (Apollo 16), in the area of

An S-IC first stage from the Saturn V rocket is lowered into position on the launch pad at Cape Canaveral in July 1967. This section of the lunar launcher was 42 metres high. (NASA/KSC)

---

24. North American Rockwell was given the task of building the S-II second stage and McDonnell Douglas the S-IVB third stage.

Guppies – or the many guises of the C-97

During the implementation of the Apollo moon programme, NASA's engineers soon ran into the problem of transporting the various elements of the huge Saturn V rocket. How could the rocket's sections be transported from the factories where they were built to Cape Canaveral in Florida? Clearly, road transport was out of the question. Shipping the sections by boat seemed too slow and expensive. The only solution appeared to be by air. At the time – this was in the early 1960s – the C-97s were beginning to be retired. Aero Spacelines, of Van Nuys, California, seized the opportunity to design a specialised version of the big four-engined plane. A first aircraft (an old Pan Am Stratocruiser) was modified by lengthening and expanding the fuselage, radically altering its shape. Thus swollen, the plane was soon nicknamed 'Pregnant Guppy', from the tropical fish – as livebearers the females are swollen up with the young inside them. The plane, which made its first flight on 19 September 1962, was followed by eight others, which, depending on the exact configurations, were named either 'Mini Guppy' or 'Super Guppy'.

1. Super Guppy (registered N941N) landing at Langley Research Center on 20 October 2000. Built in France by UTA, this aircraft made its first flight on 21 June 1983. (NASA/LRC)

2. The prototype, the 'Pregnant Guppy', had Pratt & Whitney R-4360 engines developing 3,500hp (2,607kW). It is seen here on the tarmac at NASA's Dryden Flight Research Center in October 1962. (NASA/DFRC)

3. May 1976: a Super Guppy is about to swallow the X-24B and HL-10 lifting bodies before delivering them to the US Air Force Museum at Wright Patterson, Ohio. (NASA)

4. Fitted with four 4,680hp (3,486kW) Allison 501-D22C turboprops, the Super Guppy had a cruising speed of 290mph and a range of 2,000 miles. (NASA/LRC)

5. The first Super Guppy ended its career in the early 1990s when it was put into storage at Davis Monthan base in Arizona. (J.G. Handelman)

6. The Super Guppy registered F-BPPA was one of four that were used by Airbus Industrie to carry Airbus sub-assemblies to their final assembly plants. (A. Pelletier)

7. The Super Guppy's hold can carry parts up to 7.5 metres in diameter. (NASA)

8. The front part of the Super Guppy is hinged to give easy access to the hold. (NASA/DFRC)

9. A section of the International Space Station (ISS) is loaded into a Super Guppy on 17 November 1999. (NASA/NSC)

The Lunar Roving Vehicle was a simple yet sophisticated machine. It is seen here under test in 1971. (NASA)

the Descartes crater. Making a little bit of history, they broke the moon speed record with 10.5mph. Finally came the turn of the Apollo 17 crew of Gene Cernan and Jack Schmidt.

In September 1965, at a time when the Apollo programme was mobilising the energies of some 250,000 people across the United States, the Air Force asked Boeing Aerospace to design a single-stage rocket to put small payloads into orbit. Known by Boeing as the model 946[25], the Burner II weighed around 800kg and its rocket engine had a thrust of 4.5 tonnes (44.5kN). Fourteen Burner IIs were produced before it was followed, in August 1969, by a two-stage version, the Burner IIA, of which eight were built.

---

25. The 900-series of numbers were reserved by Boeing for spacecraft. Thus the Lunar Orbiter was model 939.

Astronaut Eugene Cernan (Apollo 17) driving the Lunar Roving Vehicle on the surface of the Moon on 10 December 1972. (NASA)

Originally designated HC-1A, the CH-47A was the first production version of the Chinook. One is seen here in the company of Lufthansa 707-330B and 727-30C. (Boeing)

» Boeing broadens its range...

Looking to broaden its range, Boeing acquired, on 31 March 1960, the Vertol Corporation (formerly the Piasecki Company, started in 1940 by Frank Piasecki under the name of P-V Engineering Forum and in 1946 becoming Piasecki Helicopter Corporation)[26]. The company now became the Vertol Division of Boeing Company and Boeing moved to enlarge its factory located at Morton, near Philadelphia. Vertol's most recent helicopter production was the turbine model 107, which had made its public debut in April 1958. The first example (Vertol 107-II), for 25 passengers, entered service with New York Airways in 1961, replacing the old Vertol 44s that had gone into service in 1956. In 1965, Kawasaki bought the rights and continued production and marketing (except in North America). The US Army had ordered 10 model 107s in July 1958 under the YCH-1A designation, but in the meantime it had transferred its interest to the model 114 and the original order was reduced to just three.

As this photograph shows, the XCH-62 had unusual dimensions. (Boeing)

26. Vertol was an acronym for Vertical Take-Off and Landing.

A US Army CH-47 takes off from Muzaffarabad, Pakistan, carrying two loads of supplies for the victims of the 8 October 2005 earthquake. (DoD)

In February 1961, a naval version of the model 107 was ordered by the Marines. It entered service in early 1965, designated HRB-1 (later CH-46A) Sea Knight. In January 1964, this order was followed by another for UH-46As destined for the Navy. Vertol then won various export orders: from Canada (CH-113 Labrador and Voyager) and Sweden (HKP-4). Version CH-46D appeared in 1966, with General Electric T58-GE-10 engines of 100hp (75kW), followed by version CH-47F for the Marines. Finally, in 1975, 273 Sea Knights of various types were modernised with 1,870hp

Right up to the present day, the Boeing-Vertol CH-46 forms the major part of the Marines' helicopter fleet, although it is due to be replaced by the V-22 Osprey. Here, a CH-46 from the HC-1 Gunbearers' Squadron prepares to land on the carrier USS Nimitz during Operation Iraqi Freedom in April 2003. (US Navy)

The CH-47 Chinook is still the US Army's standard heavy transport helicopter. Here, troops from the 187th Infantry Regiment emerge from a CH-47 during Operation Swarmer, in Iraq, on 16 March 2006. (US Navy)

(1,393kW) T58-GE-16 engines, becoming version CH-46E. Over 45 years after the first order for Sea Knights, version CH-46E remains the Marine Corps' main troop-carrying helicopter.

At the same time, the US Army was starting to consider a replacement for its big Sikorsky H-37A Mojave helicopters. As the result of an invitation to tender, Boeing Vertol's model 114 was chosen and an order for five prototypes, designated YHC-1B, was signed in June 1959. The first of them, with 1,940hp (1,445kW) Lycoming T53-L-3 engines had its maiden flight on 21 September 1961. An order for five pre-production examples was signed for the 1960 financial year. These helicopters, initially designated as HC-1B and, from 1962, as CH-47A Chinook, were delivered starting in 1963, with subsequent orders taking the total number of CH-47As produced to 349. They would be followed, from 1966 onwards, by 108 CH-47Bs supplied with 2,850hp (2,123kW) T55-L-7C engines and, in 1967, by 270 CH-47Cs (model 234) with 3,750hp (2,793kW) T55-L-11C engines.

The CH-46 was sold to many export customers, including Sweden, who used ten of them, designated Hkp-4A. (DR)

This brightly decorated Boeing-Vertol brings supplies to the aircraft carrier USS Kitty Hawk on 27 March 2003. (US Navy)

A CH-46E Sea Knight from the 26th Marines Expeditionary Unit (MEU) takes part in the training of Israeli soldiers aboard USS Kearsarge in April 2005. (USMC)

The Boeing PHM-2 USS Hercules on patrol in June 1990. It was one of six of the type ordered by the US Navy. (DoD/PH1 S. Allen)

The Boeing PHM-3 hydrofoil USS Taurus at full speed. The eight Harpoon missile launchers can be seen on the aft deck. On the fore deck is the 76mm, rapid-fire gun turret. (DoD/PH1 S. Allen)

» And diversifies...

Still looking to diversify, Boeing began to show an interest in ships around 1959, when research on hydrofoils was started. The research led to the construction of an experimental boat named *Aqua-Jet*, then a second, *Little Squirt*, to demonstrate the feasibility of hydrojet propulsion. The tests were a success and, in 1965, the US Navy ordered a hydrofoil patrol boat from Boeing. Named *Tucumcari* (after a town in New Mexico), the PGH-2 gunboat was launched in July 1967. Constructed from aluminium and powered by a 3,100hp (2,310kW) turbine, it could reach a speed of 50 knots. It operated along the Vietnamese coast before serving as the prototype for a hydrofoil missile ship (PHM or Patrol Hydrofoil Missileship), on which design work got under way in November 1971. The first one, PHM-1 *Pegasus*, was launched on 9 November 1974 and was followed by five others[27]. Powered by General Electric LM-2500 gas turbines developing 18,000hp (13,410kW), these ships could reach over 50 knots. Civil versions were also developed, such as the model 929-100 launched on 29 March 1974 and put into service between Hong Kong and Macao on 25 April 1975. With two Allison 501-KF turbines producing 3,800hp (2,830kW) and with space for up to 250 passengers, it could reach 45 knots.

Boeing's efforts at diversification were not limited to helicopters and naval construction. They were also directed towards gas turbines, developed by the Industrial Products Division and designed for use in lorries, helicopters, locomotives, tractors, ships of all kinds and even racing cars.

27. PHM-2 *Hercules* launched on 13 April 1982, PHM-3 *Taurus* launched on 8 May 1981, PHM-4 *Aquila* launched on 16 September 1981, PHM-5 *Aries* launched on 5 November 1981 and PHM-6 *Gemini* launched on 17 February 1982.

The impressive sight of a 747-400 preparing to leave the Everett plant. (Boeing)

CHAPTER 6

1970-1996

From the edge of the abyss to the pinnacle

>> While it dominated the airliner market and had significant interests in other aerospace sectors, the Boeing Company restructured after 1968. In 1969, it comprised five divisions, the biggest being the Commercial Airplane Division, under the direction of E.H. 'Tex' Boullioun. The recently formed Military Aircraft Systems Division had as its principal mission the task of maintaining and modernising the B-52 and KC-135 fleets. Space activities were the province of the Aerospace Group, while the Wichita Division had been split off from the Commercial Airplane Division. Finally, Vertol Aircraft Company had become the Vertol Division.

I n the early 1970s, several factors combined to push Boeing into crisis. Activity relating to the Apollo programme had slowed appreciably and Boeing's management had hoped to offset the decline in the space programme by increasing civil aircraft sales. But this was not to be, as the air transport industry went through a crisis principally caused by excess capacity. The order books gradually emptied and deliveries soon fell in turn. In 1970, Boeing delivered 203 civil aircraft, against 291 the previous year.

Boeing's president, Thornton Arnold 'T' Wilson, found himself facing a financial crisis directly linked to the 747. Anxious not to be left behind by their rivals, many customers had wanted deliveries as quickly as

possible, causing a rise in the rate of production and, consequently, investment. In 1969, profits were down to $10 million. After 1968, orders declined steeply, falling from 316 in 1967 to 177 in 1968 and 90 in 1971. That same year, only nine 707s and seven 747s were ordered. As for 727 orders, after a peak in 1965 with 187 planes, this number was reduced by a factor of seven by 1971 with just 26 aircraft!

With misfortunes never coming singly, on 24 March 1971, Congress refused to allocate further funding to the SST, a decision that signed the programme's death warrant. Of course, the company was free to continue development at its own expense, but, in view of its limited resources, Boeing felt constrained to end it.

The Everett 747 production line. The colours on the rudders indicate which airlines the aircraft are destined for. In the foreground is a United Airlines version. (Boeing)

This fall in activity soon had repercussions on the workforce, whose numbers tumbled spectacularly. After a peak of 148,180 employees in 1967, of whom 100,874 were in the Seattle area alone, Boeing's workforce fell by two-thirds in the space of four years, reaching its lowest level in 1971 with 53,300 employees, of whom 37,200 were in the Seattle area. The situation provoked an economic crisis without precedent in the region. Thousands of former Boeing employees, unable to find work locally, left the area. The situation was such that a billboard appeared in the town with the request: 'Would the last person to leave Seattle please turn off the lights?' It was 1972 before employment started rising again and reached a new peak in 1980 with 113,172 employees (81,392 in the Seattle area). The decline in the civil aviation market in the early 1980s brought a new slowing of activity, with

the workforce again reduced, this time to 88,181 in the space of three years. Fortunately, this situation did not last and a rise in activity saw a steady increase in the workforce, which, in 1989, reached 106,670. However, in 1994, thanks to another drop in both the civil and military markets, Boeing was again forced to cut its workforce, which by 1995 had dropped to 71,834.

In this difficult context, Boeing's management undertook a further reorganisation, which was completed by 19 December 1972. This essentially amounted to a slimming operation, creating three autonomous companies, namely Boeing Commercial Airplane Company, Boeing Aerospace Company and Boeing Vertol Company. Military activities were under the aegis of Boeing Aerospace, but the Wichita plant retained its status as a division.

» Pulling out all the stops

'Diversification' was the word on everyone's lips in America's big corporations at this time. Boeing was on the edge of the abyss. In an attempt to somehow maintain the size of its business, it sought to broaden its field of activities beyond the aerospace field. On 25 May 1970, Boeing set up Boeing Computer Services (BCS), with a view to meeting its own information technology needs and to sell its services to administrative organisations and commercial enterprises. This branch built up a customer base of 2,500, including 40 banks and NASA. By March of the following year, there were teams working on irrigation projects and waste recycling in Oregon. Others were running property schemes for the Federal Department of Housing & Urban Development, and constructing a seawater desalination plant for a tourist complex. In 1971, Boeing designed and built an automated urban rapid-transit system for the University of West Virginia. Boeing Vertol won contracts for light rail vehicles in Boston and San Francisco. In July 1975, the International Oceanic Exposition at Kobe, Japan, used a rapid transit system designed by Boeing. As a way of providing more general services, such as the maintenance of vehicles on air bases, Boeing Services International (BSI) was set up in 1972. Established in 1974, Boeing Engineering & Construction (BEC) specialised in the fields of energy and the environment. This firm built some of the largest wind turbines in the world, the MOD-2, with a diameter of nearly 100 metres.

» A limited military market

Though painful, the failures of the CX-HLX and the SST were in some way beneficial to Boeing. The company was obliged to concentrate all its resources on more profitable programmes. On 8 July 1970, Boeing won the contract for an Airborne Warning and Control System (AWACS), using a 707-320 airframe and designated E-3A. With its high-tech equipment, the E-3A was the first plane to cost over $100 million each. The initial studies for such a system went back to 1963 when Boeing, Douglas and Lockheed had been invited to work on an early-warning system using the 707-320, C-141A or DC-8-62 as a platform. Lockheed had been quickly eliminated from the competition. The following year, Westinghouse Electric Corporation and Hughes Aircraft Company were in competition for the radar system.

When the Air Force launched its final invitation to tender in December 1968, Boeing put forward a proposal for an aircraft using eight General Electric TF34-GE-2 engines with 4,082kg thrust (40.1kN)[1], and

1. These engines had been designed for the carrier-borne ASM Lockheed S-3A Viking.

An E-3C Sentry from the 964th AWACS Squadron takes off from Elmendorf base in Alaska to take part in exercise 'Northern Edge' in March 2001. (DoD/SSgt W. Clark)

An E-3C from the Expeditionary Airborne Air Control Squadron (EAACS) prepares for take-off on a night mission from Tinker AFB, Oklahoma, in October 2001. (DoD/MSgt K. Reed)

A ghostly view of an E-3C undergoing night-time refuelling by a KC-135R, during Operation Enduring Freedom, October 2001. (DoD/MSgt K. Reed)

To replace the two presidential VC-137Cs, the Air Force ordered two 747-2G4Bs, designating them VC-25A. The aircraft, fitted with CF6-80C2B1 engines, can carry up to 70 passengers and 23 crew members. Seen here is the second of the two at Reno, Nevada on 18 June 2004. (R.J. Francillon)

with the rotating radar antenna mounted either on top of the fin or above the fuselage (the latter being the solution ultimately adopted). However, the two test aircraft (EC-137D) retained their original four Pratt & Whitney JT3Ds, while the decision was taken in late 1972 to equip the planes destined for NATO and the US Air Force with Pratt & Whitney TF33-PW-100/101 engines of 9,525kg thrust (93.5kN). The aircraft ordered by Saudi Arabia, Britain and France would receive CFM-56-2A-2/3 engines. The Westinghouse

AN/APY-1 system was chosen as the radar on 5 October 1972. The first flight of the E-3A was made on 21 July 1975, with deliveries to the Air Force beginning in March 1977[2]. The aircraft intended for NATO (E-3B) entered service in 1982, followed, in June 1986, by five E-3As for Saudi Arabia and, in March 1991, by the Royal Air Force's E-3Ds. Deliveries of the E-3F to the French Air Force were spread over the period from May 1991 to February 1992.

In November 1972, the Air Force put out a tender for a replacement for the Lockheed C-130 Hercules. Boeing and MDC were the finalists for this Advanced Medium STOL Transport (AMST) and, in 1973, two prototypes were ordered from each of the manufacturers. Designated YC-14, Boeing's plane had a relatively small, supercritical wing, two large CF6-50F fan jets beneath the wing and significant lift augmentation. While the prototypes were being built, Congress substantially reduced the budget allocation to the programme, which delayed the first flight until 9 August 1976. No decision was made about the competing planes and the programme was cut in 1978. As for the C-130, it got on with its job and, 30 years later, has still not been replaced.

The absence of a major programme did not mean that Boeing lacked work in the military field. The first of the three Advanced Airborne Command Posts flew on 19 June 1973. Designated E-4A, these aircraft were created using a 747 airframe and were delivered from July of the same year. Elsewhere, B-52 modernisation work was in full swing. Under the terms of a $200-million contract, the Wichita Division undertook to modify the structure of the B-52s, so as to prolong

---

2. The first E-3As were taken by the 552nd Airborne Warning & Control Wing, based at Tinker AFB, Oklahoma.

The Boeing YC-14 was in competition with the McDonnell Douglas YC-15 to replace the Lockheed C-130 Hercules, but no decision followed the trial period of the two aircraft. Here is the second prototype on display at the Le Bourget Show in 1977. (A. Pelletier)

The YC-14 short-take-off-and-landing transport had a supercritical airfoil, with the exhaust gases from the forward-mounted engines flowing over the upper surfaces. Large multi-slot flaps (partially visible here) completed the set-up. (AFFTC)

The E-30Ds are known in the Royal Air Force as 'Sentry AEW Mark 1'. Their wing span has been increased to accommodate the Loral Yellow Gate electronic surveillance pods. (MoD)

The Boeing 747 as an aircraft carrier

In the early 1970s, the arrival of heavy transports revived the dream of aerial aircraft carriers. In 1973, Boeing announced that its engineers were investigating the possibility of using a 747 to carry a dozen or so 'advanced micro fighters'. The studies, which went on until 1975, involved a variety of different configurations. It was envisaged that not only would the tiny aircraft be launched from the mother plane, but that they would also return to it, be refuelled and rearmed and launched once again. These tasks were expected to last no more than about ten minutes per plane. The micro fighters themselves were to be tailless, supersonic aircraft (Boeing model 908-625) 8.84 metres long with a wing span of 5.33 metres and weighing 3,760kg fully loaded and would be armed with a rotating 25mm cannon and air-to-air or air-to-ground missiles. Lockheed was simultaneously working on a comparable adaptation of its C-5 Galaxy.

The E-4B is the last of a small series of E-4A (747-200Bs with JT9D engines) airborne command posts, the first of which was delivered on 16 July 1973. The E-4B is distinguished by its more powerful electrical system and greater fuel capacity. It is seen here being refuelled by a KC-135 tanker in December 1984. (DoD/M. Haggerty)

The most remarkable version of the Jumbo Jet is the 747-123 used by NASA to carry the space shuttle to its launch site. Here, the 747 takes off to carry the shuttle Endeavour back to the Kennedy Space Center in Florida in May 2001. (NASA/DFRC)

their operational life. Most notably, the work involved the almost complete replacement of the wings. On 18 November 1975, Wichita delivered the first of the 80 B-52s that were to be modified to the SAC. This work eventually led to the creation, on 23 October 1979, of a new group, the Boeing Military Airplane Company, whose activities involved the production of sub-

assemblies and provision of technical support for the B-52 and KC-135A. However, under this reorganisation, Boeing Aerospace retained management over the E-3, E-4 and E-6 programmes (see page 173).

>> A new generation of airliners

At the same time, the Commercial Airplane Company was looking at the prospects for the development of the civil aviation market over the next 10 to 15 years, so as to be prepared for the future. During 1971, various airliner configurations were considered. In this way, Boeing circulated the design of a potential 'advanced transport aircraft' designated Boeing 767. It was a twin-engined plane for 200 passengers, using a swept-back, supercritical wing section and capable of flying at Mach 0.98 (high subsonic).

At this time, Boeing also signed an agreement with Aeritalia for the joint development of a four-engined STOL jet airliner to carry between 100 and 150 passengers, with entry into service planned for 1975. It soon evolved into a Quiet Short Haul (QSH) aircraft capable of operating from runways of 1,200 to 1,800 metres. The project came to an abrupt end, but the collaboration between Boeing and Aeritalia continued

Shortening the fuselage radically altered the 747SP's shape. Pan American World Airways, who were the first to use this version, began a New York to Tokyo flight in April 1976. One of Pan Am's 747SP-21s is seen at Rio de Janeiro in August 1980. (R.J. Francillon)

and was broken only in 1976. In the same spirit, Boeing signed an agreement with Japan with a view to cooperating on a small-airliner programme, the 7J7, but as with many others, nothing came of the programme. In the same year, the Commercial Airplane Company got involved in a new programme for an aircraft of advanced design, the 7X7, which was shown to the airlines in the first part of 1973. It was envisaged that the programme would be launched in early 1974 for entry into service by late 1977. But, despite the many different options suggested by Boeing, no consensus was forthcoming from among the airlines.

On 4 July 1975, American Independence Day, a completely new version of the 747 made its first flight. After unsuccessfully trying to interest the airlines in a three-engined version of the Jumbo Jet, Boeing designed a shorter version of the four-engined aircraft, with a lower passenger-carrying capacity, but an increased range. First purchased by Pan American, the 747SP (SP for Special Performance) entered service on 25 April 1976. This version did not meet with much commercial success, with only 45 planes being produced, the last of which was delivered on 9 December 1989.

It was in early 1976 that the 7N7 concept appeared. This was a design for a plane with 120 to 180 seats, using the same fuselage section as the 727/737 and as

In 1973, Boeing tried to develop an advanced-design 7X7 three-engine aircraft in collaboration with the Italian manufacturer, Aeritalia, but it attracted very little customer interest. (Aeritalia)

many other elements of those aircraft as possible. In the ensuing months, Boeing made numerous modifications to the 7N7 and 7X7 and the two projects were shown to the public for the first time at the 1977 Le Bourget Show; yet the airlines remained undecided about their needs.

The successes achieved by Airbus Industrie soon

United Airlines was the first to order 767-200s, which they put into service from September 1982. This 767-200 landing at Los Angeles International Airport in November 2000 was delivered on 11 March 1982. (R.J. Francillon)

Boeing rebuilt the prototype 767 into a test bed for the Airborne Optical Adjunct system for the US Army. It is seen here during its evaluation trials at Fort Bliss, Texas, in May 1995. (DoD/1CL J. Long)

This Boeing 767-231(PC) was delivered to Airborne Express on 14 July 2003. (R.J. Francillon)

The 767-300ER version was produced in the greatest numbers and remains in production today. It differs from the 767-300 base model in its greater fuel capacity. Pictured here is an Air New Zealand 767-319ER at Los Angeles in November 2000. (R.J. Francillon)

began to worry Boeing's directors, who saw the European plane maker as a dangerous competitor that could threaten the Seattle firm's leading position in the industry. At the time, in 1977, the Boeing catalogue consisted of the model 707, a design that was already over 20 years old, the 727, whose initial orders went back a good 15 years, and the relatively recent 737 and 747. One of the biggest users of the 727, Eastern Air Lines, with its 70 727-100s and 50 727-200s, was starting to take a serious look at their next replacement. When approached, Boeing suggested the model 7N7, a twin-engined aircraft with either CFM56s or JT10D-2s. Talks between the airlines and the manufacturer progressed slowly until Swissair and Lufthansa announced their intention to order Airbuses.

Discussions took a new turn, resulting, in February 1978, in Boeing announcing the development of a completely new family of three airliners consisting of models 757 (formerly 7N7), 767 (formerly twin-engined 7X7) and 777 (formerly three-engined 7X7). For the first time in the history of civil aviation, a manufacturer was taking the risk of launching several different aircraft simultaneously, implying

unprecedented levels of investment. Construction work on models 757 and 767 began five months apart, with the 767 leading the way. The 777 had to wait its turn.

Following the order by United Airlines for 30 planes, the 767's official launch was announced for 14 July 1978, a highly symbolic date for the French, especially as this aircraft was considered a direct competitor of the Airbus A300/310. The following September, at the Farnborough Air Show, the new plane was shown off to the press, at the same time as the 757, the 707-700 (a cargo version of the 707, with a hinged tail section, that was never built) and the 777 (now in the shape of a three-engined derivative of the 767).

The 767 was a large, twin-engined aircraft capable of carrying between 216 and 290 passengers. On 15 November 1978, American Airlines and Delta Airlines embraced this aircraft, in preference to the L-1011-600 (a twin-engined version of the Lockheed TriStar), the DC-X-200 (a twin-engined version of the MDC DC-10) and the A310. The two companies ordered, respectively, 30 and 20 767-200s. At this point, it was expected that the prototype would fly in mid-1981 and that it would receive its certificate a

The German company Condor Flugdienst currently uses nine 767-330ERs that were delivered in May 2004. (Condor)

The first 767-300 had Pratt & Whitney JT9D-7R4D engines. It made its first flight on 30 January 1986. (Boeing)

The German Lufttransport company operated three 767-3G5ERs. (Boeing)

year later. It was decided to set up the assembly line at the Everett plant, which was already building 747s. The schedule was almost met, as the prototype made its first flight on 26 September 1981 and United Airlines took delivery of its first planes on 19 August 1982. Delta received its first 767-200 on 25 October 1982 and put it into service on 15 December 1982. Although sales were significant, they were certainly not up to Boeing's expectations. Indeed, over the first five years the 767 was on the market, from 1978 to 1982, orders went into free fall, with production totals for each of the five successive years being 49, 45, 11, 5 and 2.

As with its other models, Boeing developed several versions from the basic 767-200: the 767-300 with its fuselage lengthened by 6.42 metres, allowing it to carry up to 290 passengers; the long-range 767-200ER, 300ER and 400ER; and the 767-300F cargo version. The 767-200ER was the first to be certified for so-called ETOPS (Extended range Twin engine OPerationS) that allowed the plane to be used on the North Atlantic route. Despite all this, orders for the 767 remained slow, with around 40 to 50 aircraft a year in the period from 1987 to 2003, dropping to

only ten or so in recent years. Nonetheless, by the end of 2006, total sales had reached 973 aircraft, as compared with 821 Airbus A300/310s over the same period.

The 757-200 was the most numerous version of the model 757. United Airlines, with 97 aircraft, was the second biggest user, behind American Airlines with 146 aircraft. (UAL)

The B-52 in action

Far from taking an easy retirement, the Boeing B-52 continues to be used by the US Air Force in operations worldwide. With regular upgrading, this legendary aircraft is likely to remain in service beyond 2040.

5. Specialists from the 2nd Maintenance Squadron work on the engines of a B-52 based at Andersen AFB, Guam, on 11 January 2006. (USAF/MSgt V. Gempis)

6. Captain Peter Terrebonne inspects a 2,000lb JDAM prior to a training mission at Barksdale AFB, Louisiana. (USAF/T. Wininger)

7. B-52 maintenance includes regular tyre changes, an operation that takes about 20 minutes. (USAF/TSgt J. Tudor)

8. On a winter's night in 2004, a B-52H is refuelled by a crew from the 5th Aircraft Maintenance Squadron, at Minot AFB, North Dakota. (USAF/F. Shea)

9. Mk117 750lb bombs are attached to a B-52H's bomb launcher. (USAF)

10. Like the Flying Fortresses of the Second World War, the B-52s engaged in Operation Desert Storm displayed individual insignia. This B-52G from the 379th Bombardment Wing (serial number 58-0173) has been nicknamed 'Let's make a deal'. (USAF)

1. A B-52 from the 2nd Bombardment Wing closes in on its refuelling tanker before carrying out a mission over Afghanistan during Operation Enduring Freedom, on 9 February 2006. (USAF/MSgt J. Rohrer)

2. The operator in a KC-135 Stratotanker from the 28th Expeditionary Air Refuelling Squadron prepares to lock the refuelling boom on to a B-52H's receptacle. (USAF/TSgt R. Freeland)

3. The co-pilot of a B-52 from the 40th Expeditionary Bomb Squadron in a close-support mission over Iraq during Operation Iraqi Freedom, on 17 April 2003. (USAF/TSgt R. Freeland)

4. This impressive shot taken at Barksdale AFB, on 2 February 2006, shows the variety of weaponry that a B-52 can carry. In the centre is a rotating cruise missile launcher. (USAF/TSgt R. Horstman)

The first 767-300 in the final stages of assembly at the Everett plant. (Boeing)

An Aeromexico 757-2Q8 at Los Angeles in December 2000. (R.J. Francillon)

An America West Airlines 757-225 coming in to land at Los Angeles in January 2000. Since then, this airline has rationalised its fleet and uses only Airbus A320s and A319s. (R.J. Francillon)

The first of two Avancia 757-2YOs was delivered to the Colombian company on 13 August 1992. These aircraft are still in use alongside two 757-28As and a 757-236. (Boeing)

A Condor Flugdienst 757-330 received this striking scheme for the company's jubilee. The slogan on the fuselage reads 'We love flying'. The aircraft was delivered to Condor on 28 May 2004. (Condor)

As for the 757, it was developed to satisfy the requirements of both Eastern Air Lines and British Airways as a derivative of the 727-200. On 31 August 1978, the two companies announced orders for, respectively, 21 and 19 aircraft fitted with Rolls-Royce RB211-535C engines of 17 tonnes thrust (166.4kN). This was the first time that Boeing had launched an aircraft that was not fitted with American-made engines. Other engine options, however, were available (CF6 and JT10). At this point, the 757 still included many elements from the 727-200, but by the time Eastern Air Lines confirmed its order (23 March 1979), the 757-200 had evolved substantially to include a number of new features. The characteristic T-shaped tailplane of the 727 had been abandoned for a conventional arrangement, the fuselage had been shortened and many of the 767's systems had been

adopted. In the wake of Eastern Air Lines, other companies moved to place orders, including Delta Airlines, Transbrasil and Monarch.

The first plane in the series made its first flight on 19 February 1982. The test programme got off to a perfect start and was completed earlier than scheduled. Deliveries began on 22 December 1982 and Eastern Air Lines put its first 757-200s into service on 1 January of the following year. By this time, the total number of orders had reached 107, but, as with the 767, orders for the 757 fell in 1982 to only two planes, and did not rise appreciably until 1988. A lengthened version, the 757-300, was launched in 1996, intended mainly for charter companies, but it soon interested other companies, too. It made its first flight on 2 August 1998 and the first deliveries were to the German company Condor Flugdienst on 10 March 1999.

The American Airlines 757-223 Jet Flagship received a special colour scheme. This aircraft, delivered on 15 January 1999, is fitted with Rolls-Royce RB-211-535E4 engines. (American Airlines)

The US Air Force acquired four C-32As (model 757-200), the first of which flew at Renton on 12 February 1998. This one is seen at Charleston, West Virginia, on Independence Day, 4 July 2004. (DoD/SSgt B.G. Stevens)

>> Climbing back to the top

In 1979, with a turnover of $8.1 billion, Boeing had worked its way up to second place in the American aeronautical industry behind United Technologies and ahead of LTV Corporation[3]. On 29 September 1981, Federal Express ordered 15 727-200s fitted with a cargo door and able to carry up to 26 tonnes of freight. These aircraft, the first of which flew on 28

April 1983, marked the end of the 727's career after a total of 1,831 had been delivered between 1963 and 1984.

Following the final delivery of a 727, on 18 September 1984, deliveries of 737s rose substantially, going from 67 in 1984 to 115 in 1985 and 141 in 1986. It helped, of course, that new versions were now available. Model 737-400 used the wings and CFM56 engines from the 737-300, but with a 2.9-metre fuselage extension, which provided room for 168 passengers in a high-density layout. Boeing would ultimately build 486 737-300s, with the first ones being delivered to Piedmont Airlines and entering service on 1 October 1988. The shorter 737-500 was designed at the behest of Southwest Airlines as a replacement for the 737-200. This version, powered by CFM56-3B1 engines of 8,390kg thrust (82.3kN), made its maiden flight on 30 June 1989 and was put into service in March 1990. A total of 389 planes were produced, with the last one being delivered on 26 July 1999. So ended the production career of the first-generation 737s, of which 3,132 were built, three

---

3. United Technologies' turnover was $9,053 million and LTV Corporation's was $7,997 million.

The first 737-400s at the final-assembly stage. This version was 2.9 metres longer and could carry up to 168 passengers. The second aircraft from the front in line number 3 at Renton is the first 737-400 destined for the Austrian company, Lauda Air. Also visible are 737s for Air France, Lufthansa and Aer Lingus. (Boeing)

The 737-400 uses the 737-300's engines and aerofoil, but has a longer fuselage. The Alaska Airlines 737-490 shown here (registered N792AS) is decorated with a giant salmon. The aircraft was delivered on 14 July 1997 and is still in service. (Alaska Airlines)

times the number of 707s and one and a half times the number of 727s. A new generation would soon take its place.

In 1983, the recession began to weaken. On 9 December, the 1,000th 737 left the Renton plant. By the end of the decade, Boeing aircraft formed the bulk of the airlines' fleets. In Seattle, in April 1984, Frank A. Shrontz, who had led the 707/727/737 programmes, succeeded 'Tex' Boullioun at the head of the Commercial Airplane Company. By 25 February 1985, he had taken his seat as president of the Boeing Company and from April 1986 he was chairman of the board of directors and chief executive officer until his retirement in 1996.

In 1985, Boeing undertook a major modernisation of the 747. This rejuvenation process encompassed all aspects of the plane: aerodynamics, materials, engines and equipment. Announced in May 1985, the 747-400 was available with more powerful engines such as the CF6-80, PW4056 or RB211-524. The use of new light alloys and composite materials had allowed a substantial reduction in weight and the fitting of 'winglets' and increased fuel capacity had extended the range. In its basic version, the new Jumbo could carry up to 416 passengers in three classes over a distance of 8,200 miles. The first 747-400 flew on 29 April 1988 and Northwest, the first airline to receive the new aircraft, put them into service on 9 February of the following year. Several variants were developed

at the request of the airlines: the 747-400D for Japan Air Lines and All Nippon Airways; the 747-400F cargo version; the 747-400M 'combi' and the 747-400ER and 400ERF very-long-haul aircraft. Currently, the 747-400 is the only 747 model to sell at the rate of around 15 aircraft a year and will remain so until the arrival of the 747-8 (see page 231).

The 75th 747 for Japan Airlines (JAL) was a 747-400, seen here in its final stage of assembly. This aircraft's emergence from the factory coincided with Boeing's 75th anniversary. (Boeing)

The 737-500 was developed at the request of Southwest Airlines, who wanted a replacement for their old 737-200s. Seen here is the first of the series, registered N73700. (Boeing)

A colourful paint job for this 747-481D owned by the Japanese company ANA and photographed at Tokyo-Haneda in November 2002. The 400D series aircraft were specially conceived for Japanese internal routes and can carry up to 628 passengers. (T. Wang via R.J. Francillon)

Looking to increase its range of products, Boeing acquired de Havilland Canada, on 31 January 1986, for $112 million. This company was producing a four-engined, 50-seat aircraft, the Dash 7, and Boeing's management saw a chance to get into the third-tier airline market. Unfortunately, despite heavy investment, de Havilland Canada continued to accumulate losses. Realising its error, Boeing sold the company to Canadian Bombardier in 1992.

In 1988, Boeing had risen to first place among aeronautical exporting companies. With $7.8 billion coming from exports, or 46.2% of its total turnover, it was in third place in American industry behind General Motors and Ford and well ahead of McDonnell Douglas[4]. A year later, Boeing was in first place among American aeronautical companies with a turnover of $20.3 billion, ahead of United Technologies ($19.8 billion) and McDonnell Douglas ($15 billion). Adapting, as always, to the economic climate, Boeing announced a new restructuring on 30 October 1989, in which most of the non-civil activities were placed in the Defense & Space Group.

By 17 August 1986, Boeing had delivered its 5,000th jet airliner. In 35 years of production, the Seattle manufacturer had built over 60% of the jet airliners in service in the West. As if to emphasise this, on 28 March 1990 the model 737 became the biggest-selling airliner in the world when United Airlines took delivery of the 1,832nd example, a record hitherto held by the 727 with 1,831. On 10 April 1990, the 6,000th Boeing airliner, a model 767, was delivered to Britannia Airways.

In the late 1980s, Boeing began a pilot study on an aircraft with a capacity somewhere between that of a 747-400 and a 767-300. It was a twin-engined, high-capacity, long-haul jet designated 777, by now quite unrelated to the original 777. Designed almost entirely

4. With an export turnover of $3.47 billion, MDC was in eighth place among American industries.

Norwegian has 737-36Ns with the image of a Norwegian celebrity painted on the fins. Seen here, from front to back, are the skater Sonja Henie and explorers Roald Amundsen and Thor Heyerdahl. (Norwegian)

by computer, this new-generation aircraft used state-of-the-art technology and a lot of composite materials were used in its structure (9% of the total weight). Boeing announced the programme's launch on 29 October 1990, after a firm order for 34 planes from United Airlines, in preference to the MD-11 and the Airbus A330. It turned out to be the biggest order Boeing had ever received, as United also ordered 30 747-400s at the same time.

Built at Everett, the 777-200 base version first flew on 12 June 1994, two and a half years after the Airbus A340. It had been designed to carry between 300 and 328 passengers in three classes and was offered with a range of fan-jet engines, such as the General Electric GE90-76B, Pratt & Whitney PW4074 and Rolls-Royce Trent 875-17. In addition, it had been designed from an early stage to comply with the new ETOPS

This 737-490 has been specially decorated to mark a partnership between Alaska Airlines, the Make-a-Wish Foundation and Disneyland Resorts. This was the airline's third aircraft to be decorated according to a Disney theme. (Alaska Airlines)

A United Airlines Boeing 737-522 (registered N907UA) coming in to land at Oakland, California. (R.J. Francillon)

Delivered on 5 December 1997, this British Airways 747-436 (registered G-CIVO) is fitted with Rolls-Royce RB211-524G2 engines of 26.3 tonnes thrust (258kN). (Rolls-Royce)

(Extended range Twin engine OPerationS) regulations relating to long-range twin-engined jet aircraft. The first 777-200 was delivered to United Airlines on 15 May 1995 and went into service on 7 June. As was its custom, Boeing developed a long-haul version, the 777-200ER, which, with its fuel capacity increased by 45%, could cover a distance of 9,500 miles, and a very-long-haul version, the 777-200LR, capable of flying nearly 11,000 miles non-stop. An extended version, the 777-300, for between 440 and 550 passengers, flew on 16 October 1997 and, although first ordered by All Nippon Airways, it entered service with Cathay Pacific on 27 May of the following year.

The Douglas DC-9-32 has a somewhat Lilliputian appearance against the United Airlines 747-422. The aircraft, registered N190UA, was delivered on 22 April 1993 and is currently in storage. (R.J. Francillon)

This 747-419, registered ZK-NBT, was delivered to Air New Zealand on 31 October 1990 and is still in use by the same airline. It is seen here at Los Angeles International in November 2000, alongside a Southwest 737-7H4. (R.J. Francillon)

» Boeing nicknames

Type	» Nickname	» Comments
P-26	» Pea Shooter	» From its small-calibre machine guns
Y1B-9	» Flying Panatella	» From its cigar-tube-shaped fuselage
XB-15	» Flying Barndoor	» From the large surface area of its wings
B-17	» Queen	
	» Fort	» Abbreviation of 'Fortress'
B-29	» Superfort	» Abbreviation of 'Superfortress'
	» Flying Fire Hazard	» From the tendency of its engines to catch fire
B-47	» Three Headed Monster	» From its three-man crew
B-52	» BUFF (Big Ugly Fat Fella)	» 'Fella' is often replaced by 'Fucker'
	Coconutknocker and Monkeyknocker	» From the alleged inaccuracy of its bombing, which only ever hit coconut trees or monkeys
	Cadillac	» Applied to the B-52Hs whose fan-jet engines were much quieter, like Cadillacs
KC-135	» Silver Sow	» From the size of the fuselage and the fact it was unpainted
	» Tank	» From its refuelling role
	» Stratobladder	» From its refuelling role
	» Flying Gas Station	» From its refuelling role
RC-135C	» Chipmunk	» From the large fairings on each side of its nose, resembling a chipmunk's cheeks
RC-135	» Hog Nose	» From the shape of its nose
XPBB-1	» The Lone Ranger	» There was just a solitary example of this 'Sea Ranger' seaplane
X-20	» Dinosaur	» Same pronunciation as 'Dyna-Soar'
377	» Strat	» Abbreviation of 'Stratoliner'
727	» Metal Parachute	» From its augmented-lift aerofoil
	» 3-Holer	» From its three engines
737-100	» Fat Albert	» From its podgy appearance, resembling the character from a Bill Cosby show
	» FLUF (Fat Little Ugly Fucker)	
747	» Jumbo Jet	» From its size
	» Whale	» From its size
747SP	» Fat Albert	» From its squat, compact shape
CH-46	» Phrog	» From the way it sits on the ground
CH-47	» Shithook	» Corruption of 'Chinook'

American Airlines ordered nine 777-223ERs. This version, adapted for long-haul flights, had its fuel capacity increased to 171,000 litres and the maximum take-off weight is 286.9 tonnes. (American Airlines)

A Virgin Atlantic 747-4QB, aptly registered G-VBIG, comes in to land at Oakland on 4 November 1999. Delivered on 10 June 1996, it remains in service today. (R.J. Francillon)

The 747-400F is a specialised cargo version. Here a China Airlines Cargo 747-409F comes in to land in November 2000. The aircraft, registered B-18703, was delivered on 29 August 2000. (R.J. Francillon)

United Airlines was the first company to take 777s, with a firm order for 34 planes with as many options. The 777-222s went into service from 7 June 1995. (R.J. Francillon)

» Cooperation to reduce risk

During the 1980s, Boeing, in common with other manufacturers, increasingly turned to one-off cooperation agreements when tendering for major military contracts. By this means, expertise could be pooled, while limiting the financial risks and remaining a credible bidder in the eyes of the Pentagon. Thus Boeing and Northrop cooperated as the principal sub-contractors on the stealth bomber or ATB (Advanced Technology Bomber) programme that would culminate in the well-known B-2 Spirit[5]. Likewise, the Seattle company worked in association with Bell on the JVX programme and with Sikorsky on the LHX programme (see page 197).

In the middle of the decade, the Air Force launched the Advanced Tactical Fighter (ATF) programme with a view to replacing the F-15 Eagle. The aircraft was to have a supersonic cruising speed and have a degree of stealth capability. Most of the American plane makers put forward proposals and, in July 1986, the Air Force chose Northrop and Lockheed to build two prototypes for evaluation. At this point, the two principal contractors brought in the talents of other manufacturers. Northrop chose McDonnell Douglas as a partner for the YF-23 and did the same with Boeing and General Dynamics on the design of the YF-22. After comparative tests, the YF-22 Lightning was declared the winner, on 23 April 1991. A new hurdle was cleared in the ATF programme when, on 2 August 1991, an Engineering & Manufacturing Development contract (EMD) was signed, leading to the production of the F/A-22 Raptor. Production was shared more or less equally between the Lockheed Martin Marietta plant in Georgia, General Dynamics at Forth Worth,

Lockheed, General Dynamics and Boeing collaborated on the design of the YF-22, the new Advanced Tactical Fighter for the US Air Force. (Lockheed)

Texas, and Boeing in Seattle. Among smaller programmes may be mentioned the E-6A Mercury, launched in April 1983. The Navy had decided to replace its Lockheed EC-130Q nuclear submarine communications aircraft with 707-320Cs powered by CFM F108 fan jets and with a TACAMO IV communications system. Designated E-6A, the first of these aircraft flew at Renton on 19 February 1987, with deliveries commencing in August 1989[6].

---

5. The Northrop B-2 Spirit made its first flight on 17 July 1989.

6. The first E-6As were delivered to the VQ-3 squadron based at NAS Barber's Point, Hawaii, in August 1989.

A scale model of the 777 undergoing transonic wind-tunnel tests at the Langley Research Center in February 2001. (NASA/LISAR)

The 777-200 is a medium-haul version, carrying up to 440 passengers (305 in three classes). Seen here is a Korean Air 777-285 at Oakland in the autumn of 2000. (R.J. Francillon)

The second prototype of the YF-22 in flight. It was powered by Pratt & Whitney YF119-100 engines, whereas the first prototype had General Electric YF120-100s. (Lockheed)

>> Towards heavy commercial transport

Philip M. Condit became Boeing's president on 31 August 1992 and would hold the position until 1 February 1997, when he was elected chairman of the board of directors. Under his presidency, several mergers and acquisitions were to turn Boeing into a global enterprise (see the following chapter).

At the beginning of the 1990s, Airbus began preliminary design work on a very large aircraft with 600 to 800 seats with the intention of both completing its range and breaking Boeing's monopoly in the field of high-capacity aircraft. In April 1992, McDonnell Douglas unveiled its project for a giant four-engined aircraft carrying 600 passengers, the MD-12. Bigger than the 747-400, the MD-12 required MDC to find a partner, with its development costs being estimated at $4–$5 billion. However, with the uncertain health of the airlines, the project generated no orders and was abandoned. Despite its financial problems, McDonnell Douglas passed the landmark of 2,000 twin-engined jet airliner sales on 11 June 1992. However impressive these sales may have seemed, they were still a long way behind Boeing's, with the Long Beach-based manufacturer unable to rival either them or Airbus. Its market share was diminishing dangerously and it was not until 19 October 1995 that it registered its first order for the MD-95, first offered four years previously[7].

In late 1992, Boeing announced that it would investigate the very large aircraft concept under the Very Large Commercial Transport designation in association with two members of the Airbus consortium, the German Firm DASA and the British BAe. However, in June 1994, Airbus started development work on its own large aircraft, the A33XX, while Boeing followed suit with the NLA (New Large Aircraft). In its fundamental form, the NLA would carry up to 600 passengers over a range of 9,000 miles. With a wing span of 77.7 metres and a take-off weight of over 550 tonnes, it would have been powered by engines with 30 tonnes of thrust.

At the same time, at NASA's request, Boeing was also devoting resources to preliminary studies for a new-generation supersonic airliner, the HSCT (High Speed Civil Transport), with between 250 and 300 seats and a speed of Mach 2.5. It quickly became clear that the market could not take two new planes at the same time. On 10 July 1995, Boeing decided to drop its studies for both the VLCT and the NLA and turned

---

7. Firm orders for 50 MD-95s by ValuJet with an option for a further 50.

The pilotless aircraft designed by Boeing under the Compass Cope programme was notable for its extended wing (allowing high-altitude flight) and for its dorsally mounted General Electric fan-jet. (USAF)

instead to derivatives of the 747, named 747-500X and 600X. The 747X programme was itself abandoned in January 1997, to be 'resuscitated' in November 2005 with the 747-8 (see page 231).

While all this was going on, the 737 was continuing its triumphant career. Boeing announced the launch of a new generation of 737s (given the generic name of 737-X), and on 17 November 1993 the Seattle company announced that Southwest Airlines would be taking the first batch of 63 737-700s (see page 210).

» Remote-controlled planes get off the ground

In the early 1970s, a new type of plane started to enter military thinking. These were RPVs, or Remote Piloted Vehicles, as they were then called. Because of the suitability for this kind of aircraft for high-altitude reconnaissance, the Air Force signed contracts with Teledyne-Ryan and Boeing for the construction of prototypes. Out of Boeing's Compass Cope programme emerged the YQM-94A B-Gull, a craft with a 27-metre wing span powered by a General Electric J97-GE-100 engine of 2,390kg thrust (23.5kN) that made its first flight on 28 July 1973. This prototype was wrecked on 4 August and replaced by another aircraft, which

continued the testing programme but did not make it into production.

A few years later, in 1987, Boeing designed and flew an electronic-warfare mini-RPV, designated YCEM-138A Pave Cricket, but this, too, was not put into production. Finally, on 29 March 1996, a futuristic-looking drone named Dark Star, designed in collaboration with Lockheed's famous Skunk Works, made its first flight under a programme that had been commissioned by the Defense Advanced Research Projects Agency (DARPA). Unfortunately, the first prototype crashed on its second flight, on 22 April 1996, and it was another year before a second machine was ready to take its place.

» Vertol and the hardy Chinook

After going through a bad patch, during which it, too, was forced to diversify its activities, Boeing's Vertol Division concentrated its efforts on improving the CH-47 Chinook, the first examples of which had commenced delivery in May 1967. It put forward a proposal to modernise 160 of the Army's helicopters. Designated model 347, the modernised version's prototype made its first flight on 27 May 1970, but the project was not followed up at that time.

The YUH-61A was Boeing Vertol's offering under the US Army's multi-role UTTAS helicopter programme. The first of two prototypes flew on 29 November 1974 and was handed over to the US Army for evaluation in late 1975. (Boeing)

At the same time, the US Army launched the Heavy Lift Helicopter (HLH) programme as a replacement for the Sikorsky CH-54. The Secretary of Defense at the time tried, unsuccessfully, to get the US Navy involved. Sikorsky and Boeing responded to the invitation to tender, with Vertol coming out as the winner in May 1971. The model 301 was to be powered by three Allison 501-M62B of 8,080hp (6,020kW) turning two glass-fibre rotors 28 metres in diameter. A prototype was ordered, designated XCH-62A, with the maiden flight planned for early 1976.

Construction of this 30-tonne monster, capable of carrying up to 35 tonnes, began in July 1974. However, its development proved to be difficult as well as expensive, leading Congress to vote for the cancellation of the programme on 25 July 1975. Meanwhile, the Vertol Division, which had become the Boeing Vertol Company in 1972, had taken part in two unsuccessful tenders, one, in 1973, for a new attack helicopter under the Advanced Attack Helicopter (AAH) programme[8], the other, in 1974, for a tactical

The CH-47 Chinook's carrying capacity is amply demonstrated here as it transports a Douglas C-47 belonging to the California National Guard, at Travis AFB, 6 December 2006. (USAF/D.W. Cushlan)

transport helicopter under the Utility Tactical Transport Aircraft System (UTTAS) as a replacement for the Bell UH-1 Huey. Boeing Vertol, with its model 179 (YUH-61A), was up against Sikorsky with its S.70 (YUH-60A), which, in December 1976, was declared the victor[9].

In June 1976, the Army finally decided to modernise its fleet of Chinooks so as to increase their operational capacity. The new CH-47D featured 3,750hp

Chinooks have taken part in numerous US operations around the world. Here, helicopters from the US Army's 10th Combat Aviation Brigade are on active service at Naray, Afghanistan, in January 2007. (US Army/M.J. Quaterman)

The MH-47 is a version of the Chinook designed for special operations. Here, a MH-47 from the 160th Special Operations Aviation Regiment prepares to land on the carrier USS Wasp in August 2005. (DoD/D.K. Simmons)

(2,790kW) T55-L-712 engines, advanced flight control and glass-fibre rotors. The prototype (YCH-47D) made its first flight on 11 May 1979 and 479 Chinooks were modernised under the programme, with the first being delivered on 20 May 1982. The Chinook was also widely exported and was even built under licence by Elicotteri Meridionali in Italy and Kawasaki Heavy Industries in Japan. Boeing Vertol registered its first success in the civil sector on 17 November 1978 when British Airways Helicopters Ltd ordered three model 234s, the civil derivative of the Chinook, for use over the North Sea as shuttles between Norway and the offshore oil rigs. In the ensuing years, Boeing Vertol continued to concentrate on the Chinook, developing new versions, notably the MH-47E for use by Special Operations Forces (SOF), of which the first of 26 examples appeared on 31 May 1990.

In December 1981, the Department of Defense sent out specifications for an advanced vertical-take-off aircraft, the JVX (Joint Services Advanced Vertical Lift Aircraft). During the technical validation process, it became clear that the Bell XV-15's[10] tiltrotor system

The third YV-22 (registered 163913) in hovering mode. Despite Bell's experience with convertible aircraft, particularly with the XV-15, the V-22's development proved to be troublesome. (Bell Textron)

8. The winner of the AAH programme was the Hughes AH-64 Apache.

9. The winner of the UTTAS programme was the Sikorsky UH-60 Blackhawk.

10. The Bell model 301 (XV-15) was a convertible, with the first of two prototypes flying on 3 May 1977.

The prototype of the Boeing Sikorsky RAH-66 Comanche in flight over West Palm Beach, Florida. Designed to be highly manoeuvrable, the RAH-66 also had a reduced radar and infra-red signature. Its state-of-the-art electronics allowed it to locate and 'prioritise' targets in just a few seconds. (Sikorsky)

On 28 May 1988, the first YV-22 emerged from the Arlington plant in camouflage and with the names of its future users along its sides: Marines, Air Force and Army. (Bell Textron)

was the ideal solution for the JVX. On 7 June 1982, Boeing Vertol and Bell Textron announced the formation of a joint 'Bell/Boeing Tiltrotor Team' that would undertake initial studies. Originally under the direction of the US Army, the JVX programme passed to the Navy in January 1983. A few months later, a contract was signed for the development of a convertible aircraft designated V-22 Osprey. Its in-service weight was 21 tonnes and it was powered by two rotatable Allison T406 engines of 6,150hp (4,586kN) turning two large propellers 11.58 metres in diameter. However, it was not until the autumn of 1985 that the programme received the Navy's final blessing, and six YV-22 prototypes and three static-test airframes were ordered on 2 May 1986.

Five versions were envisaged: the CV-22A for Air Force special operations, the HV-22A for Navy search and rescue (SAR) missions, the UV-22A for Army electronic warfare operations, the MV-22A assault aircraft for the Marines and the SV-22A US Navy ASM missions (this final version being soon abandoned). The start of production was planned for 1989, but the first prototype left the Arlington plant on 23 May 1988 and

When launched, the Bell-Boeing V-22 was the biggest convertible ever built. The design was evaluated on test beds such as the one pictured. (Bell Textron)

made its first flight on 19 March 1989. The following month, Secretary of Defense Dick Cheney proposed the programme's cancellation, but failed to gain sufficient support in his favour.

Unfortunately, on 11 June 1991, the fifth YV-22 was wrecked on its first flight and the following year, on 20 July, the fourth YV-22 also crashed. With the modifications required being so substantial, construction of the sixth YV-22 was halted. The programme's future came under threat but, with the arrival of a new defence secretary in 1993, further funding was allocated to development and the launch of production. On 24 March 1994, four MV-22Bs intended for production development were ordered, with the first one flying on 5 February 1997.

In 1982, the US Army invited several manufacturers to submit pilot studies under the LHX (Light Helicopter Experimental) programme with a view to acquiring 4,500 such machines. In April 1986, Boeing, in association with Sikorsky, won the development contract, beating off competition from a Bell-McDonnell Douglas consortium and, in April 1991, getting the green light to build two prototypes named

Seen head-on, with its landing gear retracted, the RAH-66 Comanche had a strange appearance. Its armament was to have been a General Electric 20mm cannon and up to 14 Hellfire anti-tank missiles. (Boeing)

The first two YV-22 Osprey prototypes undergoing final assembly at Bell. The technicians give a good idea of the size of the tilting rotors. (Bell Textron)

RAH-66 Comanche. The first of these took to the air on 4 January 1996. It featured stealth technology (giving it an unusual appearance), an airframe made entirely from composites and two LHTEC T800 engines of 1,530hp (2,053kN).

In the field of composite materials, Boeing Vertol built at its own expense an experimental tandem rotor helicopter, the model 360. When it made its first flight, on 10 June 1987, this helicopter, with a similar outline to the CH-46, was the largest in the world made from composites. Power was provided by two Textron Lycoming AL5512 engines of 4,200hp (3,139kW). However, the machine remained an experiment and it was never marketed. Also at this time, on 1 September 1987, the Vertol name disappeared, the firm henceforth being known as the Boeing Helicopter Company.

AGM-86s are installed in groups of three under the wings of a B-52 from the 319th Bombardment Wing on 13 November 1985. (DoD/B. Simonz)

Thanks to its tiny wing span, the AGM-86 cruise missile can cover considerable distances. Here, one is pictured on a test flight, on 1 February 1982. (DoD)

» New types of missile

The 1970s saw Boeing extend its activities relating to missile technology. The Air-Launched Cruise Missile, or ALCM-B programme, began in 1974. Along with nuclear submarines and ICBMs, piloted bombers were the third element on which the American deterrent strategy depended. Developed from a SCAD (Subsonic Cruise Aircraft Decoy), the ALCM was considered the way to deal with the Soviet air defence systems.

The first firing from a B-52 took place in March 1976, over New Mexico, with the first guided firings following in September of the same year. In August 1979, these AGM-86A missiles were followed by long-range ALCM-Bs (or AGM-86B) competing against a missile system offered by General Dynamics. Comparative tests lasted until 20 January 1980 and resulted in victory for Boeing with the signing of a production contract that envisaged operational service from B-52s from August 1981. The ALCM-B was a guided missile with a weight of 1,450kg and armed with a 200-kiloton nuclear warhead. Its 1,500-mile range allowed it to be launched outside the range of enemy air defence systems. Thanks to a sophisticated terrain-hugging system (TERCOM, or Terrain Contour Matching), it could fly at very low altitudes, which made it very difficult to detect on enemy radar. The B-52 could carry 20 ALCM-Bs, with 12 of them mounted on a rotating launcher inside the bomb bay.

In October 1968, having turned out 1,705 AGM-86Bs from its Kent factory in Washington State, Boeing

An AGM-86 cruise missile with wings folded is mounted under the wings of a B-52 at Hill AFB, Utah. (DoD)

A LGM-30G Minuteman III intercontinental ballistic missile is inspected in its silo at Grand Forks AFB, on 1 January 1989. (DoD/A. R. Wcheck)

A Minuteman III being fired from a silo at Vandenberg AFB, California, on 26 August 1985. (US Air Force)

began to convert some of the missiles into AGM-86Cs fitted with a conventional warhead containing 900kg of fragmentation explosive. Named Conventional ALCM (CALCM), the AGM-86C was provided with a GPS (Global Positioning System) that significantly enhanced its accuracy. The missiles were used for the first time operationally on 16 January 1991 in the initial phase of Operation Desert Storm against Iraq[11]. Elsewhere, a need to replace the SRAMs (see page 146) arose in August 1982 when the Air Force abandoned its efforts to update these missiles. Instead, in July 1983, the Defense Resources Board authorised the launch of the Advanced Air-to-Surface Missile programme (AASM), with Congress allocating funds on 20 September 1984. Boeing, Martin Marietta and McDonnell Douglas competed for the orders, with Boeing coming out as the winners. In 1985, the AASM programme was renamed SRAM II, but was cancelled on 27 September 1991 by President George Bush, along with the Minuteman III update programme, under the terms of the START (Strategic Arms Reduction Treaty) nuclear non-proliferation agreement

Boeing developed the FAADS battlefield defence system. It consists of a turret firing eight Stinger missiles. The system has been used in several foreign theatres, such as here at Ghazni, Afghanistan. The one shown here is from B Battery of the 3rd Battalion, 62nd Regiment (air defence). (US Army/C. Kaufmann)

11. That day, seven B-52Gs fired 35 AGM-86cs against the Iraqi air-defence control system.

NASA's B-52 launch aircraft

Needing to carry out flight testing on a range of craft, NASA used – and indeed still uses – a B-52 launch plane. In fact, the Dryden Flight Research Center has used three such planes over the years. A B-52A (serial number 52-0003), after being modified for the purpose by North American, was given the NB-52A designation. Taken out of service in October 1969, it was replaced by a RB-52B (serial number 52-0008), which became JB-52B, then NB-52B. It was withdrawn on 16 November 2004 and was recently replaced by a B-52H.

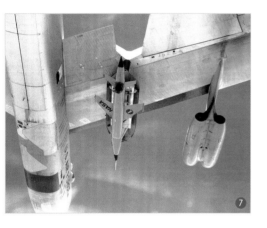

1. The X-38 seen from its NB-52B 'mothership' in November 1997. This was a forerunner of the Space Station Crew Return Vehicle. The programme was cancelled in late 2001. (NASA)

2. NASA's new B-52H on the tarmac at Dryden Flight Research Center, Edwards AFB, on 7 October 2003. (NASA)

3. The North American X-15 at high altitude just before being launched from the NB-52A in January 1965. (NASA)

4. The NB-52A flying low over the Dryden Flight Research Center on 27 March 2004, after successfully launching the second X-43A. (NASA)

5. The NB-52B, on 10 August 1971, moments after launching Northrop's M2-F3 Lifting Body. (NASA)

6. The NB-52B is ready to launch the third X-43A Hyper-X over the Pacific Ocean, on 16 November 2004. For this test, the X-43A was powered by a Pegasus booster rocket, which took it to a speed of Mach 9.8. (NASA)

7. Seen here from the chase plane, the Drone for Aeroelastic Structures Testing is attached under the NB-52B's wing. These tests took place between September 1979 and June 1980. (NASA)

8. The Highly Maneuverable Aircraft Technology programme (HiMAT) was conducted between July 1979 and January 1983 using two remote-controlled craft powered by a General Electric J85-21 engine. (NASA)

9. Spin tests using the Spin Research Vehicle (SRV) took place from November 1977 to July 1981. A model of an F-15 Eagle fighter was used in the tests. (NASA)

10. A spectacular landing during tests of the space shuttle's parachute brake. The tests were carried out at Rogers Dry Lake starting on 20 July 1990. (NASA)

Inherited from Rockwell International's Missile Systems Division, the Hellfire anti-tank missile became a part of Boeing's missile catalogue following the merger. The Hellfire can be fired from either a vehicle or a helicopter. (Rockwell International)

signed by the USSR and the United States[12]. Nonetheless, the test programme was partially completed with 16 firings between February 1992 and May 1994[13].

In addition to these programmes, Boeing designed and developed several Forward Area Air Defense Systems (FAADS), one of these being the Avenger defence system. It consisted of a turret mounted on a HMMWV[14], stabilised by gyroscopes and armed with eight Stinger FIM-92[15] ground-to-air missiles. The first

tests took place in April 1984, with the first production examples being delivered from 1 November 1988 and deployed for the first time in 1991 during Operation Desert Storm. Built at the Huntsville, Alabama, plant, more than 1,000 Avengers have been supplied to the US Army. In March 1995, they were complemented by the Bradley Linebacker system, which utilised Bradley M2 and M3 caterpillar-tracked vehicles as a platform. Put into production in November 1996, the system is provided with four Stinger missiles and a 25mm cannon.

» A major player in the conquest of space

In July 1970, despite having already signed big development contracts with North American Rockwell and McDonnell Douglas for building the space shuttle[16], NASA decided to instigate a series of complementary studies on alternative designs. It was in this context that Boeing joined with Grumman, under a contract signed on 29 December 1970, to put forward a different shuttle design. What emerged from these studies was the H33, a 90-metre-long craft comprising a 'booster', powered by 12 rocket engines and 12 Pratt & Whitney JTF-22A-4 fanjets, and an 'orbiter' fitted with three rocket engines and four JTF-22A-4s. The total take-off weight of this vehicle would have been close to 2,000 tonnes and had it actually been started in March 1972, as intended, the first orbital flight would have taken place in April 1978, but in the event nothing came of it.

Meanwhile, on 29 April 1971, the Jet Propulsion Laboratory (JPL) had made public its decision to work with Boeing on a variation of the Mariner interplanetary space probe. Christened Mariner 10[17], its mission was to fly over and photograph the surface of Venus then to continue its journey towards Mercury. Because of the position of these two planets relative to

The Mariner 10 space probe on its 'cart', ready to be placed in the launcher's nose cone. (NASA)

This computer-generated picture shows the partially assembled International Space Station. (NASA/JSC)

Launch of a Delta II rocket from Vandenberg base, California, on 14 December 2006; a reconnaissance vehicle was being put into orbit. (USAF/R. Freehand)

the Earth, launch had to take place during the fourth quarter of 1973. Fitted with two TV cameras, a radio transmitter, ultra-violet spectrometers, magnetometers and an infra-red radiometer, Mariner 10 weighed 526kg. The probe was launched from Cape Kennedy on 3 November 1973, arriving over Venus three months later (5 February 1974) and making a first pass over Mercury on 29 March 1975. Going into orbit around the Sun, the probe made two further approaches to Mercury, on 21 September 1974 and 24 March 1975.

In the ensuing years, Boeing was to become increasingly involved in a variety of space programmes. In November 1975, NASA asked Boeing to design and build two craft for the Applications Explorer Mission (AEM). The first one, designated AEM-A, and intended to study the Earth and its atmosphere, was launched

on 26 April 1978 and placed into orbit 400 miles above the Earth. The second, AEM-B, was tasked with studying concentrations of ozone and aerosols in the atmosphere and was launched on 18 February 1979. At the same time, Boeing was also involved in the development of the structure for the Hubble space telescope, for which its engineers developed new

12. The START I treaty was signed in July 1991 and came into force in December 1994. The START II treaty was signed in January 1993 and was ratified by the United States in 1996 and Russia in 2000.

13. By the time it was cancelled, the programme's costs had almost doubled, rising from $800,000 to $1.4 million and with the Air Force planning to purchase 700 examples as against the original 1,633..

14. The HMMWV, or High Mobility Multi-purpose Wheeled Vehicle, is popularly known as the 'Humvee'.

15. The Stinger was originally intended to be used by infantry, on foot.

16. Signed in July 1970, these contracts were worth a total of $2.9 million.

17. Mariner 10, sometimes written as Mariner X, followed Mariner 9, which had flown over Mars in November 1971.

An AGM-84 SLAM missile is mounted under the left wing of a McDonnell Douglas F/A-18C Hornet from the US Navy's VFA-86 Squadron, in February 1998. (DoD/B. Fleske)

On 17 December 1996, an improved version of the SLAM air-ground missile, the SLAM-ER, began deliveries to the US Navy. At the time, the Navy envisaged acquiring 700 of these missiles. (MDC)

epoxy-resin and graphite-fibre-based materials. In March 1978, Boeing received another contract, this time to build the Inertial Upper Stage (IUS), a kind of space tractor designed at the request of the Space & Missile Systems Center, and intended to place satellites in high earth orbit, or interplanetary probes into their correct trajectory. The IUS weighed almost 15 tonnes and consisted of two stages: the first stage had a rocket engine delivering 19 tonnes of thrust (188kN) and the second stage was fitted with a rocket engine of 8,160kg thrust (80kN). Its first use took place on 30 October 1982, when it was launched on a Titan 3 rocket to put two communications satellites[18] into geosynchronous orbit. This was followed, on 4 April 1983, by the first use of an IUS launched from the space shuttle Challenger to place satellite TDRS-A into orbit. Between 1982 and 1997, the IUS was used in this way 20 times.

In March 1985, Boeing began preliminary studies on the International Space Station (ISS) and, in August 1993, NASA chose Boeing to be the lead contractor in the project, which would culminate in the construction of the largest orbiting space station ever built. As big as two football pitches, the structure would be progressively assembled in sections at an altitude of 200 miles. As the lead firm in the programme, Boeing was responsible for the design, development and integration of its constituent elements, for which it had to coordinate the work of thousands of suppliers from 16 different countries. In 1993, the European Space Agency (ESA) and the Japanese Space Agency (NASDA) joined the programme. These were joined at the end of the same year by Russia, whose lengthy experience of long-duration space flight with Salyut and Mir was to make a valuable contribution.

Perhaps less spectacular and certainly less well-known to the public, the international Sea Launch programme welcomed Boeing aboard on 3 April 1995.

The Inertial Upper Stage (IUS) was developed to launch satellites into a high orbit. (NASA/KSC)

This was a completely new approach to the means of putting telecommunications satellites into orbit. The principle was to eschew land-based infrastructure, using instead a floating launch pad, which would be taken to the equator for launches and taken back to Long Beach, California, for maintenance between missions. Boeing brought to the programme all its experience of systems integration and space-project management. The project began to take shape when, in December 1995, the keel of the Sea Launch Commander was laid at Kvaerner naval dockyards and Hughes Space & Commercial Company signed a contract for a first batch of ten satellite launches.

Boeing had now regained its position as world leader of the aeronautical industry. At the end of 1996, the Boeing Commercial Airplane Group, with its 87,000 employees, was the larger of the Boeing Company's two sectors, accounting for 75% of total turnover. In the course of that year, it had received 717 orders (as against 346 the previous year), which took its rate of production up from 22.5 aircraft a month to 40 by the end of 1997. As for the Boeing Defense & Space Group, it too had increased its turnover, thanks in particular to the ISS programme and further growth would not be long in coming.

The shuttle Discovery approaching the International Space Station on 28 July 2005 and carrying the Multi-Purpose Logistics Module (MPLM) Rafaello. (NASA/MSFC)

18. These were satellites DSCS-2 and DSCS-3.

On 14 February 2004, a Delta rocket carries a military surveillance satellite and an Inertial Upper Stage as it lifts off from Cape Canaveral's launch pad no. 40. (USAF)

Sea Launch is an innovative concept in which launchers are fired from a floating pad located near the equator. (Boeing)

The interior of the International Space Station. (NASA/JSC)

The X-32A made its first flight on
18 September 2000, at Palmdale, in the
hands of Fred Knox. In its CTOL
(Conventional Take-Off and Landing)
configuration, it is powered by a Pratt &
Whitney F119 engine. It is seen here at Luke
AFB, Arizona, on 4 May 2001.
(DoD/SSgt C.J. Matthews)

CHAPTER 7

Endless horizons

>> By the early 1990s, it was becoming clear that there were more aeronautical manufacturers in the United States than the market could bear. Already, overcapacity in the aeronautical industry had seen manufacturers such as Fairchild LTV drop out. By 1992, there were only seven manufacturers who were capable of independently designing and developing advanced aircraft types: Boeing, General Dynamics, Grumman, Lockheed, McDonnell Douglas, Northrop and Rockwell. It was evident that in the short-to-medium term just three or four manufacturers were going to suffice. In the field of subcontracting, things were going the same way.

At this time, Boeing's priorities were productivity and cost control. Market pressure in the commercial aircraft field had obliged the Seattle group to reduce drastically its workforce, which had gone from 165,000 employees in 1989 to 120,000 by 1993.

>> An era of mergers

In 1993, aiming to make a comeback in the military market, Boeing had attempted a takeover bid for the aeronautical side of General Dynamics but was beaten to the post by Lockheed, who acquired it for $1.5 billion. At the time Boeing had no major military programme, bar military variants of its commercial jets, which is why its role as Lockheed-Martin's partner on the Advanced Tactical Fighter (ATF), later to become the F-22A Raptor, was of such critical importance – as was the Joint Strike Fighter (JSF) programme. Aware of

the company's vulnerability to the great cyclical fluctuations in the civil market, Boeing's management adopted a new strategy of having a presence in all of the principal aerospace markets so as to reduce their reliance on the civil sector (which at this point accounted for 75% of Boeing's turnover). The only way to achieve this was by mergers and acquisitions.

In October 1995, the announcement of a possible link between Boeing and McDonnell Douglas took the aeronautical industry by surprise, but in the end negotiations came to nothing. However, the following year McDonnell Douglas announced its intention to cooperate with Boeing on future airliner development. Were the two companies preparing the way for a merger? Whatever their reasons, a few months later Boeing announced the purchase of its St Louis competitor for $13 billion.

Meanwhile, on 6 December 1996, Boeing acquired most of the space and military activities of Rockwell

After the ban on flights instigated by the Pentagon in December 2000, tests with the Osprey resumed on 29 May 2002 at the Patuxent River naval base. (US Navy)

International Corporation[1]. The various divisions were gathered into an entity called Boeing North American Incorporated and henceforth functioned as a Boeing subsidiary. The remainder of Rockwell's activities (avionics, automation, communications, semi-conductors, etc) not included in the deal were formed into a new enterprise under the Rockwell name.

Boeing ended 1996 with a well-filled order book. That year, the Seattle company had netted 668 civil aircraft orders (against 379 the previous year), entailing an increase in monthly output from 22½ aircraft at the end of 1996 to 40 by the end of 1997. Boeing had reckoned on delivering 340 planes in 1997 (in fact, it delivered 321) and 550 planes in 1998 (the actual number was 509). The increase in orders was a direct consequence of the steady rise in passenger numbers around the world during the preceding years[2] and Boeing's commercial experts estimated that growth would continue for at least a further five years. According to them, the growth in traffic combined with the need for replacement of outdated planes would generate a market for around 17,000 new aircraft up to 2017.

In the military and space fields, 1996 had witnessed the first flight of the RAH-66 helicopter, the production launch of the V-22 Osprey (with the first deliveries expected in 1999), the continuation of the JSF programme, the starting of assembly work on the pre-production F-22As (at Lockheed-Martin) and the signing of a contract with the Air Force to develop and test, in partnership with Lockheed-Martin and TRW, an airborne laser capable of destroying ballistic missiles.

The RAH-66 Comanche's origins dated back to

21 June 1988, when the US Army had put out a tender for the design of a fast, manoeuvrable, armed reconnaissance helicopter employing stealth technology. Two pairs of manufacturers were involved: Bell/McDonnell Douglas and Boeing/Sikorsky. The selection of the latter pair was made public on 5 April 1991 and the first of the two prototypes (YRAH-66) emerged from the shops on 25 May 1995. On 4 January 1996, the first prototype made its inaugural flight, marking the start of a two-year programme to test the machine's aerodynamic and structural qualities, as well as evaluating the new 2,198hp (1,639kW) LHTEC T800-LHT-801 engines. The Comanche was the first production-series helicopter to make full use of fly-by-wire control[3]. The second prototype would make its first flight in September 1998, and tests were to be followed by an initial order for six machines.

The first MV-22B Osprey destined for the EMD, or Engineering & Manufacturing Development, establishment flew on 5 February 1997 and was delivered to the naval centre at Patuxent River, Maryland, where it was joined by other machines for EMD. In April 1997, the Defense Acquisition Board authorised a start on production of a first small batch of MV-22Bs with the first one flying on 30 April 1999.

The Marines' MV-22B Ospreys are designed to operate from type-LHA amphibious assault ships. An MV-22B is seen coming in to land on the deck of the USS Saipan, on 17 January 1999, during tests of its suitability for carrier-borne operations. (US Navy/1CL B.D. Olvey)

Tests on the RAH-66 Comanche light attack helicopter were already well advanced when the US Army cancelled the programme. (Sikorsky)

After several serious accidents during operational evaluation, flights and production were halted. The whole programme was the subject of an audit and the Ospreys were grounded for 17 months. The enquiry discovered that one of the accidents was caused by faults in both the hydraulic and electronic systems. Rectification of the problem promised to be time-consuming and the programme was substantially delayed.

» The purchase of McDonnell Douglas

On Thursday 1 August 1997, the Boeing Company merged with the McDonnell Douglas Corporation. Philip M. Condit retained his position as chairman and managing director of Boeing, while Harry C. Stonecipher, former chairman of McDonnell Douglas, became president. With the acquisition of Rockwell, this made Boeing the world's biggest aerospace manufacturer. Organisationally, the new enterprise was structured around three principal divisions: the Commercial Aviation Group, Space & Defense Systems and the Shared Services Group.

However, apart from this strategic regrouping, 1997 was not a good year for Boeing. For reasons unconnected with the McDonnell Douglas merger, the financial results for 1997 were disappointing, showing a net loss of $178 million. This was principally due to significant production difficulties in the commercial aircraft division. The measures taken to double aircraft production in response to the volume of orders had had the effect of so disrupting the Renton and Everett plants (where the 737 and 747 were built) that production was held up for a month. It required all of Alan Mulally's will and determination to bring the company safely out of the crisis. Despite these problems, Boeing managed to deliver 321 airliners in 1997, compared with 219 in the

1. This acquisition involved the following companies: Space Systems Division of Downey, California; Rocketdyne Division of Canoga Park, California; Autonetics & Missile Systems Division of Anaheim, California; North American Aircraft Division of Seal Beach, California; North American Aircraft Modification Division of Anaheim, California; Collins International Center of Richardson, Texas; Systems Development Center of Seal Beach, California; and a 50% share of Rockwell's interest in United Space Alliance, a joint venture with Lockheed-Martin Corporation of Houston, Texas.

2. Between 1992 and 1996, passenger traffic grew at 5.7% per annum.

3. Helicopters like the Dauphin 6001, the Kawasaki BK117 and the Bö 105 S3 had already made experimental use of such a control system.

previous year, an increase of 39%, and won 528 new orders to a total value of $39.1 billion. By the year's end, taking all models into account (including McDonnell Douglas's MD-80, MD-90 and MD-11) the order book was worth $93.8 billion. In achieving these figures, it is clear that Boeing had been far from inactive.

This 737-890 (registered N546AS) was delivered to Alaska Airlines on 3 February 2005. (Alaska)

» A new generation of 737s

With the Airbus A320's breakthrough in the United States, Boeing's design department had begun work on a direct competitor to the European plane, to be positioned between the 737-400 and the 757-200 in its range. In a bid to reduce development costs, Boeing tried, unsuccessfully, to link up with the Japanese on the project. Study was therefore directed towards new derivatives of the 737. In fact, they were much more than derivatives, being a completely new family of aircraft, taking the generic designation of 737X (or Next Generation 737).

In 1993, with the market more buoyant, Boeing officially announced the launch of the 737X family, Southwest Airlines being the first customer with an order for 63 of the base model, the 737-700. Though similar in appearance, the new 737s differed from the old, or standard, 737s in a number of ways, notably new aerofoils, extensive use of composite materials and new alloys aimed at weight reduction, and CFM56-7 engines that were more powerful, quieter and less-polluting than the CFM56-3s used in the previous generation. Naturally, all these changes

In an effort to improve productivity, Boeing reorganised the 737's production lines. Instead of being arranged at an angle in the assembly plant, the aircraft were built in a true line that moved forward by a few centimetres every hour. (Boeing)

brought about a significant improvement in performance.

The new-generation 737s were offered in four versions: 737-600, -700, -800 and -900, offering between 132 and 189 seats. The first 737-700 flew on 9 February 1997 and went into service with Southwest Airlines on 18 January 1998. This version was followed by the 737-800 with its fuselage lengthened by 5.84 metres, giving a capacity of up to 189 passengers. It made its first flight on 31 July 1997 and went into service with the German company Hapag-Lloyd in April 1998. Meanwhile, the first 737-600 had flown on 22 January 1998 and entered service with the Scandinavian Air System (SAS) on 25 October of that year. The last representative of the new family was the 737-900 with its even longer fuselage (2.54 metres longer), although, initially, it carried no more passengers than the 737-800 (later on, Boeing offered the 737-900ER version, which, with no increase in fuselage length and a new layout of the emergency exits, could carry 215 passengers). Alaska Airlines was the first customer with an order for ten aircraft and an option on a further ten. The new-generation 737's arrival on the market would boost the sales of this model. The 1,988th and final standard 737 emerged from the factory on 9 December 1999. Five years later, the 1,500th aircraft of the new generation – a 737-800 – would be delivered to ATA Airlines.

The 737 was not the only new aircraft of the year. On 6 January, Boeing announced the launch of a new version of the 767, the 767-400ER, specially adapted to the internal American market and having an increased payload of 46,540kg, or 129m³. The first customer for the new version was Delta Air Lines and the first aircraft flew on 9 October 1999, although, as things turned out, it was Continental Airlines who put the first 767-400ER into service, on 14 September 2000. Like the 767-200ER and 300ER, the 400ER was offered with Pratt & Whitney PW4062 or General

The 737-800 was the second version of the new-generation 737. The fuselage was lengthened by 5.84 metres and its take-off weight increased to 76.4 tonnes. It made its first flight on 31 July 1997 and FAA certification was granted on 13 March of the following year. This is an American Airlines 737-823 pictured in November 2000. (R.J. Francillon)

A longer-range version of the 767-200 was announced by Boeing in January 1983. It had an additional 14,000-litre fuel tank in the central part of the wings. Seen here is an Israeli El Al 767-27E (ER) landing at Los Angeles. (C.E. Porter via R.J. Francillon)

Two Southwest 737-7H4s: Southwest was the 737-700's first customer, announcing an order for 63 aircraft that entered service from 18 January 1998. (R.J. Francillon)

Sobelair, a subsidiary of Belgian airline Sabena, used this former Air France 767-328ER between 1996 and 2001. After a period of service with Asiana Airlines, this plane is now with Royal Air Maroc. (R.J. Francillon)

Electric CF6-80C2B8F engines and had a maximum, fully loaded range of 6,550 miles (400ER) or 7,600 miles (200ER). However, there were no takers for this version and the programme came to nothing.

These aircraft were very welcome in a growing market. Indeed, between 1993 and 1997, air travel increased by an average of 5.7% a year and experts predicted an average annual increase of around 5% over the next two decades.

»A return to the defence market

In the military field, the Information Space & Defense Systems (ISDS) group would henceforth account for 40% of Boeing's turnover. The year 1997 had been distinguished by some major events. On 7 September the F-22 Raptor had made its first flight, during which it had climbed to 4,500 metres in under three minutes. The F/A-18E/F Super Hornet and the V-22 Osprey had started production, while F-15s had been delivered to Israel, F-18s to Malaysia and Chinook helicopters to Britain. In addition, Boeing had gained the contract to modernise the NATO AWACS aircraft.

In space, where Boeing was now NASA's leading supplier, ten Delta rockets had been successfully launched and the space shuttle had been launched eight times. Finally, the International Space Station (ISS) was now 70% complete.

The following year, 1998, Boeing took the lion's share of the Air Force's major contracts. It was selected to design and develop a new satellite launcher, the EELV (Evolved Expendable Launch Vehicle). Intended to replace the Delta II rockets, it would be 25% cheaper in use. Additionally, Boeing delivered the production JDAM to the Department of Defense in June and was chosen to coordinate the new anti-missile missile under the National Missile Defense Program. Finally, the first production Super Hornet flew on 6 November at St Louis, the first aircraft in an initial batch of 12 planes.

Boeing also hoped to emerge as the winner of the competition organised for the JSF programme. 'We believe our approach to the JSF will offer an unbeatable cost/performance ratio,' claimed Boeing's management[4]. The origins of this programme dated back to 1990. In that year, the Advanced Research Project Agency (ARPA) had begun preliminary studies on an inexpensive, lightweight STOVL fighter, usable by the Air Force, Navy and Marines (the Common Affordable Lightweight Fighter or CALF). The following year, contracts for a pilot study had been signed with Lockheed-Martin and McDonnell Douglas to lead phase 1 of a development programme for a Supersonic Strike Fighter (SSF). This phase was particularly intended to test the method of powering the future

The F/A-18E Super Hornet had already made its first flight, on 29 November 1995, when Boeing bought McDonnell Douglas. This carrier-borne fighter-bomber is still in production. (US Navy)

A Delta IV is launched from Cape Canaveral, Florida, in February 2003. (DoD)

4. Quoted in Boeing's annual report for 1998.

An F/A-22 Raptor dropping a bomb at supersonic speed over the Panamint Mountain firing range, California, in July 2005. (USAF/D. Russell)

aircraft. Known as JAST (Joint Advanced Strike Technology), this idea was soon incorporated in the CALF programme and gave rise to three aircraft based on a common technology: a conventional-take-off-and-landing strike aircraft for the Air Force, a strike aircraft for the Navy with a larger aerofoil and good low-speed performance, and a short-take-off-and-vertical-landing aircraft for the Marines and the Royal Navy. Three aircraft builders presented their plans: McDonnell Douglas (in association with Northrop Grumman and British Aerospace), Boeing and Lockheed-Martin. McDonnell Douglas's proposals were rejected and, in November 1996, demonstrators were ordered from Boeing (designated X-32A for the CTOL and X-32B for the STOVL) and from Lockheed-Martin (X-35A and X-35B). A few months later, Northrop Grumman joined Lockheed-Martin, followed shortly by British Aerospace.

In the civil arena, Boeing remained the biggest supplier of airliners in the world. In 1998, out of the 12,000 jet airliners in service around the world, around 10,000 were Boeings. Beside the problems already mentioned, Boeing was also badly hit by the economic crisis in Asia.

The order book was getting empty, with the 747 programme particularly badly hit. The company was thus obliged to take steps to reduce its aircraft output

from five to two planes a month in 1999 (and then down to just one a month in early 2000). With misfortune never arriving singly, the situation was compounded by cuts in both the defence budget and at NASA. Despite the unpromising context, Boeing managed to deliver 509 airliners, compared with 321 the previous year.

An F/A-18F Super Hornet from the VFA-102 Squadron is catapulted from the deck of the carrier USS Kitty Hawk, on 28 February 2004. The Super Hornet replaced the F-14 Tomcat in the Navy's carrier-borne fleet. (US Navy)

After the purchase of McDonnell Douglas, the MD-95 became the Boeing 717-200. A total of 555 of the type were built before production ceased. (Boeing)

>> The growth of the 700 family

The MD-95 was just 14 months old at the time Boeing took over McDonnell Douglas and, once the merger was complete, Boeing rebranded the aircraft and brought it into the 700 family. Thus on 8 January 1998, the MD-95 became the model 717 (or more precisely the 717-200), taking over the KC-135 model number that had never been used for civil purposes. The first 717-200 emerged from McDonnell Douglas's Long Beach plant (now called Douglas Products Division) on 10 June 1998 and made its first flight on 2 September. Meanwhile, production of the very last

Douglas aircraft continued, with the final MD-80 going to TWA on 21 December 1999. This was followed two weeks later by the delivery of the first two 717-200s to the Bavaria International Leasing Company. By the end of 2006, Boeing had delivered 155 model 717s.

In the 757 family, a new version, the 757-300, was developed for European charter companies. It made its first flight on 2 August 1998 and had its fuselage lengthened to accommodate up to 279 passengers. Condor Flugdienst was the 757-300's first customer, with its first commercial flight taking place on 19 March 1999. On 2 May 2000, American Airlines put in an order for 20 757-300s, taking the total sales of the twin-engined jet over the 1,000 mark. Starting in 2001, 34 British Airways planes were to be rebuilt into cargo aircraft; designated 757-200 (SF) – SF for Special Freighter – these aircraft were stripped of their passenger-carrying interiors, and the first one flew on 15 February 2001. On 14 February 2002, Boeing delivered its 1,000th 757. However, orders for 757s would soon begin to slow appreciably and this slump in sales would bring about the end of production by the end of 2004.

Following the introduction of the 777-200ER the previous year, 1998 witnessed the 777-300's entry into service with Cathay Pacific in May. Development of a very-long-distance version, the 777-200LR, would start in February 2000. This version for 301 passengers was distinguished by its increased wingspan and GE90-110B1 jet engines of nearly 50 tonnes thrust. It could now cover over 10,500 miles, or 2,000 miles more than the 200ER and 300ER. However, with customers showing little enthusiasm for this version, its development was slow, the first 777-200LR not flying until 8 March 2005, followed by entry into service in the first quarter of 2006.

Financially speaking, although 1998 was an improvement over the previous year, it was still not up to the expectations of the company's management. Earnings were just over $1.2 billion and the profit margin was no more than 2.8%. Boeing therefore sought to improve productivity, particularly by taking another look at the 747 programme with a view to reducing production costs by investing £52 million in a huge employee-training programme, as well as cutting the size of the workforce. In addition, the ISDS group was reorganised by splitting it into two parts: the Military Aircraft & Missile Systems Group and the Space & Communication Group.

Despite the continuing fall in orders in 1999 (only 355), the year witnessed an improvement in results, both in turnover ($58 billion) and profits, with

The 757-300 received certification on 22 January 1999 and entered service with Condor Flugdienst in the following March. ATA Airlines took delivery of this 757-33N on 25 September 2001, but has since disposed of it. (C.E. Porter via R.J. Francillon)

deliveries also up (573 planes). Commercial aircraft now accounted for 66% of the total turnover, which ran counter to the strategy that had been pursued. The new 737's success was sustained, with 278 of these aircraft delivered during the year. On the other hand, the fate of the aircraft inherited from the McDonnell Douglas merger was sealed: Boeing announced that production of the MD-80, MD-90 and MD-11 would be halted the following year and, on 9 February, the civil helicopter sector was sold to the Dutch firm RDM[5]. As for the long-term development of the market, Boeing's commercial experts were expecting reduced annual growth of 4.7% up to 2019.

Meanwhile, Boeing had made an entry into the executive jet market with the Boeing Business Jet (BBJ) version of its 737, which rolled off the production line on 27 July 1999. This plane had been announced in

---

5. This comprised the MD 500E and MD 530F conventional helicopters, as well as the MD 520N and MD 600N models fitted with the NOTAR system.

Boeing announced the 777-300 version in June 1995 and All Nippon Airways was the first airline to use it after its certification on 4 May 1998. This Japan Airlines 777-346 was photographed at Osaka-Itami on 4 September 1999. (T. Wang via R.J. Francillon)

July 1996 and made its first flight on 22 February 1999. It was the first time that Boeing had offered an executive aircraft. 'Winglets' fitted to the wing tips had been specially developed for this version and effected such an improvement in the plane's performance that some airline companies modified their 737-700s accordingly and others ordered aircraft with this feature. Announced in October 1999, the BBJ-2 was a more spacious version, with 25% more cabin area.

However, in the military sector, turnover declined by $0.8 billion. Activity in this sector was very diverse and no single programme, other than the C-17, accounted for more than 15% of turnover. Deliveries were down in all the programmes apart from the F/A-18E/F Super Hornet, which was just going into production (with a contract worth $8.9 billion over five years for a total of 222 aircraft) and the AH-64 Apache strike helicopter. In addition, Boeing had delivered the first F-15E Eagle since 1994 to the Air Force, having in the meantime supplied 75 of the planes to Israel and Saudi Arabia. At the same time, the Navy had signed a five-year $650 million contract to continue the T-45 Goshawk trainer aircraft programme. In the missile sector, the first conventional cruise missiles (CALCM) had come off the production line at St Charles, Missouri and, on 16 October, the Air Force had announced its intention to go ahead with the launch of 19 Delta IV rockets.

Originally designed by McDonnell Douglas, the C-17A Globemaster III made its first flight on 15 September 1991. Pictured here is a C-17A from the 437th Airlift Wing based at Charleston AFB, South Carolina. (USAF/Sgt R.E. Cooley)

The situation was identical in the space sector, with a small decline in the turnover and with the ISS as the principal programme. On 27 March 1999, the first commercial launch by the Sea Launch system had been a success. The floating launch pad had arrived at its home port on 4 October 1998, travelling via the Suez Canal, the Indian Ocean and the Pacific.

Since its entry into operational service on 17 January 1995, the C-17A has taken part in all of the United States' foreign interventions. Seen here is an impressive line-up of Globemaster IIIs during Operation Iraqi Freedom. (USAF)

civil aircraft sector saw its share of total turnover drop to 61%.

Turnover in the military sector remained at the same level as the previous year, but it was even more diversified, with no programme exceeding 8% of the total. The doubling of Super Hornet deliveries could not compensate for the fall in deliveries of other equipment, the F-15E being a case in point with just five delivered. For the Department of Defense, the Joint Strike Fighter was the principal programme, where Boeing was in contention with its X-32, which, on 18 September 2000, was the first to take to the air.

Winglets were introduced on the BBJ and then offered as an option on the whole 737 range. Developed by Richard T. Whitcomb, these additions substantially increase an aircraft's range. (A. Pelletier)

From this angle the X-32A's delta wing is clearly revealed, as well as its two 'butterfly' fins. (Boeing)

» Boeing keeps on growing

Maintaining its strategy of acquisition, Boeing began the year 2000 by scooping up the space and communications activities of the Hughes Electronics Corporation for $3.75 billion. This was the company that had built the automated Surveyor lunar probes. Then, on 15 August 2000, Boeing announced the acquisition, for $1.5 billion, of Jeppesen Sanderson Incorporated, a leader in the field of navigational maps and, in October 2000, via its subsidiary, Boeing Australia, Boeing purchased Hawker de Havilland, a designer and builder of structural parts for civil and military aircraft. In the same month, Boeing announced the creation of three new business units: Connexion by Boeing, Air Traffic Management and Boeing Capital Corporation.

Despite the civil sector's fall in production (Boeing would deliver only 482 airliners in the year 2000, but received 588 orders), the firm made huge strides in productivity, notably by slashing the time required to build the 737 from 30,000 hours to 10,000. Still dominated by this model (279 aircraft delivered), the

The X-32B short-take-off-and-landing version made its first flight on 22 March 2001, with the first vertical landing occurring on 3 July. (Boeing)

An AH-64D Apache, from the 1st Infantry Division, 4th Brigade, is made ready for its next mission over Iraq, on 24 April 2004. (US Army)

Originally designed by Hughes, then built by McDonnell Douglas, the Apache is still in production and winning several export orders. Here, an AH-64D from the 1st Battalion, 101st Airborne is seen over Iraq in November 2005. (US Army)

It was followed, on 24 October 2000, by its competitor, the X-35A. On 26 October 2001, the Lockheed-Martin aircraft was declared the winner of the contest. The choice was down to political/economic considerations as much as purely technical ones. For Lockheed-Martin, the future was looking particularly auspicious, as potential orders were estimated to be around 3,000 aircraft.

>> Boeing leaves its historic cradle

For Boeing, as for many other companies, the year 2001 occurred in two parts: before 9/11 and after 9/11, whose effects would certainly be felt in the financial results for the following year. On 21 March 2001, Boeing revealed its intention to move its headquarters from Seattle to a place separate from its manufacturing bases and other activities. After much consideration, the city of Chicago was chosen and Boeing started work from its new world HQ on 4 September 2001.

On 10 July 2002, Boeing combined its space, military, governmental, information and communications activities in a single business unit under the name of Integrated Defense Systems (IDS). The products in the IDS fold included the F/A-18E/F Super Hornet, the F-15E Eagle, AV-8B Harrier II Plus, F/A-22 Raptor, C-17 Globemaster III, C-32A and C-40A, T-45 trainer system, 767 refuelling tanker, AC-130U, RAH-66 Comanche, CH-47 Chinook, AH-64D Longbow and the V-22 Osprey. The missile systems included the Conventional Air-launched Cruise Missile (CALCM), the anti-ship missile Harpoon, the Standoff Land Attack Missile Expanded Response (SLAM-ER), the Joint Direct Attack Munition (JDAM), and the new technologies intended for drones and

The T-45 Goshawk is a distant derivative of the Hawker Siddeley Hawk designed in the early 1970s. Here, a T-45C from the 1st Training Air Wing makes a touch-and-go landing on the carrier USS Harry S. Truman, on patrol in the Atlantic on 2 March 2004. (US Navy)

Also derived from a British-designed aircraft, the AV-8B Harrier is used by the Marines' attack squadrons. One is seen here being directed to its take-off spot on the flight deck of the amphibious assault ship USS Bataan on 8 January 2002, during Operation Enduring Freedom. (US Navy)

Sixty-one F-15Ds were delivered to the US Air Force, as well as 13 to Israel (under the Peace Fox programme) and 19 to Saudi Arabia (under the Peace Sun programme). Here, an F-15D from the 4th Fighter Wing (336th EFS) flies over Afghanistan on 12 April 2006, during Operation Mountain Lion. (USAF)

A pair of heavily armed F-15Ds flying over Iraq in May 2004. (USAF)

Boeing has been involved in the production of the new air superiority F-22A Raptor. One is seen here being refuelled by a KC-135R in December 2002. The replacement programme for the venerable KC-135s is also underway. (USAF)

A total of 183 F-22A Raptors are expected to be delivered to the Air Force as replacements for the F-15C Eagles. Boeing's Seattle plant is participating in the production, under Lockheed Martin's direction. (DoD)

other pilotless aircraft. Space and communications equipment included AWACS, the EC/6A/B Mercury, the ISS, Sea Launch, the space shuttle and the next generation of GPS satellites. Boeing was also coordinating the Global Missile Defense programme being developed under the Ballistic Missile Defense Organization.

By the end of 2001, Boeing had increased its turnover by 13.4% and its operating margin had further improved to 6.2%. The firm had been

The wind-tunnel model of the Sonic Cruiser has been tested up to Mach 1.08. (Boeing)

especially active in the civil sector, announcing the launch of the extra-long-range 777-300ER, delivering the 1,000th new-generation 737 as well as the first 737-900, and launching the cargo version of the 747-400ER, the 747-400ERF.

» The amazing Sonic Cruiser

Around this time, Boeing was making an impression with the announcement of a revolutionary aircraft christened the 'Sonic Cruiser', which, according to the manufacturer, would fly faster and higher than any other plane in service, giving passengers a saving of 15% to 20% in flying times. The particular feature of the aircraft was to be its very high cruising speed without actually being supersonic (dubbed 'transonic').

Right back in the early 1970s, the design office had considered a three-engined plane of this kind for 200 passengers, but along with so many other projects, it had not lasted more than a few months. The idea of a transonic plane resurfaced in 2002 when Boeing, which had just abandoned the 747X bulk carrier, aroused much interest with the unveiling of its Sonic Cruiser project. The aircraft, with its futuristic appearance, had been designed to carry 200 to 250 passengers at Mach 0.95 (or even 0.98) over distances of 7,500 miles to 10,400 miles. It made use of the so-called 'canard' configuration and it was to have two large, fan-jet engines of 40 tonnes thrust, mounted at the rear, some distance away from the fuselage.

According to the development schedule, the Sonic Cruiser would be ready to fly by July 2006 and enter service before 2009. Once again, the project failed to be realised, with Boeing announcing its abandonment in December 2002. Bearing in mind the crisis into which the airlines had plunged, this was hardly a surprise. They were now far more interested in seat cost per kilometre than high performance, however appealing that might be.

On the military equipment side, Boeing got back into the refuelling-tanker market, launching a version of the 767 for Italy and Japan. At the same time, the firm delivered four C-17A Globemaster IIIs to the Royal Air Force and won a contract to update the avionics of the Lockheed C-130 Hercules. The year 2001 also witnessed the first flight of the EA-18G Growler, derived from the F/A-18 Hornet. In addition, despite frequent updating, the Grumman EA-6B Prowler had had its day and its withdrawal was fixed for 2008. In 1993, the idea had surfaced to develop a Command & Control Warfare (C2W) version of the F/A-18F Super Hornet. While no decision was taken at the time, McDonnell Douglas made some preliminary studies on this plane. The original version was shaping up to be

Intended to replace the ageing EA-6B Prowler, the EA-18G Growler makes considerable use of the former's electronic equipment. Here, a Growler has just made a tailhook landing on the runway at the Patuxent River naval base, Maryland, on 2 August 2006. (US Navy)

very expensive and, in late 1997, the US Navy asked Boeing to work on a less costly version. The result was the EA-18G Growler, which made use of the Prowler ICAP III's electronics. The first plane flew on 15 November 2001, followed by a second on 1 December and a third on 5 April 2002. In June 2003, the US Navy announced its intention to acquire 89 EA-18Gs,

Boeing's design department came up with the futuristic 'canard' shape for the Sonic Cruiser. (Boeing)

A GMD (Ground-based Midcourse Defense) medium-range, anti-missile missile is fired from launch pad 21 at Vandenberg base on 9 January 2004. Boeing is responsible for development and systems integration, such as radar and control and communications systems. (DoD/SSgt M.A. Gilliam)

The South Korean Air Force received 40 F-15Ks between 2005 and 2008. (Boeing)

between 2008 and 2012, to equip its ten carrier-based air groups. The first test EA-18G flew in late 2006 and the first production planes were to undergo an operational evaluation in 2008 before being delivered to the fleet. The first of these aircraft was delivered to the US Navy on 25 September 2007 and went into a test regime with the VX-23 Squadron.

In the missile and launcher theatre, the first ballistic missile interception tests under the GMD or Ground-based Midcourse Defense Program (formerly the National Missile Defense Program) passed off successfully, while the Air Force signed a production contract for 11,054 JDAMs with an option for an additional 1,150. Boeing had also fitted JDAM to Israel's F-16 Falcons. The 100th Delta II rocket had also been successfully fired and the Delta IV had received certification. It carried out its first mission for the Air Force on 10 March 2003.

>> The repercussions of 9/11

As was to be expected, the attacks of 11 September 2001 could only accentuate the fall in orders that had already begun over a year before. Between 2000 and 2001, they had decreased from 588 to 314 and they continued to drop in 2002. The management decided to apply shock treatment to get out of the crisis. Starting in December 2001, 35,000 employees were laid off. The range of aircraft was rationalised to include just four base models: 737, 747, 767 and 777 (the single-aisle planes were built at Renton and the long-haul aircraft at Everett). Finally, unprofitable sites and any activities outside the core business were simply sold off: Corinth to the French firm Labinal (in March 2003), Wichita to the Canadian firm ONEX (in February 2005) and Rocketdyne to United Technologies (in February 2005). Henceforth, Boeing concentrated

Some improbable Boeing designs

As in every design bureau across the world, Boeing's engineers have worked on an incalculable number of projects. Even if it were possible, listing them all would be beyond the scope of this book. However, here is a selection of some of those projects.

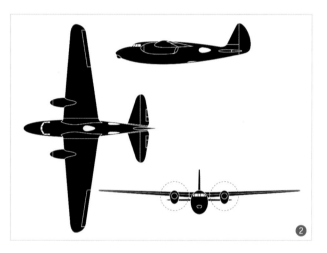

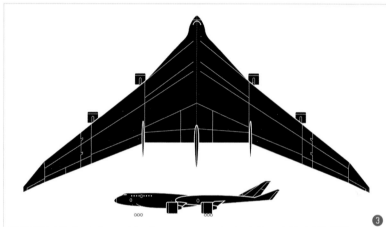

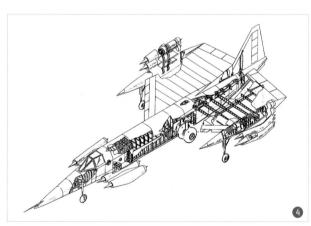

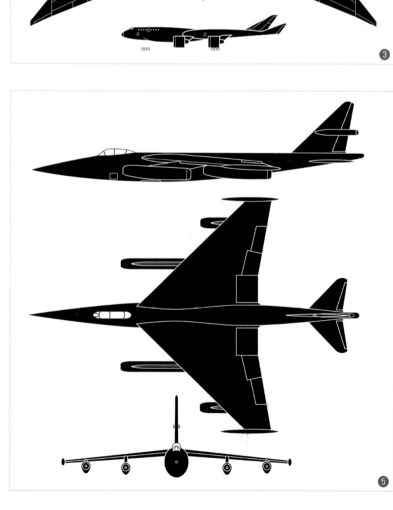

1. The ATT (Advanced Theater Transport) of 1999 was a tailless tactical transport aircraft. (Boeing)

2. The 1934 model 298 was an experimental bomber with Allison V-1710 V12 engines.

3. The 1991 model 747-XL was a 635-tonne civilian flying wing capable of carrying up to 800 passengers.

4. The 1958 model 818-102 was a single-seat interceptor powered by six jet engines.

5. The 1957 model 701-333 was one of the many configurations of the XB-59 bomber; this one had four J-73 engines.

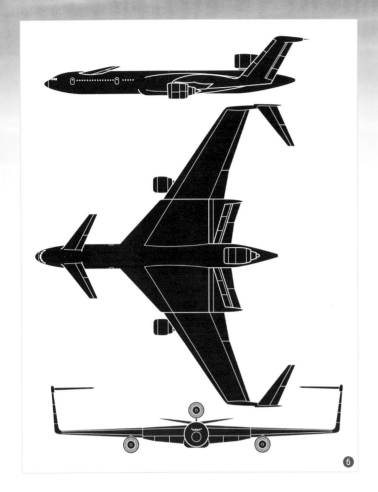

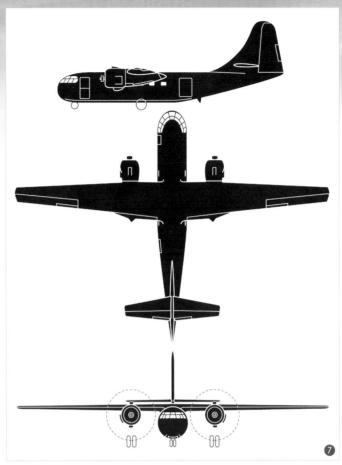

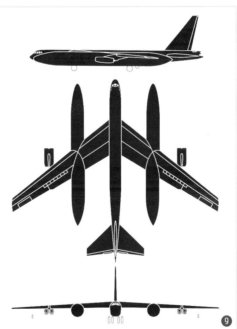

6. The 1995 model 2020A C-Wing was a project for a huge airliner carrying 650 passengers and made use of the non-planar wing concept.

7. The model 417 of 1944 was intended to knock the DC-3 off its throne.

8. The model 368 of 1943 was a fighter with a centrally mounted engine and counter-rotating propellers.

9. The 1957 model 464-245 was an extra-long-range B-52 variant with 157,000-litre external fuel tanks.

10. The model 473-48, of 1950, was one of the many pilot studies that led to the 707.

on design and final assembly of its aircraft. Thus 70% of the 787 Dreamliner's construction is sub-contracted.

In 2002, orders reached their lowest point since 1994 at 251 aircraft. At the same time, deliveries fell from 525 to 381 and earnings were just under $500 million. The civil aircraft sector's share of turnover was down to 53% of the total, while on the military side, contracts were signed for the supply of 60 C-17As to the Air Force and 40 F-15Ks to South Korea (under its F-X programme), with construction to begin in April 2003.

Reorganising once again, Boeing announced on 10 July the fusion of its space, defence, information and communication systems in a single business unit called Integrated Defense Systems (IDS). Boeing developed variants of the 737-700 for the military (the C-40A, B and C for the US Air Force and US Navy) and an airborne detection version for Australia (the 737-700 Wedgetail, the first six of which came off the Renton production line on 31 October 2002) and for Turkey, which ordered four 737 AEW&Cs (with an option on two more) on 4 July under the Peace Eagle programme. These were the most sophisticated planes to appear on the market since the introduction of the E-3 AWACS in the 1980s.

In 2003, civil aircraft orders remained at the same level, to within just two planes, but deliveries fell by a good quarter with only 281 aircraft delivered (the worst recorded result since 1993). Turnover dropped again and the operating margin slipped to no more than 0.8%. The workforce was trimmed to 157,000 compared with some 231,000 five years previously. However, forecasters remained bullish, reckoning on an annual increase in passenger traffic of 5% (6% for cargo) over the ensuing 20 years, translating into a global market of 24,000 new planes, or $1.9 trillion!

Under the Wedgetail project, 737-700 airframes were converted into flying AEW & C (Advance Early Warning and Control) platforms and fitted with Northrop Grumman MESA radar. Australia ordered four of these aircraft in December 2000. (Boeing)

» A brand-new kind of plane...

Since the time when Boeing had worked on the Compass Cope and Darkstar pilotless aircraft, the technology had progressed substantially. The military was beginning to make considerable use of such aircraft for reconnaissance missions. They now began to look at the next stage, pilotless combat planes, or Unmanned Combat Air Vehicles (UCAV). Boeing got involved in the development of such aircraft under a shared-costs programme with the Air Force and DARPA. From this emerged the X-45A, a tailless plane with a span of around ten metres and a load capacity of 1,350kg. It made its first flight on 22 May 2002, at Edwards AFB and began its test programme on 18 April 2004, during which it dropped a guided bomb while flying at over 10,000 metres. A few weeks later, work was started on assembling the operational version, designated X-45C, which was to go into competition with a similar aircraft developed by Northrop-Grumman, the X-47B.

Boeing's range of pilotless vehicles was not, however, restricted to this one plane. They had also developed a small reconnaissance vehicle named Scan Eagle, which was used by the Marines in Iraq (accumulating 3,000 hours of operational flights), a pilotless helicopter, the A160 Hummingbird, which had made its first flight, in California, on 15 June 2007, and a hybrid half-plane/half-helicopter, the X-50A Dragonfly, whose broad-bladed rotor became a fixed wing in cruising flight.

» The birth of the 787

Alan Mulally, the director of Boeing Commercial Airplanes, announced the development of a 'traditional-style', economy, medium-/long-haul aircraft with entry into service projected around 2008. Provisionally designated 7E7, this aircraft was intended as a replacement for the 757 and 767, as well as the Airbus A300 and A310. It was to make use of the new generation of more powerful but less thirsty fan-jet jet engines developed by General Electric, Pratt & Whitney and Rolls-Royce. Fuel consumption per passenger was 15%–20% less than with similarly sized conventional planes. On 16 December 2003, the board gave the go-ahead for the plane. It was not until the first order came in, on 24 April 2004 from All Nippon Airways (ANA) for 50 planes, that it received a name: the 787 Dreamliner. Once again, Boeing was thinking big.

In the context of high oil prices, the 787 promised fuel consumption 20% lower than that of its competitors. The choices announced for the 787 constituted a real break with tradition in aeronautical technology, but its design turned out to be highly complex, in particular because of the widespread use

The X-45A pilotless combat aircraft foreshadowed the definitive X-45C version, which would have a 1,500-mile range and a payload of 2 tonnes. The X-45A is seen here flying over Edwards AFB, California, in February 2005. (DARPA)

The Boeing Scan Eagle is a small battlefield reconnaissance and surveillance drone, launched using a pneumatic catapult. It also serves as a communication relay post. This one is being used in the 'Talon 2006' exercise on the Yuma Marines base, Arizona. (USMC)

To carry large sub-assemblies between the different factories involved in the 787's construction, Boeing converted some of its 747s into Dreamlifter versions. (Boeing)

Originally set up by McDonnell Douglas in April 1991, Phantom Works is today Boeing's driver of innovation. This is where the wildest dreams become reality. The organisation's mission is to come up with systems of advanced design, pushing the boundaries of technology so as to significantly improve performance, quality, construction and costs of Boeing's products and services.

With its headquarters in St Louis, Missouri, in former McDonnell Douglas territory, Phantom Works is a community of some 2,600 technicians and engineers spread throughout the entire enterprise, working on dozens of projects using shared IT systems. Once the design and development of a particular production technology or system have reached the point where they can be used in production, they are transferred to the civil and military programmes.

Among the recent output of Phantom Works is the Bird of Prey, an unusual-looking aircraft that first flew in 1996 and was instrumental in the development of stealth technology and the experimental pilotless aircraft such as the X-43 Hyper-X, X-45, X-48, X-50A Dragonfly and the Little

Boeing has been studying flying wings for some years. The X-48A seen here in the Langley Research Center's wind tunnel is the latest contribution to this research. (NASA)

Bird. Phantom Works is currently working on large flying-wing transport aircraft and, looking even further into the future, individual 'flying cars'.

The Bird of Prey was built and tested in complete secrecy over a period of several years. (USAF)

The multi-purpose, maritime Poseidon P-8A makes use of the 737-800 airframe. It is able to undertake not only reconnaissance missions but also anti-submarine and anti-surface-ship warfare. Construction began in 2007. (Boeing)

of composites (50% of the total weight), allowing a substantial saving in the plane's weight. Another new challenge was the use of a 3D digital model accessible by all the sub-contractors involved in the programme. In this way, the 6,000 engineers dispersed over 135 sites were able to work in real time. The 787 was not slow to attract customers. On 27 April 2005, Boeing announced that it had 237 options and firm orders.

Industrially, Boeing set up a production system inspired by the famous Toyota TPS (Toyota Production System). Out went the shop floor with the aircraft set out in two oblique rows. Henceforth, they were to be assembled one behind the other in a moving line, creeping forward at the rate of a few centimetres per hour, using mobile tool equipment so as to achieve maximum flexibility and the ability to have different 787 models on the same line. The big sub-assemblies built in Japan (by Kawasaki, Fuji and Mitsubishi), in Italy (by Alenia) and in the United States are assembled on the line after being transported by ship or in specially modified 747-400s named Dreamlifter (this model was certified by the FAA on 2 June 2007).

In the defence sector, 2003 was marked by an order from Japan for four 767 transport/tanker aircraft (KC-767J). At the very end of the year (29 December), contracts worth a total of $9.6 billion were signed for the production of 210 more Super Hornets and for the development of an electronic warfare version, the EA-18G. A few days before, the St Louis plant had delivered its last ASV-8B Harrier II, while the 300th Apache Longbow AH-64 strike helicopter was delivered on 20 June. An upgrading programme for the V-22 Osprey was launched, with the first modified machine being delivered to Patuxent River on 20 August 2003. Production had resumed and, by mid-2005, 63 V-22s of all types had been built. The first MV-22B would be supplied to the Marines on 8 December 2005.

Finally, 2003 ended with a change at the top. Philip M. Condit quit the post of managing director, with Harry C. Stonecipher taking his place. In 2004, the deterioration in the company's situation halted and the position stabilised. Orders and deliveries ceased their vertiginous fall (277 planes ordered; 285 delivered).

By 1 January 2008, the 787 Dreamliner had attracted 817 orders since the programme's launch in 1984. (Boeing)

Profits passed $1.8 billion and the operating margin rose to 3.8%. As for the civil aircraft sector's share of the company's overall activities, it continued to fall, stabilising at 40%.

While the 787 programme was underway, with order after order pouring in, Boeing announced, on 4 January 2004, the launch of a cargo version of the 747-400 with Cathay Pacific Airways as the first customer, and began preparations to convert at least six of its 747-400s into cargo aircraft.

As for military contracts, the Navy announced on 14 June that it had accepted Boeing's candidature for the development and production of the Multi-mission Maritime Aircraft, or MMA, intended to replace the ageing fleet of Lockheed P-3 Orions then in service. Based on the model 737-800, this aircraft was chosen in preference to Lockheed's own Orion 21, which had recently been renamed P-8A Poseidon. In the military helicopter sector, the durable Chinook family saw a new arrival in the form of the MH-47G, the first of which was handed over to the Special Forces on 7 May. However, there was bad news from the US Army when, on 23 February 2004, it cancelled the RAH-66 Comanche programme after it had swallowed up $6.9 billion. The decision stemmed from an economic survey conducted by the Army, which concluded that it was the best way to release funds for the necessary restructuring of the US Army[6].

Following this gloomy spell, 2005 marked Boeing's comeback on the aeronautical scene with a 57% leap in civil aircraft orders. That year, air traffic registered a 7.5% increase and the market for aircraft with more than 100 seats easily exceeded its previous high point of 1989 (1,587 aircraft) with 2,140 orders. With 1,028 net orders, Boeing had 48% of the market as against Airbus's 52% (1,111 orders). For Boeing, this substantially exceeded the record 1996 figure (668

The P-8A, whose prototype is seen here, will be powered, like the Wedgetail and the C-40, by two CFM56-7 engines, with equipment by Northrop Grumman, Raytheon and Smiths Aerospace. (USAF)

aircraft ordered). Furthermore, while Boeing had been overtaken by Airbus in the number of orders and deliveries, its share of the market in value terms was superior, with 55% and $112.3 billion. Airbus had made most of its sales in the single-aisle A320 segment, while Boeing had dominated the more remunerative segment for large, long-haul aircraft.

» The rejuvenated 747

As the Airbus A380 was making its demonstration tour in the Asia-Pacific area, Boeing announced the launch of the 747-8 on 14 November 2005. Two versions of this aircraft, up until then known as the 747-Advanced, were envisaged: on the one hand, the 747-8 Intercontinental passenger version; on the other, the 747-8 Freighter for cargo. The 747-8 Intercontinental is 3.6 metres longer than the 747-700 so as to carry 34 additional passengers, which makes it the only aircraft in the 400-500-seat bracket. It has a capacity of 450 passengers in three classes. This, however, is the least of its differences from its elder brother.

The 747-8 makes use of technology developed for the 787 Dreamliner, making it more economic and environmentally sound (lower noise levels and emissions). It makes use of new engines like the General Electric GEnc-2B67 with 30 tonnes of thrust (296kN), which, according to the Americans, are the best-performing engines in the world. Boeing claims that the running costs of the 747-8 will be 20% lower than those of the A380. In its cargo version, with its take-off weight of 435 tonnes, it will be able to carry

The first 787 outside the Everett plant on 8 July 2007. It was due to enter service in May 2008 with All Nippon Airways. (Boeing)

6. Despite this, the US Army plans to acquire 303 light helicopters to replace the 122 existing UH-1H and OH-58D models.

The 747-8 was to benefit from numerous improvements over the previous generation of 747s, especially in its use of composite materials and more fuel-efficient engines. The first order came from Atlas Air, for 12 of the 747-8F cargo versions, on 11 September 2006. (Boeing)

The Boeing YAL-1A is unique of its type being armed with a high-energy laser installed in the nose. It is seen here flying over Edwards AFB on 9 December 2004. (USAF)

138 tonnes of freight over a distance of 5,150 miles[7] and, if Boeing is to be believed, the 747-8 will be able to use 210 airports around the world without expensive infrastructure modifications.

In the military field, 2005 witnessed a new export success for the F-15. On 6 September, Singapore announced that it had chosen the F-15T (a similar aircraft to the F-15K apart from its radar) in preference to the Dassault Rafale as a replacement for its ancient Douglas A-4SU Skyhawks. Meanwhile, the first of four KC-767A refuelling tankers for the Italian military had made its first flight on 21 May, whilst development work was proceeding on the KC-767J version for Japan (making its first flight on 21 December 2006).

As for the ISS, assembly had begun on 28 November 1998 with the launch of a Russian Proton rocket carrying the Zarya command module. Between 1998 and 2005, 12 major sub-assemblies were launched and

The first KC-767J for the Japanese Air Self-Defence Force flew on 31 May 2005. It has since been fitted with its refuelling equipment at McConnell base in Kansas. Japan ordered three of these aircraft in April 2003. (Boeing)

assembled in space. By November 2005, the ISS had grown in weight to 183 tonnes with 425m³ of living space, and 16 countries were now involved in the programme[8]. When it is finished, the space station will weigh 420 tonnes and it is expected to be in use until at least 2016.

After a record-breaking 2005, air transport experts expected orders in 2006 to hold up, particularly in view of the high cost of aviation spirit, which encourages companies to accelerate the renewal of their fleets, and also because of the projected 5% to 6% annual increase in traffic over the next 20 years. This situation has favoured the birth of new companies, especially those in the low-cost segment of the market[9].

In addition, the market has become weighted by Asian airline companies, whose orders make up 43% of the total. Boeing has profited the most from this

situation over Airbus which, despite serious problems with the A350 and A380, was still posting good results (its second-best commercial year).The best seller of all types remains the 737, with the range being enhanced in August 2006 by a new, higher-capacity and longer-range version, the 737-900ER, which obtained its certificate on 20 April 2007, with its first customer being the Indonesian company Lion Air[10].

Over the whole of 2006, and for the first time since 2000, Boeing moved ahead of Airbus in terms of orders (1,058 net orders as against 790). On the other hand, Airbus kept its first place in deliveries (434 against 398), even though Boeing's deliveries had

---

7. The A380-800F cargo version will be able to carry 150 tonnes of freight.

8. Belgium, Brazil, Canada, Denmark, France, Germany, Italy, Japan, Netherlands, Norway, Russia, Spain, Sweden, Switzerland, United Kingdom, United States.

9. Orders from low-cost companies represent a third of total sales and a half of all medium-haul aircraft acquisitions.

10. Lion Air ordered 30 737-900ERs on 30 June 2005.

The Royal Australian Air Force ordered four C-17A Globemaster IIIs as replacements for its old Lockheed C-130 Hercules. (Australian DoD)

Boeing received a very sizeable order from the Australian company Qantas, with 45 787s purchased and an option for a further 20. In 2006 alone, the company took no fewer than 160 orders for its new aircraft and, on 31 December 2007, the 787 had amassed 817 firm orders. In the same month, using the digital model, Boeing's teams successfully achieved the first virtual construction of the 787. This virtual assembly permitted the engineers to check that the 5,000-odd elements from the different sub-contractors would fit together correctly when the real aircraft was built.

The 787's first flight, originally scheduled for August 2007, was moved forward to spring 2008 when assembly problems were encountered. With such a substantial order book, Boeing has enough work to occupy its assembly lines until 2013. As a consequence, a second assembly line, to be ready for 2011, is on the agenda, although no decision has yet been taken. Additionally, the numerous suppliers and partners will need to keep pace with this level of production. To simplify the range of options available and save customers' time, Boeing opened, in January 2007, the Dreamliner Gallery, where all the different types of equipment available (seats, materials, seat coverings, lighting, etc) are displayed along with 3D systems providing simulations. No more expensive 'à la carte' fitting-out arrangements...

increased by 37%. As for the market prospects of the civil airliner manufacturers over the next 20 years, Boeing's experts continue to see them rising. They estimate that the combination of rising air traffic and replacement of old aircraft will generate a need for 27,210 planes with a global value of $2.6 trillion[11].

In the current range of programmes, the 787 will clearly take centre stage. On 13 December 2005,

The 737's final version to date is the 737-900ER, which emerged from the Renton plant on 8 August 2006. Its first customer was Lion Air, an Indonesian airline based in Jakarta, which ordered 30 aircraft. (Boeing)

In the KC-135 replacement contest, Boeing carried out a 'dry boom' refuelling demonstration between a KC-767A destined for Italy and a B-52H from the AFFTC research centre at Edwards AFB. (DR)

Just at the moment when the 787 had its whole future ahead of it, a final page in the history of the American aeronautical industry was turned. On 13 April 2006, the very last Boeing 717 (ex-MD-95) left the Long Beach plant after a total of 16,791 aircraft had been built there, marking the end of Douglas and its aircraft.

In 2006, Boeing's military activities remained varied. On 3 March 2006, the Royal Australian Air Force announced its intention to acquire four C-17A Globemaster IIIs for its 36th Squadron based at Richmond (New South Wales). The first one arrived in Australia on 4 December 2006, going to the Amberley (Queensland) base to replace the Hercules C-130Hs that had been in service for 48 years! More recently, on 1 February 2007, the Canadian government ordered four C-17As, with the first being delivered on 12 August to the 8th Wing stationed at Trenton. However, these orders were insufficient to keep the

C-17 production line going and Boeing took steps to close it by mid-2009.

Boeing's management has its eyes on a much bigger programme that some have not hesitated to call the 'contract of the century'. This is the KC-X replacement programme for the Air Force's KC-135 refuelling tankers. After an initial invitation to tender, which was later cancelled when Congress determined that the process had not been fair[12], the Air Force repeated its request on 25 September 2006 and launched a final invitation to tender on 12 February 2007 to the two selected competitors: Boeing, with its KC-767 proposal (a derivative of the 767-200LR), and Northrop

11. These 27,210 aircraft would comprise 16,540 single-aisle planes, 6,230 twin-aisle planes, 990 heavy-haul planes and 3,450 short-haul planes. A more recent market study estimated the number of aircraft needed between now and 2025 at 28,600.

12. It was discovered that someone at the Pentagon who was responsible for procurement was also applying for a job with Boeing.

This simulation gives an idea of how the future HH-47 combat search and rescue Chinook might look (CSAR-X programme). It is due to equip the US Air Force from 2012. (Boeing)

The X-48B Flying Wing during its first flight at Edwards AFB, California, on 20 July 2007. (NASA Dryden)

Grumman-EADS, with a proposal based on the Airbus A330 (the KC-330). The winning consortium will walk away with a contract worth around $200 billion with four test aircraft and 175 production aircraft spread over 15 years starting in 2010.

On the helicopter side, the Chinook range was widened with the appearance of two new models. On 23 October 2006, the first new CH-47F made its maiden flight, with the US Army planning to acquire 55 examples to add to the 397 CH-47Ds that had been rebuilt to the CH-47F standard, and the 58 MH-58Gs that had been ordered. Additionally, the Secretary for the Air Force, Michael W. Wynne, announced on 9 November that the HH-47 version of the Chinook had been chosen (in preference to the Lockheed-Martin US101 and the Sikorsky HH-92) under the CSAR-X (Combined Search & Rescue) tender contest to replace the HH-60G Pave Hawks in service with the Air Force. If tests are satisfactory, this programme could generate orders for 141 HH-47s to be delivered between 2012 and 2019. The first delivery of a CH-47F to an operational unit took place on 14 August 2007.

The 58th Special Operations Wing based at Kirtland, New Mexico, is equipped with CV-22B Ospreys. One of the convertibles is seen being delivered on 8 July 2006. (USAF)

As for the Osprey, after a difficult development period, the year 2006 finally saw its entry into service. On 3 March, the Marines' VMM-263 Squadron became the first unit operational with MV-22s. The current requirement for the Marines is for 360 MV-22s, which will allow for the re-equipment of 16 squadrons with CH-46s and four squadrons with CH-53Ds. As for the Air Force, on 20 March 2006 it allocated the first CV22 to the 58th Special Operations Wing, based at Hurlburt Field, Florida.

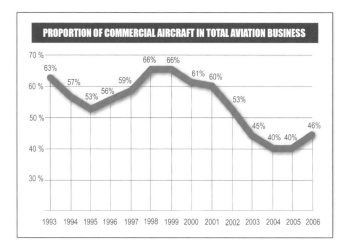

» Endless horizons

Boeing today is a global enterprise of over 153,000 employees spread across the 48 States and in 70 countries along with 6,451 suppliers working for it in around 100 countries. With a turnover of $61.53 billion in 2006, up by 15%, and a civil airliner order book worth $250 billion, ensuring at least four years of production, Boeing look to the future with serenity. By 31 December 2007, 817 orders had been received for the 787. Over 2007 as a whole, Boeing beat all its records for civil airliner orders with 1,423 aircraft, of which 850 were for the 737. Boeing currently has 3,400 orders, which is enough to ensure work for several years

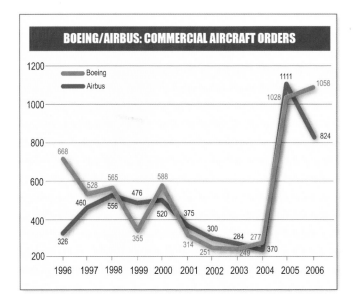

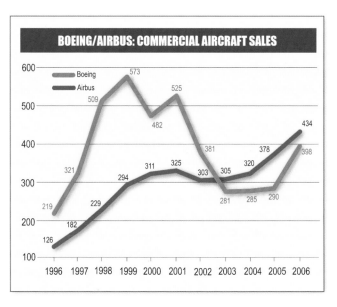

to come. The firm has consequently revised its 2008 forecast, expecting a turnover of more than $70 billion and the delivery of between 515 and 520 aircraft.

A further challenge for Boeing is located far from our planet. On 4 December 2006, NASA unveiled its programme for the establishment of a permanent base on the Moon as the first stage in a much larger project to put men on Mars from 2020. As a leader in the aerospace industry, Boeing is bound to be significantly involved with this project, which will open up limitless horizons. From the Red Barn to the Red Planet will have taken just over a century.

Boeing's past few years have been marked by substantial media coverage of two major projects: the 787 Dreamliner programme and the bid for the KC-X tanker. As for the latter project, the original February 2008 invitation to tender had resulted in the acceptance of the Grumman-Northrop/EADS bid, but this was contested, leading to the issue of a new invitation, on 25 September 2009, for the supply of 175 aircraft. There is no doubt that this would be a big challenge for Boeing as the historical provider of such aircraft to the US Air Force (with the KB-29, KB-50, KC-97 and KC-135).

The 787 faced severe setbacks caused by technical and production problems, which delayed the maiden flight by two years over the original schedule. Since the aircraft came off the construction line, the first flight had been postponed seven times, not finally taking place until 15 December 2009. It has to be said that the Chicago company had faced numerous and indeed significant problems with this programme. This was the first time that a jet airliner had made use of such a high proportion of composites (over 50% of the primary structure). The strategy of contracting out 80% of the production also demonstrated its limitations, bringing many technical problems and knock-on delays in its wake.

In the military sphere, while the tanker programme awaited the result of the new tendering process, another programme appeared to be proceeding without any problems. This was the P-8A Poseidon patrol aircraft intended to replace the Lockheed P-3 Orion, whose prototype had flown half a century before. The first two Poseidons made their maiden flights on 27 April and 5 June 2009 respectively.

Boeing was sparing no effort to sell the C-17A Globemaster III, with Qatar putting in an order for two aircraft on 21 July 2008 and the United Arab Emirates ordering six on 6 January 2010. A new version of the F-15, the F-15SE, designed for export, was unveiled on 17 March 2009, while the F-18E Super Hornet continued its career with the entry into squadron service of the first EF-18G Growler on 4 June 2008. In addition, the US Navy took delivery of its 400th Super Hornet on 24 July 2009. Finally, the venerable CH-47 Chinook helicopter was given a shot in the arm with the modernised CH-47F version, 191 of which were ordered by the US Army in August 2008 with service in the 1st Cavalry Division beginning on 18 November 2009.

The 787 was heralded as the biggest commercial success ever, with 851 aircraft ordered by 56 different airlines by the end of 2009. But this should not be allowed to overshadow the other 'members of the family', starting with the 747, which underwent rejuvenation in its 747-8 version (and should have made its first flight by the time this book appears), and the 737 which continued its remarkable success, with the landmark of 6,000 aircraft being passed on 16 April 2009. With 481 aircraft delivered in 2009, Boeing achieved the target of 480-485 deliveries it had set itself at the start of the year. As for orders, the company had taken in 263, but against this must be placed 121 cancellations. Nonetheless, the order book was still well filled, with no fewer than 3,375 aircraft to be built.

Appendices

APPENDIX 1

>> Aircraft designed by Boeing 240

APPENDIX 2

>> Performance figures and design features of
Boeing aircraft and helicopters 245

APPENDIX 3

>> Missile data 250

APPENDIX 4

>> Jet airliner orders (1958–2007) 251

APPENDIX 5

>> Jet airliner deliveries (1958–2007) 251

APPENDIX 6

>> Military aircraft deliveries (1995–2007) 252

APPENDIX 7

>> The Boeing family tree 252

APPENDIX 8

>> Boeing's financial results (1996–2007) 253

APPENDIX 9

>> Key to acronyms 253

APPENDIX 10

>> Index of aircraft mentioned in the text 254

APPENDIX 11

>> Index of persons mentioned in the text 255

Aircraft designed by Boeing

The table below is a list of the aircraft and other models designed by Boeing from its origins to the present day. Boeing began using a numbering system for its models in 1925, starting at model 40, with numbers 1–39 being applied retrospectively to the 39 types already designed, which had up to that point been identified simply by letters. Starting at this time, a number was subsequently allocated to any new aircraft design, even if it never got past the pilot-project stage. Later on, batches of numbers were allotted to specific design

studies. Thus batch 104–199 was reserved for aerofoil sections, batch 500–599 was reserved for gas turbines and 600–699 for missiles. With the proliferation of design variants, this numbering system became more complex, allowing identification of the slightest variation of a particular model. For obvious reasons of space, in this table, any aircraft that failed to proceed beyond the planning stage is referred to only by the generic model number, while aircraft that were actually built are identified by their specific model number.

Model number	Start of design work	First flight	Description / type	Usual designation & name (programme)	Ordered by/ first customer	Crew & passengers (max)	Typical engine package	Power/ thrust per engine	Status	Number built
1	1916	29/06/1916	Biplane/floatplane	B & W	–	2	1 x Hall-Scott A-5	125hp		2
1A	1966	15/07/1966	Replica	B & W 1A	Boeing	2	1 x Lycoming GO-435	170hp	Replica	1
2	1916		Biplane/floatplane	C-4	Boeing	2	1 x			1
3	1917		Biplane/floatplane	C-5, C-6 and C-11	US Navy	2	1 x Hall-Scott A-7A	100hp		3
4	1917		Basic trainer	EA	USAAS	2	1 x Curtiss OXX-3	100hp		2
5	1917		Biplane trainer	C-650-700, C-1F and CL-4S	US Navy	2	1 x Hall-Scott A-7A	100hp	Into production	52
6	1919	27/12/1919	Biplane boat plane	B-1	US Mail	1 + 2	1 x Hall-Scott L-6	200hp		1
6D	1928	04/1928	Four-seat boat plane	B-1D	Canada	1 + 3	1 x Wright J-5	220hp	Into production	2
6E		04/03/1928	Boat plane	B-1E		1 + 3	1 x P&W Wasp	410hp	Into production	6
7	1919	07/01/1920	Commercial boat plane	BB-1	A/c Mfg Co.	1 + 2	1 x Hall-Scott L-4	130hp		1
8		24/05/1920	Commercial transport	BB-L6	H. Munter	1 + 2	1 x Hall-Scott L-6	200hp		1
10	1921	05/1921	Ground-attack triplane	GA-1	USAAS	3	2 x Liberty 12A	435hp	Into production	10
10	1922		Ground-attack biplane	GA-2	USAAS	3	1 x Eng. Div. W-18	750hp	Prototypes	2
15	01/1922	02/06/1923	Fighter biplane	PW-9	USAAS	1	1 x Curtiss D-12	435hp	Into production	32
15A	10/1925	19/06/1926	Fighter biplane	PW-9A	USAAS	1	1 x Curtiss D-12C	435hp	Into production	25
15B	10/1925		Fighter biplane	PW-9B	USAAS	1	1 x Curtiss D-12D	435hp	Prototype	1
15C	06/1926	09/07/1927	Fighter biplane	PW-9C	USAAS	1	1 x Curtiss D-12D	435hp	Into production	40
15D	08/1927	28/05/1928	Fighter biplane	PW-9D	USAAS	1	1 x Curtiss D-12D	435hp	Into production	16
16	1920		Multi-purpose biplane	DH-4B, DH-4M-1, O2B-1	USAAS	2	1 x Liberty 12A	420hp	Into production	354
21	1924		Trainer biplane	VNB-1, NB-1/-4	US Navy	2	1 x Lawrance J-1	200hp	Into production	77
40	04/1925	07/07/1925	Mail transport		Boeing	1	1 x Liberty	400hp	Prototype	1
40A		20/05/1927	Mail and passenger transport		BAT	1 + 2	1 x P&W Wasp	420hp	Into production	23
40B		1928	Mail and passenger transport		BAT	1 + 4	1 x P&W Hornet	425hp	Into production	?
40C		16/08/1928	Mail and passenger transport		Pacific AT	1 + 4	1 x P&W Wasp	420hp	Into production	10
40H		1929	Mail and passenger transport		Canada	1 + 4	1 x P&W Hornet	425hp	Into production	4
40X			Passenger transport		Associated Oil	1 + 2	1 x P&W Hornet	425hp		1
40Y		10/12/1928	Passenger transport		Standard Oil	1 + 2	1 x P&W Hornet	425hp		1
42	1924		Observation biplane	XCO-7, XCO-7A, XCO-7B	USAAS	2	1 x Liberty 12A	420hp	Prototypes	3
50	09/1924	05/08/1925	Patrol boat plane	PB-1, XPB-2	US Navy	5	2 x Packard 2A-2500	800hp	Prototype	1
53		12/1925	Fighter biplane	FB-2	US Navy	1	1 x Curtiss D-12D	410hp		2
54	12/1924	01/1926	Fighter biplane	FB-4, FB-6	US Navy	1	1 x Wright P-1	450hp	Prototype	1
55	12/1924	18/1-/1925	Fighter biplane	FB-3	US Navy	1	1 x Packard 1A-1500	510hp	Prototypes	3
56	*1925*	*–*	*Observation seaplane*	*–*		*2*	*1 x Packard 1A-1500*	*500hp*	*Project*	*–*
58	06/1925	07/1926	Fighter biplane	XP-4	USAAS	1	1 x Packard 1A-1500	510hp	Prototype	1
63		04/05/1927	Torpedo biplane	TB-1	US Navy	3	1 x Packard 3A-2500	730hp	Into production	3
64		02/1926	Trainer biplane		PAT	2	1 x Wright J-3	200hp	Prototypes	2
66	11/1925	14/07/1927	Fighter biplane	XP-8	USAAS	1	1 x Packard 2A-1500	600hp	Prototype	1
67		07/10/1926	Carrier-based fighter biplane	FB-5	US Navy	1	1 x Packard 2A-1500	520hp	Into production	27
68			Advanced trainer biplane	AT-3	USAAS	2	1 x Wright Hispano E	180hp	Prototype	1
69		03/11/1926	Carrier-based fighter	XF2B-1, F2B-1	US Navy	1	1 x P&W R-1340B	425hp	Into production	33
69B			Fighter	–	Export	1	1 x P&W R-1340	425hp	Prototypes	2
72	*1927*	*–*	*Passenger transport*	*–*			*1 x Wright Whirlwind*		*Project*	*–*
73	*1926*	*–*	*Passenger transport*	*–*		*5*	*2 x Wright J-4*	*200hp*	*Project*	*–*

Model number	Start of design work	First flight	Description / type	Usual designation & name (programme)	Ordered by/ first customer	Crew & passengers (max)	Typical engine package	Power/ thrust per engine	Status	Number built
74		02/03/1927	Carrier-based fighter	XF3B-1	Boeing	1	1 x P&W R-1340	425hp	Prototype	1
77	06/1927	03/02/1928	Carrier-based fighter	F3B-1	US Navy	1	1 x P&W R-1340-80	425hp	Into production	73
80	1928	08/1928	Passenger transport	Model 80	BAT	3 + 12	3 x P&W Wasp	410hp	Into production	4
80A		1928	Passenger transport	Model 80A	BAT	3 + 18	3 x P&W Hornet	525hp	Into production	10
80B		1930	Passenger transport	Model 80B	BAT	3 + 18	3 x P&W Hornet	575hp		1
81		1928	Basic trainer	XN2B-1	US Navy	2	1 x Fairchild-Caminez	125hp		2
81A		27/12/1928	Basic trainer		BSA	2	1 x Axelson	145hp		1
81B		1929	Basic trainer		BSA	2	1 x Axelson	115hp		1
81C		1932	Basic trainer		BSA	2	1 x Kinner K-5	100hp		1
82	1927	–	Passenger transport	–		6	3 x Fairchild-Caminez	120hp	Project	–
83		25/06/1928	Fighter biplane	XF4B-1	US Navy	1	1 x P&W R-1340B	500hp	Prototype	1
89		07/08/1928	Fighter biplane	XF4B-1	US Navy	1	1 x P&W R-1340B	450hp	Prototype	1
93	03/1928	09/1928	Fighter biplane	XP-7	USAAC	1	1 x Curtiss V-1570-1	600hp	Prototype	1
95	1928	29/12/1928	Mail/freight transport	Model 95	BAT	1	1 x P&W Hornet	525hp	Into production	25
95A		1932				1	1 x P&W R-1340	500hp	Experimental	1
96	05/1928	18/11/1930	Monoplane fighter	XP-9	USAAC	1	1 x Curtiss SV-1570-15	600hp	Prototype	1
99	11/1928	06/05/1929	Fighter biplane	F4B-1, F4B-1A	US Navy	1	1 x P&W R-1340-8	500hp	Into production	27
100		06/1929	Trainer biplane		Air Commerce	2	1 x P&W R-1340	450hp	Into production	4
100A		25/07/1929	Biplane		H. Hughes	2	1 x P&W R-1340	450hp		1
100E			Biplane		Siam	1	1 x P&W R-1340	450hp		2
100F		20/06/1932	Experimental biplane		P & W	1	1 x P&W R-1535	700hp	Experimental	1
101		11/04/1929	Fighter biplane	XP-12A	USAAC	1	1 x P&W R-1340-9	525hp	Prototype	1
102	11/1928	11/04/1929	Fighter biplane	P-12	USAAC	1	1 x P&W R-1340-7	500hp	Into production	9
102B	06/1929	12/05/1930	Fighter biplane	P-12B, XP-12G	USAAC	1	1 x P&W R-1340-9	500hp	Into production	90
104 to 199			Aerofoil sections							
200		06/05/1930	Monoplane mail plane	Monomail	Boeing	1	1 x P&W Hornet B	575hp	Prototype	1
202		30/01/1930	Monoplane fighter	XP-15	USAAC	1	1 x P&W SR-1340D	525hp	Prototype	1
203	03/1929	01/07/1929	Trainer biplane		Boeing School	1 + 2	1 x Axelson	145hp	Into production	4
203A		29/08/1929	Trainer biplane		Boeing School	1 + 2	1 x Wright J-6-5	165hp	Into production	3
203B			Trainer biplane		Boeing School	1 + 2	1 x Lycoming R-680	220hp	Conversion	4
204	1929		Boat plane			1 + 4	1 x P&W Wasp	410hp	Into production	7
204A			Mail boat plane			2	1 x P&W Wasp	420hp		1
205		02/1930	Monoplane fighter	XF5B-1	US Navy	1	1 x P&W SR-1340C	485hp	Prototype	1
208	1929	–	Patrol boat plane	–		5	2 x P&W Hornet	525hp	Project	–
214		05/11/1931	Monoplane medium bomber	Y1B-9	USAAC	5	2 x Curtiss GIV-1510C	600hp	Prototype	1
215		13/04/1931	Monoplane medium bomber	XB-901, YB-9	USAAC	5	2 x P&W R-1860-13	575hp	Prototype	1
218		29/09/1930	Monoplane fighter	XP-925 and XP-925A	Boeing	1	1 x P&W R-1340D	525hp	Demonstrator	1
221		18/08/1930	Monoplane mail/passenger	Monomail	BAT	1 + 6	1 x P&W Hornet B	575hp	Prototype	1
221A		1930	Monoplane mail/passenger	Monomail	BAT	1 + 8	1 x P&W Hornet B	575hp	Prototype	1
222		30/01/1930	Fighter biplane	P-12C	USAAC	1	1 x P&W R-1340-9	450hp	Into production	96
223		1931	Carrier-based fighter biplane	F4B-2	US Navy	1	1 x P&W R-1340-8	500hp	Into production	46
226		1930	Luxury passenger transport	Model 226	Stanavo		3 x		Conversion	1
227	11/1930	02/03/1931	Fighter biplane	P-12D and XP-12H	USAAC	1	1 x P&W R-1340-17	500hp	Into production	35
234	03/1931	15/10/1931	Fighter biplane	P-12E, P-12J, YP-12K, XP-12LK, A-5, F4B-4A	USAAC/USN	1	1 x P&W R-1340-17	500hp	Into production	110
235	04/1931	1931	Carrier-based fighter biplane	F4B-3, F4B-4	US Navy	1 / 1	1 x P&W R-1340-10 / 1 x P&W R-1340-16	500hp / 500hp	Into production / Into production	21 / 92
236	06/1931	01/02/1933	Carrier-based fighter biplane	XF6B-1, XBFB-1	US Navy	1	1 x P&W R-1535-44	625hp	Prototype	1
238	1931	–	Monoplane passenger transport	–		2 + 15	3 x P&W Hornet	550hp	Project	–
239	1931	–	Passenger transport biplane	–		2 + 15	3 x P&W Hornet	550hp	Project	–
243	1931	–	Passenger transport	–	UAL		2 x		Project	–
246		14/07/1932	Monoplane medium bomber	Y1B-9A	USAAC	5	2 x P&W Y1G1SR-1860B	600hp	Into production	5
247	1932	08/02/1933	Passenger transport	Model 247	United A/L	2 + 10	2 x P&W S1D1 Wasp	550hp	Into production	60
247A		14/09/1933	Research and testing		P&W	2 + 6	2 x P&W Twin Wasp Jr	625hp	Experimental	1
247D		1934	Passenger transport	C-73	Philips Petrol.	2 + 10	2 x P&W S1H1G Wasp	500hp	Into prod.+ conv.	13
247E			Test bed		Boeing	2	2 x P&W S1H1G Wasp	500hp	Conversion	1
247Y		01/1937	Armed transport		China	2 + 6	2 x P&W S1H1G Wasp	500hp	Conversion	1
248		20/03/1932	Monoplane fighter	XP-936, XP-26, Y1P-26, P-26	USAAC	1	1 x P&W SR-1340E	522hp	Prototypes	3
251	12/1931		Fighter biplane	P-12F	USAAC	1	1 x P&W R-1340-21	550hp	Into production	25

Model number	Start of design work	First flight	Description / type	Usual designation & name (programme)	Ordered by/ first customer	Crew & passengers (max)	Typical engine package	Power/ thrust per engine	Status	Number built
256		1932	Biplane fighter	C1B	Brazil	1	1 x P&W S1D1 Wasp	550hp	Into production	14
257	*1945 ?*		*Interceptor*	*–*		*1*	*2 x stato-jet engines*			*–*
264	08/1933	20/01/1934	Monoplane fighter	XP-940, YP-29A	USAAC	1	1 x P&W R-1340-31 1 x P&W R-1340-35	550hp 600hp	Prototypes	3
266	01/1933	10/01/1934	Monoplane fighter	P-26A, P-26C	USAAC	1	1 x P&W R-1340-27	600hp	Into production	111
266A	01/1933	10/01/1935	Monoplane fighter	P-26B	USAAC	1	1 x P&W R-1340-33	600hp	Into production	25
267		1932	Biplane fighter	P-12	Brazil	1	1 x P&W S1D1 Wasp	550hp	Into production	9
272		1933	Fighter			1	1 x P&W SR-1340	550hp	Prototype	1
273	12/1932	14/09/1933	Carrier-based monoplane fighter	XF7B-1	US Navy	1	1 x P&W SR-1340-30	550hp	Prototype	1
278A		*–*	*Monoplane fighter*	*XP-32*	*USAAC*	*1*	*1 x P&W Twin Wasp*	*750hp*	*Project*	*–*
281		02/08/1934	Monoplane fighter		China	1	1 x P&W R-1340-27	570hp	Into production	12
294	04/1934	15/10/1937	Heavy bomber	XBLR-1, XB-15, XC-105	USAAC	10	4 x P&W R-1830-11	850hp	Prototype	1
298	*1934*	*–*	*Medium bomber*	*–*	*USAAC*		*2 x Allison V-1710-3*	*1,600hp*	*Project*	*–*
299	1935	28/07/1935	Heavy bomber	XB-17 Flying Fortress	USAAC	8	4 x P&W S1EG Hornet	750hp	Prototype	1
299B	01/1936	02/12/1936	Heavy bomber	YB-17, Y1B-17 Flying Fortress	USAAC	6	4 x Wright R-1820-39	850hp	Pilot production	13
299F		29/04/1938	Heavy bomber	Y1B-17A Flying Fortress	USAAC	8	4 x Wright R-1820-51	800hp	Test bench	1
299H		21/07/1940	Heavy bomber	B-17C and B-17D Flying Fortress	USAAC	8	4 x Wright R-1820-65	1,000hp	Into production	80
299M		27/06/1939	Heavy bomber	B-17B Flying Fortress	USAAC	8	4 x Wright R-1820-51	1,200hp	Into production	39
299-O		05/09/1941	Heavy bomber	B-17E, B-17F and B-17G Flying Fortress	USAAF	10	4 x Wright R-1820-97	1,200hp	Into production	12,587
299-Z	1946		Engine test bed	EB-17G, JB-17G	USAAF		4 x Wright R-1820-97	1,200hp	Conversion	2
299AB	1946		Passenger transport		TWA		4 x Wright R-1820-97	1,200hp	Conversion	2
300		*–*	*Passenger transport*	*–*			*4 x*		*Project*	*–*
307	12/1935	31/12/1938	Passenger transport	Stratoliner, C-75	Pan Am A/w	5 + 33	4 x Wright GR-1820	900hp	Into production	5
307B			Passenger transport	Stratoliner, C-75	TWA	5 + 33	4 x Wright GR-1820	900hp	Into production	5
314	1935	07/06/1938	Passenger transport seaplane	Clipper, C-98, B-314	Pan Am A/w	10 + 74	4 x Wright GR-2600	1,200hp	Into production	12
316	*1938*	*–*	*Heavy bomber*	*Y1B-20*	*USAAC*	*9*	*4 x Wright GR-2600 A73*	*1,650hp*	*Project*	*–*
320	*1938*	*–*	*Patrol seaplane*	*–*	*US Navy*	*8*	*6 x Wright GR-2600*	*1,200hp*	*Project*	*–*
322	*1938*	*–*	*Heavy bomber*	*(Programme number R-40-B)*	*USAAC*	*6*	*4 x P&W R-2100*	*1,400hp*	*Project*	*–*
326	*02/1936*	*–*	*Commercial seaplane*	*–*		*100*	*6 x*	*2,500hp*	*Project*	*–*
333	*1939*	*–*	*Heavy bomber*	*(Programme number R-40-B)*	*USAAC*	*6*	*4 x Allison V1710*	*1,150hp*	*Project*	*–*
334	*1939*	*–*	*Heavy bomber*	*(Programme number R-40-B)*	*USAAC*	*9*	*4 x P&W X-1800*	*1,850hp*	*Project*	*–*
341	*1939*	*–*	*Heavy bomber*	*(Programme number R-40-B)*	*USAAC*	*12*	*4 x R-2800-AG*	*2,000hp*	*Project*	*–*
344		09/07/1942	Patrol boat plane	XPBB-1 Sea Ranger	US Navy	10	2 x Wright R-3350-8	2,000hp	Prototype	1
345	09/1940	21/09/1942	Heavy bomber	XB-29, YB-29, B-29, B-29A and B Superfortress	USAAF	10	4 x Wright R-3350-23	2,200hp	Into production	3,974
345-2	07/1945	25/06/1947	Heavy bomber	B-50A and B Superfortress	USAAF	12	4 x P&W R-4360-35	3,500hp	Into production	371
345-9-6		23/05/1949	Heavy bomber	B-50D Superfortress	USAF	12	4 x P&W R-4360-35	3,500hp	Into production	222
345-31-26		1952	Trainer	TB-50H Superfortress	USAF	12	4 x P&W R-4360-35B	3,500hp	Into production	24
367-1-1	01/1942	09/11/1944	Cargo/troop transport	XC-97 Stratofreighter	USAAF	5 + 134	4 x Wright R-3350-57A	2,325hp	Prototype	1
367-1-2			Cargo/troop transport	XC-97 Stratofreighter	USAAF	5 + 134	4 x Wright R-3350-57A	2,325hp	Prototypes	2
367-4-6	10/1945	28/01/1948	Cargo/troop transport	YC-97A Stratofreighter	USAAF	5 + 134	4 x P&W R-4360-35A	3,000hp	Pilot production	3
367-4-7	10/1945		Troop transport	YC-97B, C-97B, C-97D Stratofreighter	USAAF	5 + 80	4 x P&W R-4360-35A	3,000hp	Pilot production	1
367-4-19		16/06/1949	Cargo/troop transport	C-97A Stratofreighter	USAAF	4	4 x P&W R-4360-35B	3,500hp	Into production	50
367-4-29			Cargo/refuelling tanker	C-97C & KC-97E Stratofreighter	USAAF	4	4 x P&W R-4360-35C	3,500hp	Into production	14
367-5-5	10/1945	11/03/1947	Cargo/troop transport	YC-97 Stratofreighter	USAF	4	4 x Wright R-3350-57A	2,325hp	Pilot production	6
367-76-29			Transport/refuelling tanker	KC-97F & KC-97G Stratofreighter	USAF	4 + 96	4 x P&W R-4360-59B	3,500hp	Into production	751
367-80	05/1952	15/07/1954	Passenger/refuelling tanker	Dash 80	Boeing	3	4 x P&W JT3	44.5kN	Demonstrator	1
368		*–*	*Fighter*	*–*		*1*	*1 propellent engine*		*Project*	*–*
374	*1942*	*–*	*Carrier-based fighter*	*–*	*US Navy*	*1*	*2 x Wright R-1820*	*1,350hp*	*Project*	*–*
377-10-19		08/07/1947	Passenger transport	Stratocruiser	Boeing	5 + 55-100	4 x P&W R-4360	3,500hp	Prototype	1
377-10-26			Passenger transport	Stratocruiser	Pan Am A/w	5 + 55-100	4 x P&W R-4360	3,500hp	Into production	20
377-10-28			Passenger transport	Stratocruiser	SAS	5 + 55-100	4 x P&W R-4360	3,500hp	Into production	4
377-10-29			Passenger transport	Stratocruiser	AOA	5 + 55-100	4 x P&W R-4360	3,500hp	Into production	8
377-10-30			Passenger transport	Stratocruiser	Northwest A/L	5 + 55-100	4 x P&W R-4360	3,500hp	Into production	10
377-10-32			Passenger transport	Stratocruiser	BOAC	5 + 55-100	4 x P&W R-4360	3,500hp	Into production	6
377-10-34			Passenger transport	Stratocruiser	United A/L	5 + 55-100	4 x P&W R-4360	3,500hp	Into production	7
390	*1943*	*–*	*Experimental*	*–*	*US Navy*	*1*	*1 x P&W R-4360-3*		*Project*	*–*
391	*1943*	*–*	*Experimental*	*–*	*US Navy*	*1*	*1 x P&W XR-4360*		*Project*	*–*

Model number	Start of design work	First flight	Description / type	Usual designation & name (programme)	Ordered by/ first customer	Crew & passengers (max)	Typical engine package	Power/ thrust per engine	Status	Number built
396	1943	–	Experimental	–	US Navy	1	1 x Lycoming O-290	125hp	Project	–
399U			Bomber	–	Export		4 x		Into production	20
400	05/1943	27/11/1944	Carrier-based fighter	XF8B-1	US Navy	1	1 x P&W XR-4360-10	3,000hp	Prototypes	3
401	1943	–	Helicopter	–		2	1 x Lycoming O-435D	212hp	Project	–
413	01/1944	–	Bomber/reconnaissance	–	USAF		4 x		Project	–
417		–	Passenger transport	–		2 + 17	2 x Wright 7BA-1	800hp	Project	–
424		–	Bomber	–	USAF				Project	–
432	12/1944	–	Bomber	–	USAF		4 x R-		Project	–
448	09/1945	–	Bomber	–	USAF		6 x R-		Project	–
449	1945	–	Interceptor	–	USAF	1	2 x Westinghouse		Project	–
450-3-3	10/1945	17/12/1947	Medium bomber	XB-47 Stratojet	USAF	3	6 x GE J35	16.7kN	Prototypes	2
450-10-9		25/06/1950	Medium bomber	B-47A Stratojet	USAF	3	6 x GE J47-GE-11	23.1kN	Pilot production	10
450-11-10		26/04/1951	Medium bomber	B-47B Stratojet	USAF	3	6 x GE J47-GE-11	23.1kN	Into production	87
450-67-27			Medium bomber	B-47B Stratojet	USAF	3	6 x GE J47-GE-23	23.2kN	Into production	202
450-126-29		08/1953	Strategic reconnaissance	RB-47E Stratojet	USAF	3	6 x GE J47-ST-25A	26.7kN	Into production	52
450-157-27			Medium bomber	B-47B Stratojet	USAF	3	6 x GE J47-GE-11	23.1kN	Into production	110
450-157-35		30/01/1953	Medium bomber	B-47E Stratojet	USAF	3	6 x GE J47-GE-25	32.0kN	Into production	1,590
450-158-36			Strategic reconnaissance	RB-47E Stratojet	USAF	3	6 x GE J47-ST-25A	26.7kN	Into production	188
450-162-48			Experimental	XB-47D Stratojet	USAF	3	2 x Wright YT-49-W-1 2 x GE J47-GE-23	9,710hp 11.7kN	Conversion	2
450-171-51		06/1955	Strategic reconnaissance	RB-47H	USAF	3 + 3	6 x		Into production	32
451	07/1946	13/07/1947	Liaison/observation	XL-15, YL-15 Scout	USAF	2	1 x Lycoming O-290-7	125hp	Into production	12
454	Fin 1945	–	Carrier-based fighter	–	US Navy	1	1 x		Project	–
457	1945	–	Interceptor	–	USAF	1			Project	–
459	12/1945	–	Carrier-based fighter	–	US Navy	1			Project	–
462	04/1946	–	Bomber	–	USAF	12	6 x Wright T-35	5,000hp	Project	–
464-67		02/10/1952	Strategic bomber	XB-52 and YB-52 Stratofortress	USAF	5	8 x P&W YJ57-8-3	38.7kN	Prototypes	2
464-201-0		05/08/1954	Strategic bomber	B-52A Stratofortress	USAF	5	8 x P&W J57-P-9W	44.5kN	Pilot production	3
464-201-3		25/01/1955	Strategic bomber	B-52B and RB-52B Stratofortress	USAF	5	8 x P&W J57-P-19W	44.5kN	Into production	50
464-201-6		09/03/1956	Strategic bomber	B-52C Stratofortress	USAF	5	8 x P&W J57-P-29W	44.5kN	Into production	35
464-201-7		04/06/1956	Strategic bomber	B-52D Stratofortress	USAF	5	8 x P&W J57-P-29WA	53.8kN	Into production	170
464-253		26/10/1958	Strategic bomber	B-52G Stratofortress	USAF	5	8 x P&W J57-P-43WB	61.2kN	Into production	193
464-259		03/10/1957	Strategic bomber	B-52E Stratofortress	USAF	5	8 x P&W J57-P-29WA	53.8kN	Into production	100
464-260		06/05/1958	Strategic bomber	B-52F Stratofortress	USAF	5	8 x P&W J57-P-43W	61.2kN	Into production	89
464-261		06/03/1961	Strategic bomber	B-52H Stratofortress	USAF	5	8 x P&W TF33-P-3	75.6kN	Into production	102
466	1947	–	Patrol	XP3B-1	US Navy		2 x Allison XT-40	5,200hp	Project	–
473	06/1947	–	Passenger transport	–	–	27	2 to 6 RR Nene	26.78kN	Project	–
474	1948	–	Bomber	XB-55	USAF		4 x Allison T-40A-2		Project	–
479	1948	–	Bomber	XB-55	USAF		4 x		Project	–
482	07/1948	–	Carrier-based fighter escort	–	US Navy	1	1 x turbine		Project	–
486	Fin 48	–	Night fighter	–	US Navy		1 x jet engine		Project	–
495	1950	–	Tactical transport	–	USAF		4 x P&W T-34P-6	5,700hp	Project	–
500/599			Gas turbines							
600/699			Missiles, rockets and satellites							
701		–	Bomber	XB-59	USAF	3	4 x GE J-73	41.3kN	Project	–
707-120		20/12/1957	Passenger transport		Pan Am	3+179	4 x P&W JT3C-6	49.8kN	Into production	63
707-120B		22/06/1960	Passenger transport		American	3+189	4 x P&W JT3D-1	75.6kN	Into production	78
707-220		11/05/1959	Passenger transport		Braniff	3+181	4 x P&W JT4A-3	70.3kN	Into production	5
707-320		11/01/1958	Passenger transport		Pan Am	3+189	4 x P&W JT4A	74.7kN	Into production	69
707-320B		31/01/1962	Passenger transport		Pan Am	3+189	4 x P&W JT3D-3	80.1kN	Into production	250
707-320C		19/02/1963	Passenger transport		Pan Am	3+219	4 x P&W JT3D-3	80.1kN	Into production	353
707-420		19/05/1959	Passenger transport		BOAC	3+189	4 x RR R.Co.12 Conway	77.8kN	Into production	37
707-700		27/11/1979	Passenger transport		–		4 x CFM56	89kN	Prototype	1
708	1953	–	Supersonic bomber	–	USAF	5	4 x		Project	–
712	06/1954	–	Interceptor	(Weapons system WS.202A)	USAF	1			Project	–
713	1954	–	Supersonic bomber	(Weapons system WS.110)	USAF		4 to 10 jet engines		Project	–
717		31/08/1956	Tanker/passenger transport	KC-135/C-135	USAF	80	4 x P&W J57-P-59W	61.2kN	Into production	806
717-200		1998	Passenger transport	717			2 x RR BR715-A1-30	82.3kN	Into production	147
720		23/11/1959	Passenger transport	720	United	3+141	4 x P&W JT3C-7	53.4kN	Into production	65

Model number	Start of design work	First flight	Description / type	Usual designation & name (programme)	Ordered by/ first customer	Crew & passengers (max)	Typical engine package	Power/ thrust per engine	Status	Number built
720B		06/10/1960	Passenger transport	720B	American	3+149	4 x P&W JT3D-1	75.6kN	Into production	89
722	1955	–	Supersonic bomber	(Weapons system WS.110)	USAF		4 to 8 jet engines		Project	–
724	1955	–	Supersonic bomber	(Weapons system WS.110)	USAF		4 to 8 jet engines		Project	–
725	1956	–	Supersonic bomber	(Weapons system WS.110)	USAF		2 to 6 jet engines		Project	--
727-100	1956	09/02/1963	Passenger transport	727-100	Eastern		3 x P&W JT8D-1	62.3kN	Into production	408
727-100C	07/1960		Combined transport		Northwest		3 x P&W JT8D-1	62.3kN	Into production	164
727-200		27/07/1967	Passenger transport	727-200	Northeast		3 x P&W JT8D-17	72.2kN	Into production	1,245
727-200F	09/1981	28/04/1983	Cargo		FedEx	3	3 x P&W JT8D-11	66.7kN	Into production	15
733		–	Supersonic transport	–		250-350	4 x GE4/J5		Project	–
737-100	11/1964	09/04/1967	Passenger transport	737-100	Lufthansa	119	2 x P&W JT8D-7	62.3kN	Into production	30
737-200		08/08/1967	Passenger transport	737-200	United	130	2 x P&W JT8D-9A	68.9kN	Into production	1,114
737-300		24/02/1984	Passenger transport	737-300	US Air	149	2 x CFM56-3B1	88.9kN	Into production	1,113
737-400		19/02/1988	Passenger transport	737-400	Piedmont	168	2 x CFM56-3B	97.8kN	Into production	486
737-500		30/06/1989	Passenger transport	737-500	United	132	2 x CFM56-3B1	97.8kN	Into production	389
737-600		22/01/1998	Passenger transport	737-600	SAS	132	2 x CFM56-7	101.1kN	Into production	56
737-700		09/02/1997	Passenger transport	737-700	Southwest	149	2 x CFM56-7	117.1kN	Into production	686
737-800		31/07/1997	Passenger transport	737-800	Hapag-Lloyd	189	2 x CFM56-7	121.6kN	Into production	834
737-900		03/08/00	Passenger transport	737-900	Alaska	189	2 x CFM-56-7	120.3kN	Into production	46
739			Reconnaissance	RC-135	USAF		4 x P&W J57	61.2kN	Into production	14
747-100	1965	09/02/1969	Passenger transport		Pan American	550	4 x P&W JT9D-7A	205.5kN	Into production	205
747SP		04/07/1975	Passenger transport		Pan American	360	4 x P&W JT9D-7A	206.8kN	Into production	45
747-200		11/10/1970	Passenger transport		KLM	550	4 x P&W JT9D-74R4G2	241.9kN	Into production	393
747-300		10/12/1982	Passenger transport		Swissair	544	4 x GE CF6-80C2B1	245.9kN	Into production	81
747-400		29/04/1988	Passenger transport		Northwest	660	4 x GE CF6-80C2B1F	199.3kN	Into production	623
751			Passenger transport	767	–		4 x		Project	–
757-200	1978	19/02/1982	Passenger transport	757-200	Eastern	239	2 x P&W PW2037	162.8kN	Into production	993
757-300		02/08/1998	Passenger transport	757-300	Condor	279	2 x P&W PW2040	178.4kN	Into production	55
761			Passenger transport	757	–		2 x		Project	–
767-200	1978	26/09/1981	Passenger transport	767-200	United	255	2 x P&W PW4062	281.6kN	Into production	247
767-300		30/01/1986	Passenger transport	767-300	Japan A/L	290	2 x P&W PW4062	281.6kN	Into production	646
767-400		09/10/1999	Passenger transport	767-400	Delta	409	2 x P&W PW4062	281.6kN	Into production	37
777-200		12/06/1994	Passenger transport	777-200	United A/L	440	2 x P&W PW4077	342.9kN	Into production	434
777-300		16/10/1997	Passenger transport	777-300	ANA	550	2 x P&W PW4098	436.5kN	Into production	65
787	1984	2008	Passenger transport	Dreamliner	ANA	210-330	2 x RR Trent 1000	330kN	Into production	–
804	1957	–	Supersonic bomber	(Weapons system WS.110)	USAF	4	6 jet engines		Project	–
806	04/1957	–	Carrier-based bomber	(Programme number TS-149)	US Navy				Project	–
815	1958	–	Tactical transport	–	US Army		2 x RDa.7		Project	–
818	1958	–	STOL fighter	–	USAF	2	2 x P&W JTF10A-1	44.5kN	Project	–
818	1962	–	Fighter	(Programme TFX)	USAF/USN	2	2 x P&W TF30		Project	–
820	1958	–	Heavy transport	–	USAF		4 jet engines		Project	–
835	10/1959	–	Missile-launcher	(Programme number TS-151)	US Navy				Project	–
837	1965	–	Variable geometry, battlefield support	–	US Army	2	2 x		Project	–
901		28/07/1973	Drone	YQM-94 Compass Cope	USAF	0	1 x GE J97-GE-100	23.4kN		
907		–	Passenger transport	–		600	8 x		Project	–
908	1972	–	Carrier-based mini-fighter	–	USAF	0	1 x GE YJ101	42.3kN	Project	–
909	12/1971	–	Light fighter	–	USAF	1	1 x		Project	–
922	1962	–	Space shuttle	–					Project	–
929			Boat	Jetfoil						
939			Space probe	Lunar orbiter		0				
953	1972	09/08/1976	STOL tactical transport	YC-14A	USAF	3 + 150	4 x GE CF6-50D	226.8kN	Prototypes	2
979	1931	–	Space shuttle	F-1 Flyback					Project	–
2020		–	Passenger transport	C-Wing					Project	–
2707		–	Supersonic transport	–		250-350	4 x GE4/J5		Project	–

APPENDIX 2

Performance figures and design features of Boeing aircraft and helicopters

>> 1. Boeing models

Boeing model	User designation	Propulsion (number x type)	Power (hp/kN)	Maximum wingspan (m)	Length (m)	Height (m)	Wing surface (m²)	Empty weight (kg)	Full weight (kg)	Maximum speed (mph @ m*) (Mach)	Cruising speed (mph) (Mach)	Service ceiling (m)	Range (m)	Armament, cargo or number of passengers
1	B&W	1 x Hall-Scott A-5	125hp	15.85	9.50	–	52.20	951	1,268	75	67	–	317	1 passenger
1A	B&W	1 x Lycoming GO-435	170hp	15.85	9.50	–	53.88	952	1,270	75	67	–	311	1 passenger
3	C-5	1 x Hall-Scott A-7A	100hp	13.36	8.23	3.83	44.55	860	1,085	73	65	1,980	199	1 passenger
4	EA	1 x Curtiss OXX-5	100hp	14.88	7.57	–	43.11	724	990	67	60	2,130	280	1 passenger
5	C-650	1 x Hall-Scott A-7A	100hp	13.36	8.23	3.83	44.55	860	1,085	73	65	1,980	199	1 passenger
6	B-1	1 x Hall-Scott L-6	200hp	15.32	9.53	4.06	44.28	1,087	1,744	90	80	4,050	398	2 passengers
6D	B-1D	1 x Wright J-5	220hp	12.10	9.37	3.66	43.29	1,106	1,559	95	80	3,650	174	3 passengers
6E	B-1E	1 x Pratt & Whitney Wasp	410hp	12.10	9.75	3.66	43.29	1,400	2,061	115	105	3,650	451	3 passengers
7	BB-1	1 x Hall-Scott L-4	130hp	13.87	8.43	3.55	36.27	918	1,222	84	75	3,050	497	2 passengers
8	BB-L6	1 x Hall-Scott L-6	200hp	13.64	8.92	3.30	41.85	748	1,192	99	90	4,570	4,362	2 passengers
10	GA-1	1 x Liberty 12A	435hp	19.96	10.24	4.34	91.44	3,549	4,723	105	95	2,920	348	8 x 7.62mm and 1 x 37mm
10	GA-2	1 x Engineering Division W-18	750hp	16.46	11.20	3.66	76.59	2,930	3,937	113	100	3,650	199	6 x 7.62mm and 1 x 37mm
15	XPW-9	1 x Curtiss D-12	435hp	9.75	7.14	2.49	23.40	878	1,348	154 @ 2,000	142	6,700	391	1 x 12.7mm and 1 x 7.62mm
15	PW-9	1 x Curtiss D-12	435hp	9.75	7.14	2.49	23.40	878	1,286	159 @ 3,000	142	6,400	391	1 x 12.7mm and 1 x 7.62mm
15A	PW-9A	1 x Curtiss D-12C	435hp	9.75	7.14	2.49	23.40	878	1,378	163 @ sl	142	6,400	391	1 x 12.7mm and 1 x 7.62mm
15C	PW-9C	1 x Curtiss D-12C	435hp	9.75	7.14	2.49	23.40	878	1,438	163 @ sl	142	6,400	391	1 x 12.7mm and 1 x 7.62mm
15D	PW-9D	1 x Curtiss D-12D	435hp	9.75	7.14	2.49	23.40	878	1,378	152 @ 1,500	142	5,550	391	1 x 12.7mm and 1 x 7.62mm
16	DH-4	1 x Liberty 12A	420hp	13.05	9.12	2.94	39.60	1,331	2,082	118	104	3,900	329	4 x 7.62mm, 181kg of bombs
21	VNB-1	1 x Lawrance J-1	200hp	11.23	8.76	3.50	30.96	967	1,285	99	90	3,100	298	–
40	–	1 x Liberty	400hp	12.25	10.11	3.73	49.23	1,551	2,489	135	110	4,810	696	450kg of mail
40A	–	1 x Pratt & Whitney Wasp	420hp	12.25	10.11	3.73	49.23	1,599	2,718	128	105	4,420	652	2 passengers, 540kg of mail
40B-4	–	1 x Pratt & Whitney Hornet	525hp	12.25	10.11	3.73	49.23	1,686	2,752	137	125	4,900	534	4 passengers, 225kg of mail
40C	–	1 x Pratt & Whitney Wasp	420hp	12.25	10.11	3.73	49.23	1,595	2,752	125	105	4,420	572	4 passengers
42	XCO-7A	1 x Liberty 12A	420hp	13.72	8.89	3.25	39.60	1,407	2,113	122	110	3,970	416	4 x 7.62mm
50	PB-1	2 x Packard 2A-2500	800hp	26.67	18.10	6.35	162.09	5,232	12,150	112	94	2,740	2,498	3 x 7.62mm, 181kg of bombs
53	FB-2	1 x Curtiss D-12D	435hp	9.75	7.14	2.49	23.40	1,055	1,425	164 @ sl	–	5,550	391	1 x 12.7mm and 1 x 7.62mm
54	FB-4	1 x Wright P-1	450hp	9.75	7.14	2.49	23.40	878	1,286	160 @ sl	142	6,860	435	1 x 12.7mm and 1 x 7.62mm
55	FB-3	1 x Packard 1A-1500	510hp	9.75	7.14	2.49	23.40	1,083	1,453	165 @ sl	142	7,040	379	1 x 12.7mm and 1 x 7.62mm
58	XP-4	1 x Packard 1A-1500	510hp	9.75	7.29	2.69	28.78	1,230	1,634	162	137	6,700	373	2 x 7.62mm
63	TB-1	1 x Packard 3A-2500	730hp	16.76	12.44	4.11	78.12	2,555	4,433	115	99	3,810	876	2 x 7.62mm, 1 torpedo
64	–	1 x Wright J-3	200hp	11.23	7.73	3.38	30.96	969	1,286	98	84	2,280	249	1 passenger
66	XP-8	1 x Packard 2A-1530	600hp	9.16	6.95	3.27	22.53	964	1,322	166 @ 1,500	148	7,000	323	1 x 12.7mm and 1 x 7.62mm
67	FB-5	1 x Packard 2A-1500	520hp	9.75	7.26	2.88	22.41	1,115	1,474	163 @ 1,500	150	6,700	416	1 x 12.7mm and 1 x 7.62mm
68	AT-3	1 x Curtiss D-12	435hp	9.75	7.14	2.49	24.15	862	1,123	129	–	–	–	1 pilot
69	XF2B-1	1 x Pratt & Whitney R-1340B	425hp	9.16	7.01	3.12	22.54	900	1,272	154	130	6,800	329	1 x 12.7mm and 1 x 7.62mm
69	F2B-1	1 x Pratt & Whitney R-1340B	425hp	9.16	6.98	3.14	22.54	902	1,272	158 @ sl	132	6,550	317	1 x 12.7mm and 1 x 7.62mm
74	XF3B-1	1 x Pratt & Whitney R-1340-80	425hp	9.16	6.95	2.74	21.83	870	1,232	155	131	6,490	336	2 x 7.62mm, 56kg of bombs
77	F3B-1	1 x Pratt & Whitney R-1340-80	425hp	10.05	7.56	2.79	25.54	988	1,336	157	131	6,550	342	1 x 12.7mm and 1 x 7.62mm
80	–	3 x Pratt & Whitney Wasp	410hp	24.38	16.73	4.47	109.80	4,182	6,920	128	115	4,270	541	12 passengers, 450kg of cargo
80A	–	3 x Pratt & Whitney Hornet	520hp	24.38	17.22	4.65	109.80	4,794	7,927	138	130	4,270	460	18 passengers, 407kg of cargo
81	XN2B-1	1 x Fairchild-Caminez	125hp	10.67	7.82	3.40	27.40	748	987	104	86	3,660	336	1 passenger
83	XF4B-1	1 x Pratt & Whitney R-1340B	500hp	9.14	6.27	2.92	21.13	755	1,160	169	142	8,200	522	1 x 12.7mm and 1 x 7.62mm, 54kg of bombs
93	XP-7	1 x Curtiss V-1570-1	600hp	9.75	7.31	2.74	23.40	1,070	1,479	163 @ 1,500	134	6,440	249	1 x 12.7mm and 1 x 7.62mm
95	–	1 x Pratt & Whitney Hornet	525hp	13.49	9.73	3.68	45.52	1,448	2,645	142	120	4,870	516	–
96	XP-9	1 x Curtiss SV-1570-15	600hp	11.12	7.67	2.99	19.50	1,211	1,643	213 @ 3,600	180	8,170	423	2 x 7.62mm, 111kg of bombs

*@ sl: at sea level

>> 1. Boeing models (continued)

Boeing model	User designation	Propulsion (number x type)	Power (hp/kN)	Maximum wingspan (m)	Length (m)	Height (m)	Wing surface (m²)	Empty weight (kg)	Full weight (kg)	Maximum speed (mph @ m*) (Mach)	Cruising speed (mph) (Mach)	Service ceiling (m)	Range (m)	Armament, cargo or number of passengers
99	F4B-1	1 x Pratt & Whitney R-1340-8	500hp	9.14	6.27	2.92	21.13	890	1,236	176 @ 1,800	140	8,200	373	1 x 12.7mm and 1 x 7.62mm, 54kg of bombs
100	–	1 x Pratt & Whitney Wasp	450hp	9.14	6.12	2.92	21.13	819	1,225	166	140	7,300	600	–
102	P-12	1 x Pratt & Whitney R-1340-7	500hp	9.14	6.27	2.92	21.13	797	1,091	171 @ 1,500	135	8,200	522	1 x 12.7mm and 1 x 7.62mm, 54kg of bombs
102B	P-12B	1 x Pratt & Whitney R-1340-9	500hp	9.14	6.12	2.92	21.13	882	1,091	169 @ 1,500	135	8,200	522	1 x 12.7mm and 1 x 7.62mm, 54kg of bombs
200	Monomail	1 x Pratt 1 Whitney Hornet B	575hp	18.02	12.56	–	49.70	2,155	3,624	158	135	4,270	528	6.2 m³ of mail
202	XP-15	1 x Pratt & Whitney SR-1340D	525hp	9.29	6.40	2.84	14.61	931	1,246	190 @ 2,400	160	8,090	416	2 x 7.62mm (not fitted)
203	–	1 x Axelson B	145hp	10.36	7.42	2.59	27.87	859	1,189	108	92	3,960	398	1–2 passengers
204	–	1 x Pratt & Whitney Wasp	410hp	12.10	9.93	3.66	43.66	1,494	2,238	115	95	2,740	348	4 passengers
205	XF5B-1	1 x Pratt & Whitney SR-1340C	485hp	9.29	6.40	2.84	14.61	936	1,274	190 @ 2,400	145	8,050	690	1 x 12.7mm and 1 x 7.62mm, 227kg of bombs
214	Y1B-9	2 x Curtiss V-1570-29	600hp	23.39	15.70	3.86	86.58	3,884	6,147	173 @ sl	147	5,850	497	4 x 7.62mm, 996kg of bombs
215	YB-9	2 x Pratt & Whitney R-1860-13	575hp	23.39	15.70	3.86	86.58	–	5,736	163 @ sl	137	5,910	1,119	4 x 7.62mm, 996kg of bombs
218	XP-925	1 x Pratt & Whitney R-1340D	500hp	9.14	6.12	2.92	21.13	886	1,222	195 @ 2,440	–	–	–	–
221	Monomail	1 x Pratt & Whitney Hornet B	575hp	18.03	12.55	3.81	49.70	2,263	3,629	158	137	4,480	541	6 passengers
222	P-12C	1 x Pratt & Whitney R-1340-9	450hp	9.14	6.12	2.97	21.13	880	1,193	178 @ 2,400	141	8,000	578	1 x 12.7mm and 1 x 7.62mm
223	F4B-2	1 x Pratt & Whitney R-1340-8	500hp	9.14	6.12	2.99	21.13	935	1,267	186 @ 1,800	158	8,200	404	1 x 12.7mm and 1 x 7.62mm, 210kg of bombs
227	P-12D	1 x Pratt & Whitney R-1340-17	500hp	9.14	6.12	2.97	21.13	887	1,201	178 @ 2,100	150	7,740	472	1 x 12.7mm and 1 x 7.62mm
234	P-12E	1 x Pratt & Whitney R-1340-17	500hp	9.14	6.22	3.15	21.95	914	1,225	189 @ 2,100	160	9,570	584	2 x 7.62mm, 111kg of bombs
235	F4B-3	1 x Pratt & Whitney R-1340-10	500hp	9.14	6.22	3.15	21.13	991	1,315	187 @ 1,800	160	8,380	584	1 x 12.7mm and 1 x 7.62mm, 105kg of bombs
235	F4B-4	1 x Pratt & Whitney R-1340-16	500hp	9.14	6.22	3.15	21.13	991	1,315	187 @ 1,800	160	8,380	584	1 x 12.7mm and 1 x 7.62mm, 105kg of bombs
236	XF6B-1	1 x Pratt & Whitney R-1535-44	625hp	8.68	6.73	3.22	23.41	1,281	1,680	200 @ 1,800	170	7,440	522	2 x 7.62mm, 227kg of bombs
246	Y1B-9A	2 x Pratt & Whitney R-1860-11	575hp	23.42	15.85	3.66	86.58	–	6,487	186	165	6,320	541	2 x 7.62mm, 1,087kg of bombs
247	247	2 x Pratt & Whitney Wasp S1D1	550hp	22.55	15.65	4.70	77.68	3,805	5,730	182	155	5,600	485	10 passengers, 180kg of mail
247A	247A	2 x Pratt & Whitney SGR-1535	625hp	22.55	15.65	5.00	77.68	4,066	5,619	198	170	6,920	646	6 passengers
247D	247D	2 x Pratt & Whitney S1D1	560hp	22.55	15.72	3.70	77.68	4,142	6,183	200	189	7,740	746	10 passengers, 180kg of mail
248	Y1P-26	1 x Pratt & Whitney R-1340-21	550hp	8.22	7.16	2.36	13.93	939	1,243	210 @ 6,100	190	9,360	354	1 x 12.7mm and 1 x 7.62mm, 102kg of bombs
251	P-12F	1 x Pratt & Whitney R-1340-19	500hp	9.14	6.22	3.15	21.95	2,923	1,237	194 @ 3,000	165	9,570	298	2 x 7.62mm, 111kg of bombs
264	YP-29	1 x Pratt & Whitney R-1340-35	600hp	8.94	7.59	2.33	16.40	1,138	1,596	250 @ 3,000	212	7,920	522	1 x 12.7mm and 1 x 7.62mm, 77kg of bombs
266	P-26A	1 x Pratt & Whitney R-1340-27	600hp	8.50	7.18	3.04	13.88	996	1,340	234 @ 1,800	199	8,350	360	2 x 7.62mm, 91kg of bombs
266A	P-26B	1 x Pratt & Whitney R-1340-33	600hp	8.50	7.23	3.07	13.84	1,044	1,388	235 @ 1,800	200	8,230	323	2 x 7.62mm, 91kg of bombs
266	P-26C	1 x Pratt & Whitney R-1340-27	570hp	8.50	7.23	3.17	13.84	1,058	1,395	235 @ 2,300	200	8,230	634	1 x 12.7mm and 1 x 7.62mm, 91kg of bombs
273	XF7B-1	1 x Pratt & Whitney SR-1340-30	550hp	9.72	8.40	2.26	19.78	1,262	1,657	239 @ 3,000	200	8,900	752	2 x 7.62mm
294	XB-15	4 x Pratt & Whitney R-1830-11	850hp	45.41	26.69	5.51	258.27	17,082	32,030	200 @ 1,500	152	5,760	513	2 x 12.7mm, 4 x 7.62mm, 3,625kg of bombs
299	XB-17	4 x Pratt & Whitney S1EG	750hp	31.62	20.95	4.57	131.92	9,811	14,692	236	140	7,500	3,107	5 x 7.62mm, 2,175kg of bombs
299B	Y1B-17	4 x Wright R-1820-39	1,000hp	31.62	20.82	5.58	131.92	11,083	15,800	256 @ 4,270	217	9,330	1,373	5 x 7.62mm, 3,625kg of bombs
299O	B-17E	4 x Wright R-1820-65	1,200hp	31.62	22.50	5.84	131.92	15,075	24,009	317 @ 4,570	224	11,150	2,001	1 x 7.62mm, 8 x 12.7mm, 1,812kg of bombs
299O	B-17F	4 x Wright R-1820-97	1,200hp	31.62	22.78	5.84	131.92	15,402	25,595	299 @ 1,500	160	11,430	1,305	10 x 12.7mm, 2,718kg of bombs
299O	B-17G	4 x Wright R-1820-97	1,200hp	31.62	22.65	5.84	131.92	16,369	29,671	287 @ 1,500	150	10,850	2,001	11–13 x 12.7mm, 4,077kg of bombs
307	Stratoliner	4 x Wright GR-1820	900hp	32.69	22.66	6.32	138.05	13,730	19,026	246 @ 5,270	220	7,980	2,386	33 passagers, 5 crew members
314	Clipper	4 x Wright GR-2600	1,200hp	46.33	32.31	8.68	266.35	22,771	37,372	193 @ 3,000	183	4,080	3,498	40–74 passagers, 10 crew members

*@ sl: at sea level

›› 1. Boeing models (continued)

Boeing model	User designation	Propulsion (number x type)	Power (hp/kN)	Maximum wingspan (m)	Length (m)	Height (m)	Wing surface (m²)	Empty weight (kg)	Full weight (kg)	Maximum speed (mph @ m*) (Mach)	Cruising speed (mph) (Mach)	Service ceiling (m)	Range (m)	Armament, cargo or number of passengers
344	XPBB-1	2 x Wright R-3350-8	2,000hp	42.58	28.88	10.67	169.64	16,934	45,811	219 @ 1,370	158	5,760	3,965	4 x 12.7mm, 9,060kg of bombs
345	B-29	4 x Wright R-3350-23	2,200hp	43.05	30.17	8.46	161.56	31,533	47,565	365 @ 7,620	220	9,700	5,829	12 x 12.7mm, 1 x 20mm, 9,060kg of bombs
345-2	B-50A	4 x Pratt & Whitney R-4360-35	3,500hp	43.05	30.17	9.95	159.80	36,716	76,425	385 @ 7,620	235	11,280	4,648	12 x 12.7mm, 1 x 20mm, 9,060kg of bombs
345-9-6	B-50D	4 x Pratt & Whitney R-4360-35	3,500hp	43.05	30.17	9.95	159.80	–	78,473	400	–	–	–	12 x 12.7mm, 1 x 20mm, 9,060kg of bombs
367-4-6	YC-97	4 x Wright R-3350-57A	2,325hp	43.05	33.63	10.13	161.46	31,616	54,360	346 @ 7,620	–	8,750	3,107	135 troops, 5 crew members
367-4-19	C-97A	4 x Pratt & Whitney R-4360-35A	3,500hp	43.05	33.63	11.66	161.46	–	77,112	350	–	–	–	135 troops, 5 crew members
367-4-29	KC-97E	4 x Pratt & Whitney R-4360-35C	3,500hp	43.05	35.97	11.66	161.46	–	79,380	350	–	–	–	5 crew members
367-76-29	KC-97G	4 x Pratt & Whitney R-4360-59B	3,500hp	43.05	35.79	11.66	164.34	37,372	79,275	375	300	9,200	4,300	96 troops, 5 crew members
367-76-29	YC-97J	4 x Pratt & Whitney YT-34P-5	5,700hp	43.05	33.63	11.66	161.46	32,701	79,275	416 @ 7,770	–	10,670	2,299	5 crew members
367-80	Dash 80	4 x Pratt & Whitney JT3	44.5kN	39.52	38.84	11.58	222.97	41,730	86,070	582 @ 7,620	550	13,100	3,542	3 crew members
377	Stratocruiser	4 x Pratt & Whitney R-4360	3,500hp	43.05	33.63	11.66	159.79	35,750	61,155	375	340	9,750	4,200	55-100 passagers, 5 crew members
400	XF8B-1	1 x Pratt & Whitney XR-4360-10	3,000hp	16.45	13.18	4.95	45.46	6,437	9,302	432 @ 8,000	190	11,430	1,305	6 x 12.7mm, 2,900kg of bombs
450-3-3	XB-47	6 x General Electric J35	16.7kN	35.36	32.92	8.53	132.66	34,428	56,625	578	–	11,580	3,996	2 x 12.7mm, 9,965kg of bombs
450-157-35	B-47E	6 x General Electric J-47-GE-25	32.0kN	35.36	32.92	8.53	132.66	35,582	93,635	606 @ 4,970	557	12,340	4,039	2 x 20mm, 4,530kg of bombs
450-171-51	RB-47H	6 x General Electric J-47-GE-25	32.0kN	35.36	32.64	8.53	132.66	35,867	104,326	594 @ 4,970	494	13,710	1,749	no armament
451	YL-15	1 x Lycoming O-290-7	125hp	12.19	7.69	2.74	24.99	683	928	119	101	5,000	249	2 crew members
464-67	XB-52	8 x Pratt & Whitney YJ57-8-3	38.7kN	56.39	46.53	14.71	371.61	72,480	176,670	556	521	11,900	5,201	4 x 12.7mm, 4,530kg of bombs
464-201-3	RB-52B	8 x Pratt & Whitney J57-P-19W	44.5kN	56.39	47.73	14.71	371.61	78,148	190,512	629 @ 6,000	521	14,420	8,140	4 x 12.7mm, 19,050kg of bombs
464-201-6	B-52C	8 x Pratt & Whitney J57-P-29W	44.5kN	56.39	47.73	14.71	371.61	78,308	204,120	629 @ 6,000	521	14,420	7,854	4 x 12.7mm, 19,050kg of bombs
464-201-7	B-52D	8 x Pratt & Whitney J57-P-29WA	53.8kN	56.39	47.73	14.71	371.61	74,610	204,117	629 @ 6,150	521	14,120	7,854	27,215kg of bombs
464-259	B-52E	8 x Pratt & Whitney J57-P-29WA	53.8kN	56.39	47.73	14.71	371.61	78,346	226,664	629 @ 6,000	521	14,080	7,854	4 x 12.7mm, 19,050kg of bombs
464-260	B-52F	8 x Pratt & Whitney J57-P-43WB	61.2kN	56.39	47.73	14.71	371.61	78,087	204,120	639 @ 6,000	523	14,020	8,898	4 x 12.7mm, 19,050kg of bombs
464-253	B-52G	8 x Pratt & Whitney J57-P-43WB	61.2kN	56.39	48.03	12.40	371.61	71,935	204,117	636 @ 6,250	523	11,700	8,898	4 x 12.7mm, 12 AGM-86, 22,680kg of bombs
464-261	B-52H	8 x Pratt & Whitney TF33-P-3	66.9kN	56.39	48.56	14.71	371.61	75,297	221,357	630 @ 6,000	523	14,080	8,898	1 x 20mm, 20 AGM-86, 22,680kg of bombs
707-120		4 x Pratt & Whitney JT3C-6	49.8kN	39.88	44.22	11.79	226.03	53,524	111,584	621 @ 7,600	572	11,430	2,834	165-179 passengers
707-120B		4 x Pratt & Whitney JT3D	75.6kN	39.88	44.04	12.80	233.19	57,833	117,027	626 @ 7,000	618	12,800	4,076	142-189 passengers
707-220		4 x Pratt & Whitney JT4A-3	70.3kN	39.88	44.22	12.80	226.03	55,338	116,573	623 @ 7,600	602	12,800	2,361	142-181 passengers
707-320		4 x Pratt & Whitney JT4A-3	74.7kN	43.41	46.61	12.70	268.67	64,682	136,531	623 @ 7,600	604	11,340	4,785	141-189 passengers
707-320B		4 x Pratt & Whitney JT3D-3	80.1kN	44.41	46.61	12.93	273.32	67,132	148,325	626 @ 7,000	606	10,970	6,195	141-189 passengers
707-320C		4 x Pratt & Whitney JT3D	80.1kN	44.41	46.61	12.93	273.32	70,352	148,325	628 @ 7,000	600	11,735	3,157	141-219 passengers or 50m³ of cargo
707-420		4 x Rolls-Royce R.Co 12 Conway	77.8kN	43.41	46.61	12.70	268.67	64,682	143,335	623 @ 7,100	432	11,700	6,065	141-189 passengers
717	KC-135A	4 x Pratt & Whitney J57-P-59W	61.2kN	39.88	41.52	11.68	226.03	44,605	118,388	597 @ 9,300	506	15,240	8,675	37,650kg of fuel
720		4 x Pratt & Whitney JT3C-7	53.4kN	39.88	41.68	12.66	233.19	50,258	103,873	626 @ 7,100	601	11,700	2,834	131-141 passengers
720B		4 x Pratt & Whitney JT3D	75.6kN	39.88	41.68	12.66	233.19	52,163	100,698	611 @ 7,100	557	–	3,797	137-149 passengers
727-100		3 x Pratt & Whitney JT8D-1	62.3kN	32.92	40.54	10.36	153.29	36,512	77,000	630 @ 6,800	570	11,000	3,107	131 passengers
727-200		3 x Pratt & Whitney JT8D-17	72.2kN	32.92	46.68	10.36	153.29	44,575	83,714	630 @ 6,700	599	12,800	2,796	189 passengers
737-100		2 x Pratt & Whitney JT8D-7	62.3kN	26.52	28.57	11.28	85.66	25,773	50,283	586 @ 7,160	575	10,670	1,150	99-107 passengers
737-200		2 x Pratt & Whitney JT8D-9A	68.9kN	28.35	30.48	11.23	91.04	27,918	57,984	586 @ 7,160	575	10,670	2,131	115-130 passengers
737-300		2 x CFM56-3B1	88.9kN	28.88	33.40	11.12	105.44	31,438	62,967	–	0.462	–	1,864	128-149 passengers
737-400		2 x CFM56-3B	97.8kN	28.88	36.45	11.12	105.44	33,386	68,176	–	0.462	–	2,486	146-170 passengers
737-500		2 x CFM56-3B1	97.8kN	28.88	31.01	11.12	105.44	31,983	60,555	–	0.462	–	2,728	110-132 passengers
737-600		2 x CFM56-7	101.1kN	35.78	31.24	12.55	124.60	36,870	66,000	0.51	0.488	11,920	3,511	110-132 passengers
737-700		2 x CFM56-7	117.1kN	35.78	33.63	12.55	124.60	37,920	70,080	0.51	0.488	11,430	3,865	126-149 passengers

*@ sl: at sea level

>> 1. Boeing models (continued)

Boeing model	User designation	Propulsion (number x type)	Power (hp/kN)	Maximum wingspan (m)	Length (m)	Height (m)	Wing surface (m²)	Empty weight (kg)	Full weight (kg)	Maximum speed (mph @ m*) (Mach)	Cruising speed (mph) (Mach)	Service ceiling (m)	Range (m)	Armament, cargo or number of passengers
737-700C		2 x CFM56-7	121.6kN	34.32	33.63	12.55	124.60	–	77,560	–	0.48	–	3,691	120-149 passengers
737-700ER		2 x CFM56-7	117.1kN	35.78	33.63	12.55	124.60	–	77,565	–	0.48	–	6,338	48-126 passengers
737-800		2 x CFM56-7	121.6kN	35.78	39.47	12.55	124.60	41,480	79,010	0.509	0.48	10,730	3,517	162-189 passengers
737-900ER		2 x CFM56-7	120.3kN	35.78	42.11	12.55	124.60	–	85,130	–	0.48	–	3,679	180-215 passengers
747-100		4 x Pratt & Whitney JT9D-7A	205.5kN	59.64	70.51	19.33	510.97	167,980	333,400	595 @ 9,100	0.52	13,700	6,089	366-452 passengers
747SP		4 x Pratt & Whitney JT9D-7A	206.8kN	59.64	56.31	19.94	510.97	151,257	317,100	619 @ 9,145	–	13,700	7,656	331-440 passengers
747-200		4 x Pratt & Whitney JT9D-74R4G2	241.9kN	59.64	70.66	19.33	510.97	173,770	374,850	606	0.52	12,190	7,892	366-452 passengers
747-300		4 x General Electric CF6-80C2B1	245.9kN	59.64	70.54	19.33	510.97	178,255	374,850	619	0.53	–	7,705	412-496 passengers
747-400		4 x General Electric CF6-80C2B1F	199.3kN	59.64	70.66	19.40	520.25	182,253	378,182	612	0.53	12,500	1,802	568 passengers
747-400	Freighter	4 x General Electric CF6-80C2B5F	276.2kN	64.44	70.66	19.40	520.25	–	396,900	–	0.525	–	5,114	112,630kg of cargo
747-400	Combi	4 x General Electric CF6-80C2B5F	276.2kN	64.44	70.66	19.40	520.25	–	396,890	–	0.53	–	8,302	266 passengers + cargo
747-400ER		4 x General Electric CF6-80C2B5F	276.2kN	64.44	70.66	19.40	520.25	–	412,776	–	0.531	–	8,824	416-524 passengers
747-400ER	Freighter	4 x General Electric CF6-80C2B5F	276.2kN	64.44	70.66	19.40	520.25	–	396,900	–	0.531	–	5,114	112,630kg of cargo
747-8		4 x General Electric 2B67	296.2kN	68.50	74.22	19.35	–	–	435,456	–	0.531	–	5,139	450 passengers
757-200		2 x Pratt & Whitney PW2037	162.8kN	38.05	47.32	13.56	185.25	57,266	115,680	0.53	0.50	11,675	4,487	200-228 passengers
757-200	Freighter	2 x Pratt & Whitney PW2040	178.4kN	38.05	47.32	13.56	185.25	–	115,668	–	0.50	–	3,623	39,780kg of cargo
757-300		2 x Pratt & Whitney PW2040	178.4kN	38.05	54.43	13.56	185.25	86,954	123,600	–	0.50	11,340	3,909	243-280 passengers
767-200ER		2 x Pratt & Whitney PW4062	281.6kN	47.57	48.51	15.85	283.35	84,460	179,170	–	0.50	10,760	7,594	181-255 passengers
767-300ER		2 x Pratt & Whitney PW4062	281.6kN	47.57	54.94	15.85	283.35	167,829	186,880	–	0.50	10,270	7,022	218-351 passengers
767-400ER		2 x Pratt & Whitney PW4062	281.6kN	51.92	61.37	16.86	–	–	204,120	–	0.50	–	6,494	245-375 passengers
767	AWACS	2 x General Electric CF6-80CB6FA	273.6kN	47.57	48.51	15.85	283.35	–	174,633	500	–	12,220	5,754	21 crew members
777-200		2 x Pratt & Whitney 4077	342.9kN	60.96	63.73	18.52	427.8	138,073	247,210	0.54	0.52	13,100	5,997	305-440 passengers
777-200ER		2 x Pratt & Whitney 4090	400.9kN	60.96	63.73	18.52	427.8	151,185	297,560	–	0.52	13,100	8,892	301-440 passengers
777-200LR		2 x General Electric GE90-110B1	490.4kN	64.80	63.73	18.58	427.8	145,149	347,458	–	0.52	–	10,837	301 passengers
777-300		2 x Pratt & Whitney 4098	436.5kN	60.96	73.86	18.52	427.8	158,122	299,370	0.55	0.52	–	6,854	368-550 passengers
777-300LR		2 x General Electric GE90-115B	513.5kN	64.80	73.86	18.57	427.8	–	351,540	–	0.52	–	9,066	365 passengers
787-3		2 x RR Trent 1000	330kN	51.82	56.69	17.07	–	149,685	165,108	–	0.53	–	3,511	290-330 passengers
787-8		2 x RR Trent 1000	330kN	60.05	56.69	17.07	–	154,221	219,540	–	0.53	–	9,445	210-250 passengers
787-9		2 x RR Trent 1000	330kN	63.40	62.79	17.07	–	176,901	244,940	–	0.53	–	9,787	250-290 passengers
2707-200		4 x General Electric GE4/J5	–	32.23	96.93	14.02	836.13	–	305,775	–	1.67	–	4,039	250-350 passengers
2707-300		4 x General Electric GE4/J5P	–	43.18	85.34	15.27	734	–	288,030	1.68 @ 22,250	1.67	–	–	–

Boeing aircraft with no known model number

–	MB-3A	1 x Wright-Hispano H-2	300hp	7.92	6.10	2.34	21.23	777	1,150	138 @ 2,000	125	5,940	–	1 x 12.7mm and 1 x 7.62mm
–	HS-2L	1 x Liberty	360hp	22.58	11.89	4.44	72.27	1,975	2,914	85	–	–	572	1 x 7.62mm, 208kg of bombs
–	PB2B-1	2 x Pratt & Whitney R-1830-92	1,200hp	31.70	19.81	5.64	130.06	8,512	15,009	187 @ 2,130	–	4,810	2,691	2 x 12.7mm, 3 x 7.62mm, 1,812kg of bombs
–	YC-14	4 x General Electric CF6-50D	226.8kN	39.32	40.13	14.73	163.69	53,227	113,700	503	449	13,700	3,188	150 men or 12,230kg of cargo
–	QSRA	2 x AVCO Lycoming YF-102	333.6kN	22.40	28.42	–	55.74	16,670	27,180	–	184	–	–	2 crew members
–	E-6A	4 x CFM F108-CF-100	106.8kN	45.16	46.61	12.93	283.35	78,378	155,128	610 @ 9,150	524	12,800	1,150	–
–	Bird of Prey	1 x Pratt & Whitney JT15D-5C	12.9kN	7.00	14.30	–	–	–	3,350	300	–	6,100	–	–
–	X-32	1 x Pratt & Whitney SE614	155.7kN	10.97	13.72	–	54.81	10,000	22,680	1.0	–	–	690	–
–	X-36	1 x Williams F112	3.1kN	3.18	5.54	0.94	–	494	576	0.4	–	–	–	pilotless

*@ sl: at sea level

>> 2. Models designed by Stearman

Stearman model	User designation	Propulsion (number x type)	Power (hp / kN)	Maximum wingspan (m)	Length (m)	Height (m)	Wing surface (m²)	Empty weight (kg)	Full weight (kg)	Maximum speed (mph@ m*) (Mach)	Cruising speed (mph/h)	Service ceiling (m)	Range (m)	Armament, cargo or number of passengers
A-75	PT-13A	1 x Continental R-670-5	220hp	9.80	7.54	2.94	27.68	881	1,195	125	96	4,115	–	1 passenger or trainee
A75N-1	PT-17	1 x Continental R-670-5	220hp	9.80	7.54	2.94	27.68	875	1,193	135	-	4,025	–	1 passenger or trainee
E-75	N2S-5	1 x Continental R-670-17	220hp	9.80	7.63	2.79	27.68	877	1,230	124	106	3,415	–	1 passenger or trainee
A75L3	–	1 x Lycoming R-680-B4D	225hp	9.80	7.60	2.90	27.68	878	1,232	159	125	4,270	413	1 passenger or trainee
76C	–	1 x Wright R-975E-3	420hp	9.80	7.60	2.80	27.68	1,130	1,655	156	135	6,340	503	1 x 7.62mm
X-90/91	XBT-17	1 x Pratt & Whitney R-985-AN-1	450hp	10.90	8.46	–	18.58	1,397	1,882	190	160	6,100	–	1 passenger or trainee
X-100	XA-21	2 x Pratt & Whitney R-2180-7	1,150hp	19.81	16.15	4.27	56.39	5,788	8,270	257 @ 1,500	200	6,100	1,199	6 x 7.62mm, 1,225kg of bombs
X-120	XAT-15	2 x Pratt & Whitney R-1340-AN-1	1,550hp	18.18	12.90	3.98	42.46	4,826	6,511	207 @ 1,500	185	5,760	851	1 x 7.62mm, 453kg of bombs

>> 3. Helicopters and convertibles

Vertol model	User designation	Propulsion (number x type)	Power (hp)	Maximum wingspan (m)	Length (m)	Height (m)	Wing surface (m²)	Empty weight (kg)	Full weight (kg)	Maximum speed (mph @ m*)	Cruising speed (mph)	Service ceiling (m)	Range (m)	Armament, cargo or number of passengers
107	CH-46D	2 x General Electric T-58-GE-10	1,400hp	15.54	25.40	5.09	379.3	5,825	10,435	162	155	4,260	236	–
107	CH-113	2 x General Electric T-58-GE-8B	1,250hp	15.24	25.40	5.09	379.3	5,104	9,706	168	157	4,115	690	25 armed troops
107	–	2 x General Electric CT-58-110	1,250hp	15.24	13.59	5.13	379.3	4,530	8,370	162	155	4,170	143	25 passengers
114	CH-47A	2 x Lycoming T55-L-5	2,200hp	18.02	29.90	5.67	509.6	8,133	12,882	150 @ sl	150	3,810	963	44 armed troops
114	CH-47B	2 x Lycoming T55-L-7C	2,850hp	18.29	30.18	5.67	525.3	8,788	14,220	180 @ sl	162	3,780	1,255	44 armed troops
114	CH-47D	2 x Lycoming T55-L-712	3,750hp	18.29	30.14	5.68	526.3	10,615	19,178	185 @ sl	138	3,215	1,255	44 armed troops
114	CH-47F	2 x Lycoming T55-L-714	4,867hp	18.29	30.18	5.78	526.3	12,210	24,494	167	165	2,575	264	33 to 55 armed troops
179	YUH-61A	2 x General Electric T700-GE-700	1,500hp	14.94	18.14	4.62	175.3	4,302	8,485	184	154	1,960	544	10 armed troops
234ER	–	2 x Lycoming AL5512	4,075hp	18.29	30.14	5.68	526.3	12,020	22,000	167 @ 600	155	4,570	957	17 to 44 passengers
301	XCH-62	3 x Allison T701-AD-700	8,079hp	28.04	49.95	11.77	1,235	29,485	67,130	175	-	-	1,740	12 passengers, 35 tonnes
360	–	2 x Lycoming AL5512	4,200hp	–	15.54	5.91	–	–	13,835	270	208	-	-	–
–	CV-22	2 x Allison T406-AD-400	6,150hp	11.58	17.48	5.38	210.7	15,032	21,545	435	317	7,925	590	24 armed troops
–	RAH-66A	2 x LHTEC T800-LHT-801	1,430hp	11.90	14.28	3.39	111.2	3,942	7,812	201	190	-	1,448	1 x 20mm, 14 Hellfire or 28 Stinger

>> 4. Models acquired through the McDonnell Douglas merger

Model	User designation	Propulsion (number x type)	Power (hp / kN)	Maximum wingspan (m)	Length (m)	Height (m)	Wing surface (m²)	Empty weight (kg)	Full weight (kg)	Maximum speed (mph@ m*) (Mach)	Cruising speed (mph)	Service ceiling (m)	Range (m)	Armament, cargo or number of passengers
717-200	–	2 x Rolls-Royce BR715-A1-30	82.3kN	28.45	37.81	8.92	92.97	30,785	49,845	–	0.47	-	1,647	106 passengers
–	MD-11	3 x General Electric CF6-80C2D1F	273.6kN	51.70	61.62	17.62	338.9	181,437	273,314	0.5 @ 9,450	-	-	7,873	298 passengers
–	F-15E	2 x Pratt & Whitney F100-PW-220	105.7kN	13.05	19.45	5.63	56.5	14,515	36,740	1.5	-	18,290	2,762	1 x 20mm, 10,432kg of external load
–	F/A-18E/F	2 x General Electric F404-GE-400	78.7kN	13.62	18.31	4.88	46.4	13,274	23,540	1.0	0.6	15,240	2,072	1 x 20mm, 7,030kg of external load
–	Harrier II Plus	1 x Rolls-Royce Pegasus 11	95.9kN	9.25	14.55	3.56	21.4	6,743	14,062	0.5	-	-	1,802	1 x 25mm, 6,000kg of external load
–	T-45	1 x Rolls-Royce F405-RR-401	26kN	9.39	11.99	4.27	17.7	4,461	6,386	621 @ 2,440	-	12,190	–	1 trainee
–	C-17A	4 x Pratt & Whitney F117-PW-100	179.9kN	51.74	53.04	16.79	353.1	125,645	265,351	0.54	0.48	12,500	2,759	54 troops or 61 tonnes of cargo
–	AH-64D	2 x General Electric T700-GE-701C	1,940hp	14.63	17.73	4.95	168.1	5,352	10,107	162 @ sl	162	4,170	249	1 x 30mm, 16 x Hellfire

*@ sl: at sea level

Missile data

>> Features of Boeing missiles

Date	Designation	Name	Length (m)	Span (m)	Diam. (m)	Weight (kg)	Speed (mph, Mach)	Range (km)	Propulsion (manufacturer – type) >> Thrust (kN)	Warhead	Explosive power
1946	SAM-A-1	GAPA	6.40	2.70	0.25	2,700	Mach 2.5	56	Solid-fuel rocket + ram-jet >> n/a	High explosive	n/a
1951	CIM-10A	Bomarc	14.20	5.54	0.89	7,020	Mach 2.8	400	Booster: Aerojet LR59 >> 156 – Cruise: Marquardt RJ43 >> 51	Nuclear W-40	7–10kt
1955	CIM-10 B	Bomarc	13.70	5.54	0.89	7,250	Mach 3.0	710	Booster: Thiokol M51 >> 222 – Cruise: Marquardt RJ43 >> 53	Nuclear W-40	7–40kt
1958	LGM-30A	Minuteman I	16.40	-	1.70	29,400	14,976	10,100	1st stage.: Thiokol M55 >> 933 – 2nd stage.: Aerojet M56 >> 267 3rd stage.: Hercules M57 >> 156	Nuclear W-59	1.2Mt
1962	LGM-30B	Minuteman I	17.00	-	1.70	29,400	14,976	9,600	1st stage.: Thiokol M55 >> 933 – 2nd stage.: Aerojet M56 >> 267 3rd stage.: Hercules M57 >> 156	Nuclear W-56	2Mt
1962	LGM-30F	Minuteman II	17.60	-	1.70	33,100	14,976	11,300	1st stage.: Thiokol M55 >> 933 – 2nd stage.: Aerojet SR19-AJ-1 >> 268 3rd stage.: Hercules M57 >> 156	Nuclear W-56	2Mt
1965	LGM-30G	Minuteman III	18.20	-	1.70	35,300	14,976	13,000	1st stage.: Thiokol M55 >> 933 – 2nd stage.: Aerojet SR19-AJ-1 >> 268 3rd stage.: Aerojet/Thiokol SR73 >> 153 – Booster : Rocketdyne SR14 >> 1.4	Nuclear W-62	170kt
1966	AGM-69A	SRAM	4.83	0.76	0.44	1,010	Mach 3.5	170	Lockheed SR75-LP-1 >> n/a	Nuclear W-69	200kt
1968	AGM-84D[1]	Harpoon	3.85	0.91	0.34	540	Mach 0.85	220	Teledyne/CAE J402-CA-400 >> 3.0	High explosive	221kg
1968	AGM-84E[1]	SLAM	4.45	0.91	0.34	620	Mach 0.85	100	Teledyne/CAE J402-CA-400 >> 3.0	High explosive	
1968	AGM-84H[1]	Harpoon	4.37	2.43	0.34	725	Mach 0.85	280	Teledyne/CAE J402-CA-400 >> 3.0	High explosive	360kg
1970	AGM-86B	ALCM	6.32	3.66	0.62	1,450	Mach 0.6	2,400	Williams F107-WR-101 >> 2.7	Nuclear W-80	150kt
1971	AGM-114B/C[3]	Hellfire	1.63	0.33	0.18	45.7	Mach 1.3	n/a	Thiokol M120E1 >> n/a	Anti-tank HE	8kg
1991	AGM-114F[3]	Hellfire	1.80	0.33	0.18	48.6	Mach 1.3	n/a	Thiokol M120E1 >> n/a	Anti-tank HE	7kg
1991	AGM-114K[3]	Hellfire II	1.63	0.33	0.18	45.7	Mach 1.3	n/a	Thiokol M120E1 >> n/a	Anti-tank HE	9kg
1992	AGM-114L[3]	Hellfire II	1.78	0.33	0.18	50	Mach 1.3	n/a	Thiokol M120E1 >> n/a	Anti-tank HE	9kg
1982	UUM-125	Sea Lance	6.25	-	0.53	1,400	Mach 1.5	185	Hercules EX116 >> n/a	Nuclear W-89	200kt
1984	AGM-130A[2]	-	3.92	1.50	0.46	1,320	High subsonic	65	Alliant Techsystems SR122 >> n/a	Bomb Mk.84	906kg
1986	AGM-131A	SRAM II	3.18	-	0.39	900	Mach 2+	400	Thiokol >> n/a	Nuclear W-89	200kt
	GBU-15	-	3.92	1.49	0.46	1,110	High subsonic	n/a	None	Mk.84	907kg
	GBU-31	JDAM	3.88			968		24	None	Mk.84	907kg

1. Originally McDonnell Douglas; 2. Originally Rockwell International; 3. Originally Rockwell/Martin. HE: High explosive; n/a: data not available.

>> Boeing pilotless aircraft data (UAV, UCAV, RPV...)

Date	Designation	Name	Length (m)	Span (m)	Height (m)	Weight (kg)	Speed (mph, Mach)	Range (m or h)	Propulsion	Power/ thrust (kW, kN)
1971	YQM-94A	-	12.20	27.40		6,520	Mach 0.6	30h	General Electric J97-GE-100	23.4kN
1976	YGQM-94B	B-Gull	15.20	27.40		7,800	Mach 0.6	942m	General Electric TF34-GE-100	26.7kN
1984	YCGM-121A	Pave Tiger	2.59	2.13		120	115	497m	Cuyuna 438 cm^3	21kW
1987	YCEM-138A	Pave Cricket	2.12	2.57		n/a	199	n/a	Cuyuna 438 cm^3 + solid-fuel booster	21kW
1995	-	Heliwing	2.44	5.18	2.29	658	92	n/a	Williams WTS124	179kW
1996	X-36A	-	5.55	3.15	0.95	565	Mach 0.35	45 min	Williams Research F112	3.1kN
1998	X-40A	-	6.70	3.50	2.17	1,200	99	n/a	None	-
2001	X-37	-	8.38	4.57	2.75	5,443	Mach 25	n/a	Rocketdyne AR2-3	31.2kN
2001	X-43A	-	3.70			1,300	Mach 9.8			
2001	A.160	Hummingbird	10.67	10.97				2,796m		
2002	-	ScanEagle	1.22	3.05		15.4	80	30h	Insitu VSC-001-0	n/a
2002	X-45A	-	8.08	10.29	1.85	6,804	Mach 0.95	497m	Honeywell F124	28.1kN
2002	X-45C		11.89	14.93			Mach 0.80		General Electric F404-GE-102D	
2003	X-50	Dragonfly								
2007	X-48B	-		6.4						

n/a: data not available

APPENDIX 4

Jet airliner
orders » 1958-2007

Year	707	717	727	737	747	757	767	777	787	Total
1958	31	-	-	-	-	-	-	-	-	31
1959	17	-	-	-	-	-	-	-	-	17
1960	62	-	80	-	-	-	-	-	-	142
1961	76	-	37	-	-	-	-	-	-	113
1962	17	-	10	-	-	-	-	-	-	27
1963	42	-	20	-	-	-	-	-	-	62
1964	71	-	83	-	-	-	-	-	-	154
1965	135	-	187	83	-	-	-	-	-	405
1966	101	-	149	35	83	-	-	-	-	368
1967	87	-	125	61	43	-	-	-	-	316
1968	40	-	66	49	22	-	-	-	-	177
1969	12	-	64	28	30	-	-	-	-	134
1970	13	-	48	21	20	-	-	-	-	102
1971	9	-	26	48	7	-	-	-	-	90
1972	18	-	119	14	18	-	-	-	-	169
1973	12	-	92	42	29	-	-	-	-	175
1974	16	-	88	47	29	-	-	-	-	180
1975	9	-	50	35	20	-	-	-	-	114
1976	4	-	113	39	14	-	-	-	-	170
1977	14	-	133	37	42	-	-	-	-	226
1978	6	-	125	145	76	38	49	-	-	439
1979	1	-	98	78	72	-	45	-	-	294
1980	21	-	68	95	49	64	11	-	-	308
1981	-	-	38	121	233	3	5	-	-	190
1982	5	-	11	71	14	2	2	-	-	105
1983	15	-	1	64	24	26	20	-	-	150
1984	-	-	-	131	23	2	15	-	-	171
1985	-	-	-	274	42	45	38	-	-	399
1986	6	-	-	212	84	13	23	-	-	338
1987	11	-	-	177	66	46	57	-	-	357
1988	-	-	-	312	49	148	83	-	-	592
1989	-	-	-	241	56	166	100	-	-	563
1990	11	-	-	111	122	95	52	28	-	419
1991	-	-	-	70	31	50	65	24	-	240
1992	-	-	-	114	23	35	21	30	-	223
1993	-	-	-	101	2	33	54	30	-	220
1994	-	-	-	67	16	12	17	-	-	112
1995	-	42	-	169	32	13	22	101	-	379
1996	-	-	-	438	60	59	43	68	-	668
1997	-	-	-	314	36	44	79	55	-	528
1998	-	41	-	353	15	50	38	68	-	565
1999	-	-	-	237	35	18	30	35	-	355
2000	-	21	-	373	26	43	9	116	-	588
2001	-	3	-	188	16	37	40	30	-	314
2002	-	32	-	162	17	-	8	32	-	251
2003	-	8	-	206	4	7	11	13	-	249
2004	-	8	-	152	10	0	9	42	56	277
2005	-	-	-	574	48	-	19	155	232	1,028
2006	-	-	-	733	72	-	8	77	160	1,050
2007	-	-	-	850	25	-	36	143	369	1,423
2008	-	-	-	488	4	-	29	54	94	669
2009	-	-	-	197	5	-	7	30	24	263

APPENDIX 5

Jet airliner
deliveries » 1958-2007

Year	707	717	727	737	747	757	767	777	Total
1958	8	-	-	-	-	-	-	-	8
1959	77	-	-	-	-	-	-	-	77
1960	91	-	-	-	-	-	-	-	91
1961	80	-	-	-	-	-	-	-	80
1962	68	-	-	-	-	-	-	-	68
1963	34	-	6	-	-	-	-	-	40
1964	38	-	95	-	-	-	-	-	133
1965	61	-	111	-	-	-	-	-	172
1966	83	-	135	-	-	-	-	-	218
1967	118	-	155	4	-	-	-	-	277
1968	111	-	160	105	-	-	-	-	376
1969	59	-	114	114	4	-	-	-	291
1970	19	-	55	37	92	-	-	-	203
1971	10	-	33	29	69	-	-	-	141
1972	4	-	41	22	30	-	-	-	97
1973	11	-	92	23	30	-	-	-	156
1974	21	-	91	55	22	-	-	-	189
1975	7	-	91	51	21	-	-	-	170
1976	9	-	61	41	27	-	-	-	138
1977	8	-	67	25	20	-	-	-	120
1978	13	-	118	40	32	-	-	-	203
1979	6	-	136	77	67	-	-	-	286
1980	3	-	131	92	73	-	-	-	299
1981	2	-	94	108	53	-	-	-	257
1982	8	-	26	95	26	2	20	-	177
1983	8	-	11	82	22	25	55	-	203
1984	8	-	8	67	16	18	29	-	146
1985	3	-	-	115	24	36	25	-	203
1986	4	-	-	141	35	35	27	-	242
1987	9	-	-	151	23	40	37	-	260
1988	-	-	-	165	24	48	53	-	290
1989	5	-	-	146	45	51	37	-	284
1990	4	-	-	174	70	77	60	-	385
1991	14	-	-	215	64	80	62	-	435
1992	5	-	-	218	61	99	63	-	446
1993	-	-	-	152	56	71	51	-	330
1994	1	-	-	121	40	69	41	-	272
1995	-	-	-	89	25	43	37	13	207
1996	-	-	-	76	26	42	43	32	219
1997	-	-	-	135	39	46	42	59	321
1998	-	-	-	281	53	54	47	74	509
1999	-	12	-	320	47	67	44	83	573
2000	-	32	-	281	25	45	44	55	482
2001	-	49	-	299	31	45	40	61	525
2002	-	20	-	223	27	29	35	47	381
2003	-	12	-	173	19	14	24	39	281
2004	-	12	-	202	15	11	9	36	285
2005	-	13	-	212	13	2	10	40	290
2006	-	5	-	302	14	-	12	65	398
2007	-	-	-	330	16	-	12	83	441
2008	-	-	-	290	14	-	10	61	375
2009	-	-	-	372	8	-	13	88	481
Total	-	-	-	6,250	1,418	1,049	982	836	13,531

Military aircraft deliveries » 1995-2007

» Military aircraft deliveries

Year	C-17A	C-32A	C-40A	KC-767/ AWACS	F-15E	F/A-18C/D	F/A-18C/D (kits)	F/A-18E/F	T-45TS	CH-47	AH-64	Total
1995	6	-	-	-	5	43	3	-	15	-	-	72
1996	6	-	-	-	11	32	9	-	9	-	-	67
1997	7	-	-	-	19	46	20	-	11	1	2	106
1998	10	4	-	2	39	29	-	1	16	18	5	124
1999	11	-	-	2	35	25	-	13	12	14	11	123
2000	13	-	-	-	5	16	-	26	16	7	8	91
2001	14	-	4	-	-	-	-	36	15	11	7	87
2002	16	-	3	-	3	-	-	40	14	7	15	98
2003	16	-	1	-	4	-	-	44	12	-	-	77
2004	16	-	3	-	3	-	-	48	7	-	3	80
2005	16	-	2	-	6	-	-	42	10	-	12	-
2006	16	-	1	-	12	-	-	42	13	2	31	117
2007	16	-	3	-	12	-	-	44	9	10	17	111
2008	16	-	-	2	14	-	-	45	7	12	3	99

NB : As The Boeing Company and McDonnell Douglas Corporation merged on 1 August 1997, the figures before this date are for the two companies combined.

» Satellite and launcher deliveries

Year	Delta II	Delta III	Delta IV	BBS satellites
1995	3	-	-	-
1996	11	-	-	-
1997	12	-	-	-
1998	13	1	-	-
1999	11	1	-	-
2000	10	-	-	5
2001	12	-	-	7
2002	3	-	1	6
2003	4	-	2	3
2004	4	-	-	2
2005	2	-	-	3
2006	2	-	3	4
2007	3	-	-	3
2008	2	-	-	1

The Boeing family tree

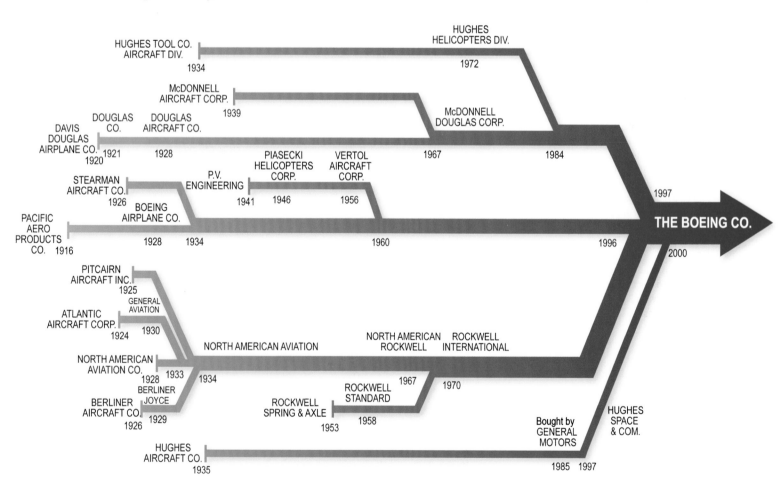

APPENDIX 8

Boeing's financial results ≫ 1996-2007

Year	Turnover ($ millions)	Net profit ($ millions)	Operating margin (%)	Order book ($ millions)	R & D ($ millions)	Workforce (year end)
1996	35,453	1,905	6.0	114,173	1,633	211,000
1997	45,800	- 178	- 0.6	121,640	1,924	238,000
1998	56,154	1,216	2.8	112,896	1,895	231,000
1999	57,993	2,309	5.5	99,248	1,341	197,000
2000	51,119	2,128	6.0	120,600	1,441	198,000
2001	57,970	2,827	6.2	106,591	1,936	188,000
2002	53,831	492	6.4	104,173	1,639	166,000
2003	50,256	718	0.8	104,812	1,651	157,000
2004	52,457	1,872	3.8	109,600	1,879	159,000
2005	53,521	2,572	5.1	160,473	2,205	153,300
2006	61,530	2,215	4.9	174,300	3,257	154,000
2007	66,387	4,074	8.8	224,400	3,850	158,500
2008	60,909	2,672	6.5	278,575	3,768	162,200

APPENDIX 9

Key to acronyms

AAH	Advanced Attack Helicopter
AASM	Advanced Air-to-Surface Missile
ABL	Air Borne Laser
ADC	Air Defense Command
AFB	Air Force Base
AFSC	Air Force Systems Command
AFSOC	Air Force Special Operations Command
ALCM	Air-Launched Cruise Missile
AMC	Air Materiel Command
AMST	Advanced Medium STOL Transport
ARDC	Air Research & Development Command
ARPA	Advanced Research Project Agency
ARS	Air Refueling Squadron
ATB	Advanced Technology Bomber
ATF	Advanced Tactical Fighter
ATT	Advanced Theater Transport
AWACS	Airborne Warning & Control System
BAe	British Aerospace
BAT	Boeing Air Transport
BAH	British Airways Helicopters Ltd
BBJ	Boeing Business Jet
BCS	Boeing Computer Services
BEC	Boeing Engineering & Construction
BOAC	British Overseas Airways Corporation
BoMi	Bomber Missile
BSI	Boeing Services International
B&W	Boeing & Westervelt
CAA	Civil Aeronautics Authority
CALCM	Conventional Air-Launched Cruise Missile
CALF	Common Affordable Lightweight Fighter
CSAR	Combat Search And Rescue
CSRL	Common Strategic Rotary Launcher
CTOL	Conventional Take Off & Landing
C2W	Command & Control Warfare
DOC	Direct Operating Cost
DoD	Department of Defense
DPC	Defense Plant Corporation
EELV	Evolved Expendable Launch Vehicle
EMD	Engineering & Manufacturing Development

EPF	Emergency Plant Facilities
ESA	European Space Agency
ETOPS	Extended range, Twin engine, Operations
FAADS	Forward Area Air Defense System
FDAF	Fleet Air Defense Fighter
GAPA	Ground-to-Air Pilotless Aircraft
GPS	Global Positioning System
HLH	Heavy Lift Helicopter
HLS	Heavy Logistics System
HMMWV	High Mobility Multipurpose Wheeled Vehicle
HSCT	High Speed Civil Transport
ICAP	Improved Capability
ICBM	Inter Continental Ballistic Missile
IDS	Integrated Defense Systems
ISS	International Space Station
IUS	Inertial Upper Stage
JAST	Joint Advanced Strike Technologies
JATO	Jet Assisted Take Off
JDAM	Joint Direct Attack Munition
JHMCS	Joint Helmet Mounted Cueing System
JPL	Jet Propulsion Laboratory
JSF	Joint Strike Fighter
LHTEC	Light Helicopter Turbine Engine Company
LHX	Light Helicopter Experimental
LRV	Lunar Roving Vehicle
LSSM	Local Scientific Survey Module
MATS	Military Air Transport Service
MDC	McDonnell Douglas Corporation
MIT	Massachusetts Institute of Technology
MMA	Multi-mission Maritime Aircraft
MOLAB	Mobile Lunar Laboratory
NDAC	National Defense Advisory Commission
NASA	National Aeronautics & Space Administration
NASDA	National Space Development Agency
NAT	National Air Transport
NATO	North Atlantic Treaty Organisation
NLA	New Large Aircraft
PAA	Pan American Airways
PAT	Pacific Air Transport
PHM	Patrol Hydrofoil Missileship

PW	Pursuit Water-cooled
QSH	Quiet Short Haul
RANSA	Rutas Aereas Nacionales SA
RoBo	Robot Bomber
SAC	Strategic Air Command
SCAD	Subsonic Cruise Aircraft Decoy
SLAM-ER	Stand off Land Attack Missile-Expanded Response
SOF	Special Operations Forces
SOR	Specific Operational Requirement
SRAM	Short-Range Attack Missile
SSF	Supersonic Strike Fighter
SST	Super Sonic Transport
START	Strategic Arms Reduction Treaty
STOL	Short Take Off & Landing
STOVL	Short Take Off & Vertical Landing
SUD	Stretched Upper Deck
TAC	Tactical Air Command
TCA	Trans Canada Airlines
TDRS	Tracking & Data Relay Satellite
TERCOM	Terrain Contour Matching
TFX	Tactical Fighter Experimental
TWA	Trans World Airlines
UAL	United Air Lines
UA&TC	United Aircraft & Transport Corporation
UAV	Unmanned Aerial Vehicle
UCAV	Unmanned Combat Air Vehicle
USAAF	US Army Air Forces
USAAC	US Army Air Corps
USAAS	US Army Air Service
USAF	US Air Force
UTTAS	Utility Tactical Transport Aircraft System
VAL	Varney Air Lines
VLCT	Very Large Commercial Transport
WADC	Wright Air Development Center
WS	Weapons Systems

Index of aircraft mentioned in the text

BAC   PAGES
Guppy »   162-163

Airbus
A300 »   178
A310 »   178
A320 »
A330 »   235
A340 »   187
A350 »   233
A380 »   233
A3XX »   192
KC-330 »   235

BAC
111 »   154

Bell
UH-1 »   194
BoMi »   137
XV-15 »   195

Bell-Boeing
V-22 »   195-197, 208-209, 229, 237

Boeing
AH-64D »   218
AV-8B »   218
ATT »   224
B & W »   10-15
B-1 »   17-30
B-1E »   30
B-17B »   50, 53-54
B-17C »   50, 53-54, 71
B-17D »   73
B-17E »   71, 74
B-17F »   64, 72-77, 80-82, 85
B-17G »   6, 68, 74, 78-85, 123
B-17H »   85
B-29 »   83, 86-94, 99, 105-107, 189
B-47 »   7, 110-116, 124, 189
B-50 »   103, 105, 108-109
B-52 »   6, 118-123, 134-135, 144-146,
176, 180-181, 189, 198, 200-201, 235
BB-1 »   17
BBJ »   235
Bird of Prey »   228
C-4 »   14
C-5 »   15
C-6 »   15
C-17A »   216, 221, 234-235
C-32A »   183
C-40 »   226
C-75 »   67
C-97 »   100, 103, 162
C-135 »   130-132
C-700 »   15-16
CX-HLS »   152
Dash 80 »   124-129
Dyna-Soar »   137-138
EA »   16
EA-18G »   221-222
EB-47 »   115
E-3A/B/C/D »   130, 173-175
E-4A/B »   174, 176
E-6A »   191
EC-135 »   142-143
EC-137 »   174
F-15D »   219
F-15K »   223
FA-18 »   212-213, 216
F/A-22 »   213, 219-220

FB-1 »   20
FB-5 »   24
FB-6 »   24
F2B-1 »   24, 27
F3B-1 »   24-25, 27
F4B-1 »   27
F4B-2 »   24-25
F4B-3 »   27
F4B-4 »   27
Flying Fortress »   see B-17
GA-X »   17
GA-1 »   16-17
GA-2 »   16-17
HC-97 »   104
HSCT »   192
IM-99 »   117-118
JB-17G »   85
KB-29 »   107, 110
KB-47 »   114, 116
KB-50 »   108
KB-97 »   104-105, 129
KC-135 »   116, 130-133, 140, 142-144,
176, 189, 219, 235
KB-767 »   229, 233, 235
MB-3A »   18-19
MMA »   231
Model 15 »   21
Model 21 »   21
Model 40 »   23-24
Model 40A »   21-24
Model 40B »   23-24
Model 54 »   see FB-6
Model 58 »   see XP-4
Model 66 »   see XP-8
Model 74 »   see F3B-1
Models 80 and 80A »   4, 30-32, 238
Model 83 »   27
Model 89 »   27
Model 93 »   see XP-7
Model 200 »   33
Model 204 »   see B-1E
Model 221 and 221A »   34
Model 226 »   31
Model 236 »   see XF6B-1
Model 246 »   see Y1B-9A
Model 247 »   31, 40-46
Model 247D »   44
Model 247Y »   44
Model 294 »   48
Model 298 »   224
Model 299 »   50-51, 85
Model 300 »   50
Model 307 »   54-56, 67
Model 314 »   57-60, 67-70
Model 326 »   60
Model 333 »   86
Model 334 »   86
Model 341 »   87
Model 344 »   69
Model 367 »   124-125, 129
Model 368 »   225
Model 377 »   100-104, 126, 189
Model 417 »   116, 225
Model 424 »   110
Model 431 »   116
Model 432 »   110-111
Model 446 »   111
Model 448 »   111
Model 450 »   111
Model 451 »   116
Model 462 »   118
Model 464 »   119, 225

Model 473 »   123, 225
Model 701 »   224
Model 707 » 125-132, 138-141, 165, 178
Model 713 »   135
Model 717 »   214, 235
Model 720 »   126, 128, 130, 141, 149
Model 722 »   135
Model 725 »   135
Model 727 » 148-150, 155, 165, 178,
183-184, 189, 238
Model 733 »
Model 737 » 154-158, 184-187, 189, 193,
210-211, 216-217, 220, 226, 229, 233-
234, 238
Model 747 » 152, 155-156, 158-159, 170-
172, 175-177, 185-190, 192-193, 220,
231-232, 238
Model 747XL »   224
Model 747 Dreamlifter »   227, 229
Model 757 »   179, 182-184
Model 767 »   9, 176, 178-179, 182, 211
Model 777 » 178, 187-188, 190-191, 220
Model 787 » 223, 227, 229-231, 234, 237
Model 7J7 »   177
Model 7N7 »   177-178
Model 7X7 »   177-178
Model 804 »   136
Model 818 »   147, 224
Model 2020 »   225
Model 2707 »   150-152
Monomail »   see model 200
NB-1 »   20-21
NB-2 »   21
NB-52 »   120, 200-201
NKC-135 »   142-143
NLA »   192
PW-9 »   19-20, 27
P-8A »   229, 231
P-12 »   26-29
P-26 »   4, 35-39, 46, 57, 189
P-2B »   106
Poseidon »   229
QB-17L »   84
QB-47 »   115
RAH-66 » 195, 197-198, 208-209, 231
RB-47 »   113-114, 129
RB-50 »   108
RC-135 »   132, 144, 189
SB-17G »   85
SB-29 »   107
Sonic Cruiser »   220-221
SST »   150-153
Stratocruiser »   see Model 377
Stratofortress »   see B-52
Stratofreighter »   see C-97
Stratojet »   see B-47
Stratotanker »   see KC-135
Super Clipper »   60
Superfortress »   see B-29
T-45 »   218
TB-1 »   24
TB-47 »   115
TFX »   146-148
VC-25 »   138, 174
VC-137 »   138, 238
VLCT »   192
WB-29 »   106
WB-50 »   142-143
WC-135 »   144
X-20 »   137, 189
X-32A »   206, 213, 217-218
X-45 »   227-228

X-48 »   228
X-50 »   228
XBLR-1 »   48-49
XB-15 »   47-50, 53, 58, 83, 86, 189
XB-29 »   88-90, 105
XB-40 »   79
XB-44 »   105, 107
XB-47 »   110-112, 115
XB-52 »   118-119
XC-97 »   94-95
XC-105 »   83
XC-108 »   84
XF2B-1 »   24
XF8F-1 »   94
XPBB-1 »   69, 189
XP-4 »   24
XP-7 »   27
XP-8 »   24
XP-9 »   36
XP-26 »   36
XP-29A »   36
XP-936 »   36
XP-940 »   36
XTB-1 »   27
YAL-1A »   232
YB-40 »   79, 84
Y1B-9A »   34-35, 42, 49, 189
Y1B-17 »   51-54, 63
YB-52 »   121
YC-14 »   174
YC-97 »   98, 100-101
YCEM-138A »   193
YF-22 »   191-192
YQM-94A »   193

Boeing Vertol
CH-46 »   166-167, 189, 237
CH-47 »   165-166, 189, 193-194, 237
CH-113 »   166
HH-47 »   236
HKP-4 »   167
MH-47 »   231
Model 107 »   166
Model 114 »   166
Model 347 »   193
XCH-62 »   165, 194
YUH-61A »   194

Convair
B-36 »   118
Model 22 »   129

Curtiss
HS-2L »   15, 17

de Havilland
DH-4 »   16
DH-4M »   19
DH-88 Comet »   44-45

Douglas
A-20 »   67
B-18 »   52, 54
Boston III »   66
C-133 »   152
DB-1 »   50, 52
DB-7B »   66-67
DC-1 »   43
DC-2 »   44-45
DC-3 »   43, 46, 116
DC-4 »   128
DC-6 »   128
DC-7 »   103, 123, 128

Index of persons mentioned in the text

DC-8 ›› 103, 123, 128, 173
DC-9 ›› 154, 155
DC-X-200 ›› 178
F6D Missileer ›› 147
M-1 ›› 21
Model 2067 ›› 148

General Dynamics
F-111 ›› 151
FB-111 ›› 145

Lockheed
C-130 ›› 174, 191, 235
C-141 ›› 152, 173
L-1011 ›› 178
P-38 ›› 151
X-35 ›› 213

Martin
B-10 and B-12 ›› 35, 46, 50
Model 123 ›› 35
Model 146 ›› 50
TA ›› 13
T3M ›› 24

McDonnell-Douglas
C-17A ›› 216
MD-11 ›› 210
MD-12 ›› 192
MD-80 ›› 210
MD-90 ›› 210
MD-95 ›› 214

North American
PBJ-1 ›› 69
XB-70 ›› 151

Republic
F-105 ›› 133, 146

Sikorsky
S-42 ›› 46

Stearman
Model 70 ›› 61
Model 73 ›› 61
Model 75 ›› 61
Model 76 ›› 63
Model 200 ›› 116
Model X-90 ›› 70
Model X-100 ›› 70, 95
Model X-120 ›› 70, 95
PT-13 ›› 61
PT-17 ›› 62-63
XA-21 ›› 70
XL-15 ›› 116
XPT-943 ›› 61

Sud Aviation
Caravelle ›› 154

Thomas Morse
MB-3 ›› 18-19

Tupolev
ANT-4 ›› 31
Tu-4 ›› 109
Tu-124 ›› 154

Verville
VCP-R ›› 18

Waco
CG-4A ›› 67

PAGES

ALLEN, Edmund T. 'Eddie' ›› 33, 49, 55, 88-90
ALLEN, William McPherson 'Bill' ››99-100, 125, 136, 144
ANDERS, William ›› 161
ANDREWS, Frank (Major-General) ›› 54
ARMSTRONG, Neil ›› 161
ARNOLD, H. 'Hap' (General) ›› 27, 52, 91-92

BARKER, Hugh ›› 23
BARR, Julius ›› 55
BEALL, Wellwood E. ›› 57
BERLIN, Claude ›› 15
BIFFLE, Ira ›› 23
BLACK, Hugo ›› 46-47
BLUMENTHAL, Vaughn ›› 119
BOEING, Bertha ›› 13, 23, 126
BOEING, William Edward 'Bill' ›› 11-19, 21, 24, 31-32, 46-47, 132, 238
BORMAN, Frank ›› 161
BOULLIOUN, E. H. 'Tex' ›› 171, 185
BOYD, George ›› 44

CARLSEN, Art ›› 119
CERNAN, Gene ›› 164
CHENEY, Dick ›› 197
CHURCH, Ellen ›› 33
CLARK, Jack ›› 61
COLLINS, Fred ›› 54
CONDIT, Philip M. ›› 192, 209, 229
COOK, William ›› 152
CORKILLE, John D. (Major) ›› 49, 53
CRAIG, Marlin ›› 86

DANIELS, Bebe V. ›› 27
DUKE, Charles ›› 161

EADS, Jane ›› 23
ECHOLS, Oliver ›› 86, 88
EISENHOWER, Dwight D. ›› 75, 138
EGTVEDT, Clairmont L. 'Claire' ›› 14-15, 19, 41, 45-48, 52, 63, 67, 71
EMERY, E. G. ›› 50
EVEREST, F. F. (General) ›› 146

FARLEY, James ›› 47
FOLEY, Edgard N. ›› 14
FOULOIS, Benjamin D. ›› 47-48
FRYE, Jack ›› 43, 54

GOLDSMITH, Louis ›› 42
GOODMANSON, Lloyd ›› 136
GOTT, Edgar N. ›› 14-15, 19

HAGE, Robert E. ›› 123
HARTNEY, Harold Evans ›› 18
HAYNES (Major) ›› 50
HEARST, W. Randolph ›› 45
HEATH, Ed ›› 12
HILL, Ployer P. (Major) ›› 52
HISCOCK, Thorpe ›› 24
HOOVER, Herbert ›› 46
HUBBARD, Eddie ›› 15-16, 22
HUGHES, Howard ›› 55-56

JACOBSEN, Al ›› 125
JAY, W. Kenneth ›› 32
JOHNSON, Lindon ›› 150
JOHNSON, Philip Gustav ›› 14, 16, 19, 21, 41, 47, 63, 71, 92
JOHNSTON, Alvin M. 'Tex' ›› 126-127
JONES, Wesley ›› 22

KELLY, Clyde ›› 21
KENNEDY, John F. ›› 145, 161
KILNER, Walter ›› 86
KNIGHT, Jack ›› 23
KNUDSEN, William S. ›› 65

PAGES

LEMAY, Curtis (Major-General) ›› 92, 119, 121
LEWIS Jr., Fulton ›› 46
LOESCH, R. L. 'Dix' ›› 126
LOVELL, James ›› 161

McNAMARA, Robert S. ›› 137, 147-148
McPHERSON ROBERTSON, Sir ›› 45
MARONEY, Terah ›› 12
MARSHALL, George C. ›› 86
MARTIN, George ›› 110, 137
MARTIN, Glenn Luther ›› 13
MINSHALL, R.A. ›› 48
MONTEITH, Charles 'Monty' ›› 33, 41, 50
MULALLY, Alan ›› 209
MUNTER, Herb ›› 13-14

NEW, Harry S. ›› 22
NICHOLS, Reeder ›› 45
NORTHROP, John Knudsen 'Jack' ›› 32

OLDS, Robert (Colonel) ›› 86
ORTIZ, Roberto M. ›› 54

PANGBORN, Clyde E. ›› 45
PAULHAN, Louis ›› 12
PENNELL, Maynard ›› 120, 125
PICKFORD, Mary ›› 45
PRATT, Conger (General) ›› 48

REED, Al ›› 89
RENTSCHLER, Frederick B. ›› 31-32, 41, 47
RENTSCHLER, Gordon S. ›› 32
RICKENBACKER, Eddie ›› 43
ROBBINS, Robert ›› 90, 112
ROBERTSON, C. T. ›› 44
ROBINSON, C. Eugene ›› 22
ROOSEVELT, Eleanor ›› 58
ROOSEVELT, Franklin D. ›› 47, 49, 65, 71

SARABIA, Francisco ›› 50
SCHAEFER, J. E. ›› 61
SCHAIRER, George ›› 110, 119
SCHMIDT, Jack ›› 164
SPAATZ, Tooey (General) ›› 52
STACE, D. F. (Lieutenant) ›› 19
STONECIPHER, Harry C. ›› 209, 229
SWEENEY, Charles W. (Major) ›› 92

TIBBETS, Paul W. (Colonel) ›› 92
TOWER, Leslie R. ›› 42, 52
TURNER, Roscoe ›› 45
TYNDALL, Frank (Captain) ›› 20

VAN DUSEN, C. A. ›› 48
VON KARMAN, Theodor ›› 110
VOUGHT, Chance Milton ›› 31

WARDEN, Peter (Colonel) ›› 119-120
WELLS, Edward Curtiss ›› 50, 52, 74, 88, 120
WESTERVELT, George Conrad ›› 12-13
WILLIAMS, Dick ›› 52
WILSON, Thornton Arnold 'T' ›› 171
WITHINGTON, H. W. 'Bob' ›› 120, 136
WOLFE, Kenneth (Brigadier-General) ›› 91
WONG, Tsu ›› 14

YOUNG, John ›› 161

ZIPP, Harold ›› 61

>> Bibliography

There is an abundance of literature devoted to Boeing and its aircraft, particularly in the case of the manufacturer's more famous aircraft. The bibliography that follows makes no claims to be exhaustive; it is aimed at the reader who seeks further information on some of the matters dealt with in this book.

General works

BROOKS (Peter W.), *The Modern Airliner*, Putnam, London, 1961.
DAVIES (R. E. G.), *A history of the world's airlines*, Oxford University Press, 1964.
FRANCILLON (René), *Du Comet à l'A380 – Histoire des avions de ligne à réaction*, Larivière, Clichy, 2005.
HUDSON (Kenneth) and PETTIFER (Julian), *Diamonds in the sky – A social history of air travel*, Bodley Head, BBC, London, 1979.
JUPTNER (Joseph P.), *US civil aircraft*, seven volumes, Aero Publishers, Fallbrook, 1967.
MORRISON (Wilbur H.), *Point of no return – The story of the 20th Air Force*, Times Books, New York, 1979.
PATTILLO (Donald M.), *Pushing the envelope: the American aircraft industry*, University of Michigan Press, 1998.

Works on the Boeing Company

BAUER (Eugene E.), *Boeing in peace and war*, TABA Publishing, Inc., 1990.
BAUER (Eugene E.) and DEMISCH (Wolfgang), *Boeing, the first century and beyond*, Taba Publishing, 2006.
BOWERS (Peter M.), *Boeing aircraft since 1916*, Putnam, London, 1966, 1968, 1982 and 1989.
JOHNSTON (A. M.), *Tex Johnston, jet-age test pilot*, Smithsonian, Washington DC, 1991.
LEE (David), *Boeing, from Peashooter to Jumbo*, Chartwell Books, 1999.
MANSFIELD (Harold), *Vision, the story of Boeing*, Popular Library, New York, 1966.
MUNSON (Kenneth) and SWANBOROUGH (Gordon), *Boeing, an aircraft album*, Ian Allan, London, 1972.
NEWHOUSE, John : *Boeing versus Airbus* (Alfred A. Knopf, 2007).
REDDING (Robert) and YENNE (Bill), *Boeing, planemaker to the world*, Bison books, London, 1983.
RODGERS (Eugene), *Flying High: The story of Boeing and the rise of the jetliner industry*, Atlantic Monthly, 1996.
SERLING (Robert J.), *Legend & legacy – The story of Boeing and its people*, St Martin's Press, New York, 1991.
TAYLOR (Michael J.), *Planemakers No. 1: Boeing*, Jane's, London, 1982.
WELLS GEER (Mary), *Boeing's Ed Wells*, University of Washington Press, 1992.
YENNE (Bill), *The Story of the Boeing Company*, Zenith Press, St Paul, Minnesota, 2005.

Works on aircraft types

COOK (William H.), *The Road to the 707: the inside story of designing the 707*, TYC Publishing Co., 1991.
FRANCILLON (René), *Boeing 707, pioneer jetliner*, MBI, Osceola, Wisconsin, 1999.
HILL (Malcolm L.), *Boeing 737*, Crowood Press, 2002.
JENKINS (Dennis R.), *Boeing 747*, Airliners Tech Vol. 6, Specialty Press, Minnesota, 2000.
KLAAS (M. D.), *Last of the flying Clippers: the Boeing 314 story*, Schiffer Publishing Co., 1998.
LERT (Frédéric), *Boeing B-52, 50 ans d'opérations*, Éditions Larivière, Docavia no 55, Clichy, 2005.
LLOYD (Alwyn T.), *Boeing's B-47 Stratojet*, Specialty Press, Minnesota, 2005.
SUTTER (Joe) and SPENCER (Jay), *747, creating the world's first Jumbo Jet*, Harper Collins Publishers, 2006.
VAN DER LINDEN (Robert F.), *The Boeing 247, the first modern airliner*, University of Washington Press, Seattle, 1991.
VERONICO (Nicholas A.), *Boeing Stratocruiser*, Airliners Tech Vol. 9, Specialty Press, Minnesota, 2001.
WOLF (William), *Boeing B-29 Superfortress, the ultimate look: from drawing board to VJ-Day*, Schiffer Publishing Ltd, Atglen, PA, 2005.
YENNE (Bill), *Inside Boeing: building the 777*, MBI Publishing Co., 2002.

Various documents and articles

Boeing Company's Annual Reports for the years 1995 to 2006.
RUST (Kenn C.), *Early Airlines*, AAHS-Journal, Santa Ana, California, 1985–1987.

Websites

General sites:
http://www.boeing.com (Boeing official site).
http://www.boeingstore.com (Boeing official site).
http://www.aia-aerospace.org (Aerospace Industries Association site).
http://historylink.org (Encyclopaedia on the State of Washington).
http://archives.seattletimes.nwsource.com (Website devoted to the history of Seattle).
http://www.museumofflight.org (Museum of Flight's website).
http://home.hccnet.nl/p.w.riool/mainb.html (Lists of all Boeing's products).
http://www.rosietheriveter.org (Website devoted to 'Rosie the Riveter').
http://www.strategic-air-command.com (Website devoted to the SAC).
http://www.leeham.net (Intelligence for the Aviation Industry).

Sites devoted to particular aircraft:
http://www.b737.org.uk (Boeing 737 website).
http://www.b17.org (B-17 website).
http://www.allaboutguppys.com (Site devoted to Guppies).
http://www.ovi.ch/B377 (Website about 377 Stratoliner).
http://www.jsf.mil (Website on Joint Strike Fighter).

>> Acknowledgements and photographic credits

The author expresses his thanks to long-time friends and correspondents, as well as to occasional contributors who have assisted in the preparation of this work, or whose photographic collections have been used in the illustrations: Peter M. Bowers (deceased), Tony Butler, Robert L. Cavanagh (deceased), Jim Dunn, Pierre Gaillard, Harm Hazewinkel, Gary Killion, William T. Larkins, Herbert Leonard, Merle C. Olmsted, C. E. Porter and Jerry Scutts. He especially wishes to thank his old partner in crime, René J. Francillon for his encouragement and for the time he has willingly spent reading the text and for his many helpful comments.

The author would also like to thank the following organisations, enterprises and airlines: AAHS, AFFTC, Alaska Airlines, American Airlines, AEDC, Australian DoD, Beech, Bell-Textron, Boeing Company (Mary Kane, Mike Lombardi), Condor, EADS, General Motors, Lockheed, Lufthansa, Martin, MDC, NASA/DFRC, NASA/LaRC, NASA/KSC, NASA/LISAR, NASA/JSC, PAA, Rockwell International, Sikorsky, United Airlines, US Air Force, US Army, US Navy, US Department of Defense.

Every effort has been made to locate copyright holders. We apologise in advance for any unintended errors or omissions, which we would be happy to correct in any future edition. Our hope is that the current edition may reveal the names of any other copyright holders, to whom we extend the usual rights.